Theology as Wisdom

A CONTRIBUTION TO TEACHING LIVING THEOLOGY

Silas B. Dias, PhD

Ad Verbum Books

Silas B. Dias/Ad Verbum Books

27 Reading Street

Swindon, Wiltshire/SN1 5BS, United Kingdom

www.asasparaoreino.org

Book Layout ©2017 BookDesignTemplates.com

Theology as Wisdom/ Silas B. Dias. —1st ed.

ISBN 978-1544941158

Contents

Soli Deo Gloria

"Theological education is the process through which the church is forged in faith and informed of it in order to articulate it in word and deed, with biblical integrity and theological, historical, ethical and spiritual vitality, going beyond its geographical, social, psychological, cultural, political, economical and religious frontiers."

– ORLANDO COSTAS (1942-1987).

Acknowledgement

I am profoundly grateful to my mentor, Prof. Abraham van de Beek, for his constant inspiration and wisdom. I also want to express my gratitude and appreciation to Prof. Eddy Van der Borght and Prof. Hans de Wit for their insights, corrections and encouragement along the way.

I also express my gratitude to Eleazar Ferreira, the President of UNIFIL, for his support and encouragement, as well as to Prof. Osni Ferreira, the chancellor of UNIFIL, for his assistance and counsel throughout my studies.

I am grateful to my ministry colleagues at Londrina Philadelphia Independent Presbyterian Church for their spiritual and financial support during my time abroad.

I am indebted to the International Reformed Theological Institute for their substantial financial assistance, which made this project possible.

A special word of thanks goes to my wife Janeide and our children, Kleber and Helen, the delight of our home, who endured patiently with me while I was away immersed in books and hidden in library corridors.

I am grateful to my PhD colleagues, especially Bambang Subandrijo, a fine Indonesian brother.

I also thank my editors who volunteered to help me with the English language, and also my co-workers at the Multifocal Institute for their support.

To the Triune God, above all, be all praise and glory forever.

Introduction

THE CRITIQUE OF THEOLOGICAL education is as old as theological education itself. The history of theological schools is one of constant reform. In times of societal instability, theological education is more challenged than usual and often reaches a critical state.

Such a crisis is visible in different parts across the church. Traditional ecclesial praxis, pastoral activity, issues related to liturgy, the ministry, spirituality and the relationship of the church to what is called the "world" in all its dimensions (social, economic, political, and so forth) have undergone profound changes over the last decades. Most theological schools are not adequately equipped to cope with the new challenges. The methods that have been employed to shed light on theological education seem to a large extent to have lost the power to organize their actions and guide their reflections.

The aim of the present study is to search possibilities and contributions to new approaches in theological education that may facilitate the formation of thinkers and practitioners of living and contextual theology. And also it has the aim to propose an integration between theology and life, content and context, which can be called wisdom.

Theology is, by its very nature, a careful articulation of God's revelation to humankind as recorded in the Scriptures. Since the church addresses the world on the basis of the counsel of God, it follows that theology is intrinsic to this task. Faith and society are closely linked in the theological task.

One of the intended functions of theological education is to develop the ability to reflect upon and apply contextual models of theological teaching. Jon Sobrino states:

> *The academic teaching process goes through three phases: in the first phase we teach what we do not know; in the second phase we teach what we know or suppose we know and finally, in the third phase, we start to learn by teaching.[1]*

The present research focuses especially on the third phase, as proposed by Sobrino.

The present crisis in theological parameters includes the realm of systematic theology as well as the entire field of theological education *per se*. Schools cannot afford to work with separate theological courses as they used to do in the past. Academic integration is in the order of the day and it must be sought through a hermeneutical process that reflects upon the reality in which the church lives and operates. This is especially urgent in times of flexibility and constant adaptation to change at the local and global levels.

Theological instruction essentially consists of processes of change. Such change goes beyond information to reach the person's inner being as a process that involves the transformation of the self, which lasts a lifetime. Therefore, theological education must go beyond the cognitive communication of truth in order to reach into the recesses of the soul; it must inquire, create possibilities,

---

[1] J. Sobrino, *Christology at the Crossroads, a Latin American Approach*. London: SCM Press, 1978, 1.

propose solutions and stimulate reflection vis-à-vis new living contexts.

Theology in my home country Brazil, for instance, operates in a context of enormous societal problems, with exclusion, poverty and conflicts, which are increased by the growing globalization. Theology cannot do without taking this reality into account because it is about the liberating power of the gospel. The debate about how this challenge should be approached has developed in Latin America for several decades now, but the answers have taken different directions. Some theologians stress the importance of societal contexts, others stress the experiences and expressions of personal faith and still others focus on the importance of tradition. Academic theological discourse should integrate all these approaches. It should bridge between reason and faith, academicism and spirituality, theology and ethics.

As the debate promotes new discoveries and elements regarding theological education, the question remains: How should we harmonize a sober rationality with a burning faith rooted in a revelation that often transcends empirical verification — all in light of the burning problems, challenges and hopes of the people at large and the church in particular?

We need to describe, analyze and look for new possibilities of theological teaching in the context of our contemporary societies. This new theology should be able to cope with the challenges of our time while firmly rooted in the tradition of the Christian faith. Academic formation should go hand in hand with personal and societal transformation.

In Brazil, for instance, the teaching of Theology in Protestant schools and seminaries is deeply rooted in Reformed Theology. This tradition was introduced by North

American missionaries steeped into the Reformed tradition and with connections to Pietism. This kind of teaching had little contact with the social/cultural context beyond the walls of the training schools. On the other extreme, there are institutions that focus on Liberation Theology. Since these are context-driven, they pay little attention to the historical roots of the Reformed tradition and the Christian tradition in general, with notable exceptions, such as Gustavo Gutiérrez.

Gustavo Gutiérrez, a classic Liberation theologian, appeals to elementary aspects of the Christian tradition and faith in his writings, especially in the first part of his Theology of Liberation, which discusses the task of theology. The oft-quoted quip that "Liberation Theology opted for the poor whereas the poor opted for the Pentecostal churches"[2] does have a grain of truth in it. Liberation theologians have repeated the same pattern set by their Reformed colleagues in that they often fail to reach the majority of the population who are social outcasts and live in abject poverty precisely because these people feel more at home with a spirituality that stresses personal faith and Pentecostal enthusiasm.

On the Protestant side, the question of theological education in Brazil has three basic dimensions or problems, which can be described as follows:

(a) The first dimension is of a *technical* order. The Protestant schools emulate the model that is present worldwide: the fragmentation of the subjects treated in the teaching of theology. There is a lack of integration between the disciplines and applied contents.

---

[2] D. E. Miller and T. Yamamori, *Global Pentecostalism: The New Face of Christian Social Engagement,* Berkeley: University of California Press, 2007, 215. See also David Tombs, "Latin American Liberation Theology: Moment, Movement, Legacy" in Patrick Claffey and Joe Egan (eds.), *Movement or Moment? Assessing Liberation Theology Forty Years after Medellin,* Studies in Society, Theology and Culture, vol. 1, Bern: Peter Lang, 2009, 45.

(b) The second dimension has to do with their *ideological* position. The majority of the Churches of Protestant origin is characteristically indisposed against Roman Catholic theology; far from displaying an ecumenical attitude, they have become extremely denominational.

(c) Finally, there is a problem of lack of *contextuality* in most handbooks. Students are taught from theological manuals that are uprooted from the Brazilian context(s).

The need for contextual studies, therefore, is in the order of the day for any theological education program that seeks to address both local and national contexts in this regard.

In Brazil, for instance, we have many textbooks are rooted in the Reformed tradition and have made an excellent contribution to theological teaching in Brazil, however, they lack a didactic and critical adaptation to the Brazilian context. This is a gap that Liberation Theology has long proposed to fill. Its novel method and especially its content were constructed from a solid interaction with the historical and social realities of the Latin American continent, specifically from the perspective of marginalized segments of society. Seen through the lenses of the poor, the Christian faith, according to Liberation theologians, should aim at the transformation of social, economic and political structures in favor of a more egalitarian society.

So we come to our main quest: How can theology contribute to bridging the gap between tradition and context? This also implies a related question: How can theology contribute to bridging the gap between traditional churches and seminaries?

The proposal of this reflections is to answer these questions by a theology of wisdom, because in wisdom practical experience and scholarly reflection are intertwined on behalf of life in peace and justice.

To answer those questions, we have to take in account the work that has been done recently in this field. There are some authors who help us to find our way. Nonetheless, I will not give an overview of everything that is written about wisdom, theology and education. That would not only be impossible but also hardly relevant for this book. I just want to refer to those authors who are directly relevant for my own reflections. Their works constitutes the scholarly context in which my reflections are situated.

In Theologia: The Fragmentation and Unity of Theological Education,[3] Edward Farley (1983) makes several proposals for a new method of teaching theology, which he describes as a way of wisdom. He especially critiques the theological fragmentation that started with the Enlightenment and influences theological education to the present day. He focuses on a real "Theological Encyclopedia".[4]

Farley is also the author of *The Fragility of Knowledge: Theological Education in the Church and the University (1988).*[5] His concept of applied theology in this work is of direct relevance to theological education. Also in this work he is especially concerned with the fragmentation of theological teaching in the present encyclopedic model.

Among the authors relevant to my research, Max Stackhouse, in his *Apologia: Contextualization, and Mission in Theological Education* (1988),[6] discusses the task of theological education in the contemporary world. His line of thinking is closely related to Edward Farley's, insofar as it discusses the contextualization of theological education.

---

[3] E. Farley, *Theologia: The Fragmentation and Unity of Theology Education*, Philadelphia: Fortress Press, 1989.

[4] Farley, *Theologia*, 25.

[5] E. Farley, *The Fragility of Knowledge: Theological Education in the Church and the University*, Philadelphia: Fortress Press, 1988.

[6] M. L. Stackhouse and others, *Apologia: Contextualization, Globalization, and Mission in Theological Education*, Grand Rapids: Eerdmans, 1988.

The Catholic theologian Bruno Forte[7] also contributes to a basic understanding of theology as wisdom. In *Constructing Local Theologies,*[8] Robert J. Schreiter emphasizes the need to build theology from a local perspective without losing sight of the global perspective. Peter C. Hodgson, *God's Wisdom: Toward a Theology of Education*[9] discusses theology as *sophia* and education as *paideia*.

Nelly P. Stromquist,[10] in Education in a Globalized World, discusses the connection between economic power, technology and knowledge. She contributes to a didactic transposition from the field of education in general to theological education proper.

In view of his academic seriousness, it is imperative to pay attention to Gerhard von Rad's *Wisdom in Israel.*[11] Von Rad's work displays clarity in the way he focuses on wisdom as an integrating paradigm for a people's faith — which generates the theme of the present research.

Of direct importance for theology in Latin America is the work of Gustavo Gutiérrez.[12] He also stresses theology as wisdom. Actually, it can be argued that the rediscovery of theology as wisdom in the Latin American context started with Liberation theology. Gutiérrez must be noted for having

---

[7] B. Forte, *Teologia como Companhia, Memória e Profecia*, São Paulo: Paulinas, 1991.

[8] R. Schreiter, *Constructing Local Theologies*, London: SCM press, 1985.

[9] P. C. Hodgson, God´s Wisdom: Toward a Theology of Education. Louisville, KY: John Knox Press, 1999.

[10] Stromquist is professor at Rossier School of Education and an affiliated scholar in the Center for Feminist Research, both at the University of Southern California. Her book, Education in a Globalized World (Lanham, MD: Rowman & Littlefield, 2002), offers a powerful introduction to the relationship between education and globalization. She argues that new technologies and communication practices have promoted the Western belief that market forces can take over governmental responsibilities regarding the promotion of social welfare and the inclusion of diverse cultures in mainstream society.

[11] G. von Rad, Wisdom in Israel, London: SMC Press, 1972.

[12] G. Gutiérrez, A Theology of Liberation: History, Politics and Salvation, Maryknoll, NY: Orbis Books, 2000, 4.

brought social themes into the theological arena together with issues that relate with a spirituality that takes into account the problems of common (lay) men and women.

The realities of human existence must be integrated with theological education if pastoral preaching and action want to become effective and relevant to our audiences. Theology as wisdom must be developed from this perspective and as such it always will be contextual as well as scriptural.

Definition: Theology as Wisdom

Theology as wisdom seeks to understand the needs of the present so that the church, as the people of God, may be able to serve their fellow human beings in the concrete reality of life. This calls for a discussion of theological issues that contemplate human life at a personal level as well as institutionally. The reality of faith must both penetrate and be informed by the reality of the world if it is to become relevant both contextually and scripturally.

To explore theology as wisdom according to a long biblical and theological tradition, as a contribution to present day theological teaching is a great challenge within the Brazilian reality, as well as in all southern hemisphere countries, where the reality tragically consists of an excluding social context for many people. It is a challenge to contribute to a spiritual and ethical transformation in the context of the gigantic social, and economic problems, and new transformations in this field due to the process of increasing globalization. An identity for theology and its voice in the current context is sought so that it can effectively contribute to a life with transformation and to the pastoral formation of the Christian communities.

CHAPTER 1

Theology in Context

THEOLOGY IS BOUND by time and space. Theological education out of context is alienation. The beginning of every theological investigation requires a minimum of contextual analysis. Theology finds itself at the crossroads of two moments – the original source of faith and its tradition, and the geographical and cultural context it is applied to.

According to Batista Libânio and Afonso Murad, classical theology is aware of the loci theologici – the theological places. These were elaborated mainly by Melchior Cano,[13] in the wake of Aristotle. They function as points of view and critical criteria in theological epistemology and methodology. The sources of this classic theology were limited to authorities: Scripture, the Apostolic Fathers, dogmas, councils and theologians.[14] Libânio and Murad refer to the fact that modernity has taught us to look for the locus *theologicus* in the human experience as a "place of

---

[13] Melchior Cano, De locis theologicis, Salamanca: M. Gastius, 1563.

[14] J. Batista Libânio and Afonso Murad, Introdução à Teologia, São Paulo: Loyola, 1998, 34.

meaning."[15] They state: "Wherever history, life, adventure and human [relationships] are to be found, their ambiguity becomes the 'theological place' of a new and diversified theology."[16]

In present postmodern times, human life has found a privileged place in the theological discussion. Mundane issues of life become places where the theologian discovers the acts of God and, therefore, the possibility of theologizing for the community of the faithful and society at large.

By using both the classic loci tradition and present day sensitivity to human existence in contextual experience, the theological inquiry can be greatly enriched. Theologians are uniquely placed to bring together their brothers and sisters around a common search for answers to their contemporary problems. Theologizing, then, becomes a common ground where all participants are free to share their pain and doubts and only then will the theologian share relevant stories from the Bible. In their personal and collective journey, human beings dig into the Word of God to find illumination for their lives.

In Latin American countries, urban violence is a serious problem. The phenomenon of social exclusion generates violence, which plagues the major cities. According to the anthropologist Alba Zaluar, in Brazil, for instance, authorities and the media tend to see violence as an issue directly related to the absence of the police on the streets. However, Zaluar[17] points out that this perception overlooks contributing social factors to the problem of violence, as follows:

A growing rift between the rich elite and the poor

---

[15] Libânio and Murad, Introdução, 34.

[16] Libânio and Murad, Introdução, 35.

[17] A. Zaluar, "Para não dizer que não falei de samba: Os enigmas da violência no Brasil", in: L. M. Schwarz (org.), História da vida privada no Brasil 4: contrastes da intimidade contemporânea, São Paulo: Companhia de Letras, 1998, 270-276.

An increase in white-collar crime that goes unpunished

A culture of violence which is found at all levels of society

Distrust of government institutions, especially those that are supposed to execute justice and promote peace

Increasing corruption scandals that undermine trust in political representatives and the institutions associated with them (especially both houses of Congress).

Rural Exodus and the Problems of Urbanization in South America

The urbanization issues that challenged Protestant theology and their opposition to Liberation Theology had two important consequences. First, since traditional Protestantism avoided facing social themes in their theological discourse, their gains in contextualization in the rural areas turned into losses because it did not adapt to the new urban reality; besides, the rise of Protestant theologians who were critical of social issues in the cities was distrusted by common believers. As a consequence, the Protestant church lost much of its impact in attending to the needs of the people. The ecumenical movement filled this void in later years by being vocal about social problems and calling for prophetic actions, which, nonetheless, did not fit into the religious framework of the majority of Protestant leaders.

A second consequence was that the void left by the conservative Protestant churches quickly became an open space, which was filled by the charismatic movement in its effort to reach the masses. The Protestant Church, even after failing to articulate an appropriate response to the social issues demanded by the national context, insisted on a theological discourse that hardly reached the people on the streets. By maintaining a conservative theology with an emphasis on doctrine and rituals, they reduced the availability of space for sacred symbols and mysticism. Most of the religious symbols and practices that had been associated with the rural context were lost in the city and the church leadership grew suspicious of the unknown. Consequently, many churches in the historical Protestantism groups in Brazil lost a significant segment of their membership, shied away from social religious involvement and reduced their religious expressions. This retreat became a fertile ground for the growth of Pentecostal churches, which, though not presenting an elaborated discourse on social issues, did recover the sacred and the mystic by way of vivid expressions of spirituality and social enthusiasm in their public meetings.

The Pentecostal Message and the Challenge of Post-Modern Spirituality

Demonizing the city and blaming Satan for its evils is one of several preaching themes that can be heard from Pentecostal pulpits. Unemployment, violence and homelessness, thus identified, actually promote a spirituality of fear.[18] According to Proença and Souza, besides demonizing society these preachers tend to over-value their personal or denominational worth by building ecclesiastical "kingdoms" that magnify themselves.[19] In their preaching and practice, however, these (neo) Pentecostal leaders end up by fostering a strong dependency on their personal charismas in their attempt at superseding the Reformed emphasis on the priesthood of all believers.[20]

Symptomatically, various churches in the city make use of television and radio programs as vehicles to provide a

[18] Proença and Souza, Formação e Desenvolvimento, 41-61.
[19] Proença and Souza, Formação e Desenvolvimento, 60.
[20] Proença and Souza, Formação e Desenvolvimento, 60.

complex religious "menu" that has met with a growing audience. For decades, denominational loyalty has fallen into disrepute, denominationalism itself undergoing an apparent decline, whereas this sort of religious smorgasbord in on the increase. The marketing of religiosity is a fact and apparently it is irreversible.

The context given requires a deep resistance against apathy which in the words of Sung, "border on cynicism facing the suffering of so many, revealing a profound spiritual and ethical crisis affecting the world today."[21]

The trivialization of social justice has a counterpart in the religious preaching according to the taste of the individual. In the end, such customized sermons foster and feed a spirit of narcissism, which is a far cry from the true gospel. This trend can only be reversed by a rethinking of our theological programs. A permanent renewal of our theological curricula is necessary so that truly biblical and contextual theological models can be proposed, with a multi-disciplinarian approach and content within practical, ethical and mature spiritual guidelines.

Theological Education in the New Century

The beginning of the 21st century coincided with a crisis in theological institutions as a direct result of the profound changes that society at large has been facing. They live beyond the great social gaps, with exclusions and still with changes that come from globalization, such as the increasing lack of commitment to a belief system on the part of many seekers as well as a personal construct of spirituality vis-à-vis the existing religious market options.

---

[21] J.M. Sung, Cinismo e solidariedade na globalização. Espaços 8(1): 2000, 38.

The phenomenon of globalization, however it is defined, has had a strong influence on the mindset and behavior of the population, Christians included. Such issues as the questioning of authority and the grand discourses – largely associated with religious, social and political structures – has favored people's alienation from their immediate neighbors. People mistrust each other and take corruption and the deterioration of social mores for granted. Individualism is on the rise just as commitment to a religious cause/community (in the case of Christian believers) dwindles as time passes. The privileged classes hold on to their economic status, being more content with a discourse that affirms their exclusivist values than otherwise.

The pace of these social changes has not been matched by the existing theological training programs, especially in the confessional schools. On the other hand, the pulpits send out a message that alienates the believers from their fellow human beings. Standard preaching largely ignores the sociopolitical and structural factors that foster injustice and degrades the average human being. The average Christian, for his part, is clueless when it comes to developing a conscious attitude of service and involvement with the welfare of society at large.

Liberation Theology

In the context of the last decades of the twentieth century, courses in theology were under the impressive strength of Latin American theologians. This resulted in one of the most creative theologies that arose in the twentieth century, known as Liberation Theology although more correctly would be to speak of liberation theologies because they do not present a monolithic form but with different perspectives.[22]

It is a fact that Liberation Theology brought an irreversible contribution to the contemporary theological task. Its postulates and hermeneutics have been criticized by many and rejected by some but they cannot in any way be ignored.

Origins of Liberation Theology

Having received its name by the Peruvian Gustavo Gutiérrez , Liberation Theology is more than a school of thought – it is a movement of the Spirit that overlaps with, enriches, corrects and challenges the great Christian traditions, be they Catholic, Orthodox or Protestant, in thought, piety and pastoral practice.

The names of Leonardo Boff, Jon Sobrino, Juan Luis Segundo, Frei Beto, José Miguez Bonino, Rubem Alves, Enrique Dussel, Galileia, Julio de Santa Ana, José Comblin and many others constitute a "cloud of witnesses" that help Latin Americans, professional theologians as well as the laity, to interpret and live a reality that is at the same time both painful and hopeful, full of dark portents and encouraging signs.[23]

According to Jon Sobrino, Liberation Theology is not a fad:

The oppression of the peoples in the third world – and the corresponding dehumanization of the first world – has not disappeared but continues to grow... Although there is oppression, there must be a theology and spirituality of liberation in which they confess themselves to be followers of Jesus and believers

---

[22] D. L. Migliore, Faith Seeking Understanding. Grand Rapids, Michigan: Eerdmans, 2002, 156.

[23] F. J. Pagura, "Formación espiritual contextual" in: Vida y Pensamiento, Vol. 8, No. 2, 1988, [Seminario Biblico Latinoamericano, São José, Costa Rica], 8.

*in the God of Jesus. A theology of liberation has become part
of history and is here to stay. They will change their forms and
hues and should improve their quality and overcome their limitations. However, the reality that gave life remains, and so it
should remain.*[24]

Episcopalian Enrique Anelelli sums up the spirituality
of Liberation Theology in that it always [attunes] one ear
to the Gospel and the other to the people. The methodology of Liberation Theology stands out as a re-reading of
the Gospel side by side with an objective knowledge of the
context it addresses. Any reading of the Bible that ignores
the questions and the heart cries of the people is doomed
to betray the Gospel. A contextualized theology, which is
a requirement of the biblical text, will bring forth a concrete commitment to the needs of the people in solidarity
with their experience of faith.

The context provides the ingredients for a methodological approach as far as the theological task is concerned.
Therefore the synthesis that bothered to elaborate and
that is still in gestation in Latin America is of a prayer in
action, within an action and with the action. It is not to
pray on the one hand and act on the other, nor a life of
prayer without a concrete commitment to the liberation
of those who are socially, politically or economically oppressed unless to pray in the same process of liberation
which experiences a relationship with God and meeting
with fellow beings; a practice that at the same time is a
compromised spirituality. That commitment is born from
prayer and the prayer flourishes from the heart of the
commitment.

Theological education to be practiced in this context is
the methodological challenge to make structural changes,
for example to speak of a Christology "from below" with a

---

[24] J. Nestor, Hacia una Espiritualidad de la Liberación, Santander: Sal Terrae, 1987, 14-15.

contextual character. On Latin American soil, a genuine theological education must have its roots in life, compared to community and corporate reality. This model should not be imposed on students but to be exposed as a new way of thinking about theology: theology and life, spirituality and contextual reality.

Under these changes the development of new curriculum in theological education was questioned, creating new disciplines and seeking to articulate innovative titles for these new disciplines that reality demands.

Methodologically, Clodovis Boff emphasizes the unlimited field what can be "theological" as everything has to do with God so everything has to do with theology. Thus the principle of legitimacy of the "liberation theology" is in fact exactly the maximum size of the field that can be theological in general.

According to Boff, theology is the supreme sphere of human cognition; it is "wisdom in an absolute sense. For theology is the very point of view of God who communicates... with human beings by means of revelation; [his message is] received by faith and [is actualized by way of] pneumatic illumination. Such a condition gives theology a unique status and dignity among all [spheres of] knowledge."[25]

Although Liberation Theology has strong Roman Catholic roots, there was also a Protestant development toward a contextual theology of social transformation in Latin America which antecedes the 1968 Medellin episcopal conference. Protestant theologians such as Rubem Alves, José Miguez Bonino and Richard Shaull had proposed contextual approaches to theology earlier on.[26]

---

[25] C. Boff, Teoria do Método Teológico, Petropolis: Vozes, 2007, 51.

[26] Rubem Alves, especially, should be noted in this regard. His doctoral dissertation, titled Towards a theology of liberation: an exploration of the encounter between the languages of humanistic messianism and messianic humanism (Princeton Theological Seminary, 1968, 298 pp.), which dealt with

ISAL (Church and Society in Latin America), founded in 1961 under the influence of European critical theologians and the ecumenical movement, was a major contribution to the development of Liberation Theology from a Protestant perspective. It was strongly impacted, among others, by Moltmann's *Theology of Hope.*

The Protestant version of Liberation Theology, however, never gained grounding in Protestant communities. An Evangelical critique of ISAL, often centering on its ideological emphases, was initially voiced at the first continental consultation of the Latin American Theological Fraternity (FTL), which took place in Cochabamba, Bolivia, in 1970. Pedro Arana stated that ISAL represented a humanist perspective on Theology, which was disconnected from the Sacred Scriptures and sought the revelation of God only in man and history.[27] René Padilla, one of the founders of FTL, saw at the outset of Liberation Theology a reversal of what a sound theology should be: "Instead of showing the pertinence of Revelation to revolution, it made revolution the source of Revelation. The result is a secularized gospel whose dominant voice coincides with the voice of Marxism."[28] Actually, Padilla later changed his perception of Liberation Theology, as he began to understand it from the perspective of the Kingdom of God. Theologians like Alves and others also were influenced by Richard Shaull's "theology of revolution," which pointed toward a radical transformation of society in its values and ethics rather than in promoting revolution at gunpoint.

---

similar issues, was published in 1971 by Corpus Books as Theology of Human Hope.

[27] E. Núñez, Teologia de la Liberación: Una Perspectiva Evangélica. Miami: Caribe, 1987, 73.

[28] Núñez, Teología, 75.

The Ethos of Liberation Theology

Liberation Theology per se does not intend to be a theology for the poor but a theology of the poor. According to Leonardo Boff, only those who understand the inhuman situation of poverty in which millions of Latin Americans live will be able to understand Liberation Theology. He underscores that the Latin American people by and large are victims of unjust wages, unemployment and sub-employment and have to struggle through issues related to malnutrition, high rates of child mortality, inadequate housing and health problems on a daily basis.[29]

The articulation of Liberation Theology is characterized by (a) an awareness of human misery; (b) an ethical indignation regarding poverty; (c) the practice of solidarity.[30] As a result, praxis and personal involvement with contextual reality come before theoretical theological proposals. In other words, Liberation Theology goes beyond mere theorizing to suggest and promote transformative actions in human history aimed towards its intended goals.

Typically, Liberation Theology proposes a three-stage intervention process of transformation: socio-analytical intervention, hermeneutical intervention and practical pastoral intervention. The key to the first is to perceive reality, the second involves "judging" it, and the third calls for action as a practical response to the two initial steps. The first step is to know those questions of live, and therefore to there amongst the poor, where they are articulated and call for an urgent answer. Liberation Theology, therefore, is always dynamic in both its analysis and proposed action.

---

[29] L.Boff and C. Boff, Da Libertação: O Sentido Teológico das Libertações Sócio-Históricas, Petrópolis: Vozes, 1982, 12.

[30] L. Boff and C. Boff, Da Libertação, 14.

By focusing on oppression and poverty, Liberation Theology presses theological education toward proposing practical steps to alleviate perceived social evils. Theology, as the saying goes, is supposed to have its feet firmly grounded on the soil of human reality. Liberation theologians emphasize that the human being is not just a soul; the human person has basic needs— such as food, shelter, good health, etc. — that must be met with dignity. This social framework (i.e., personal needs in context) is what constitutes the "concrete" material reality which Liberation theologians refer to in their writings. Therefore, Liberation Theology emphasizes reading the Scriptures in order to discover what God has to say about our complex social situation, as means to helping people to understand theology as an instrument of social transformation. Liberation theologians seek to awaken people's consciousness about their sociopolitical needs and, in the process, to help them realize that theology is concerned with practical life. Salvation, for that matter, involves the whole human being as he/she lives in his/her "concrete" reality.

Liberation Theology: The Protestant Critique

Protestant fundamentalists critique Liberation Theology as a human construction of the faith that does not ground itself in divine revelation. Emilio Núñez, for example, remarks that "the church —whether Catholic or Evangelical— needs constant renewal." The question for Núñez is "whether the renewal proposed by Liberation theologians adjusts itself to the principles of the Scriptures."[31]

In order to understand the dismissal of Liberation Theology by the majority of Brazilian Protestant churches it is necessary to consider the context in which it thrived.

---

[31] Núñez, Teología, 225.

Their opposition to Liberation theology's postulates and methods, to a great extent, has to do with the phenomenon of urbanization —which was especially prominent in the middle of the twentieth century—and its effect on the Protestant movement.

Although social concerns drew the attention of noted intellectuals in all walks of life, Liberation Theology's stress on social issues encountered strong opposition, especially after the installation of a military dictatorship in 1964, which lasted over two decades. During that period, classical Protestantism migrated to the cities. Having initially achieved significant growth in the rural areas, it was forced to undergo change due to the issues posed by the growing rural exodus to the cities.

Protestantism did grow in urban centers as a direct result of this social phenomenon. People who were forced to move to urban centers were uprooted from their social and religious roots and needed to settle in the new environment. The theological discussion about social and political issues, which was typical of liberation theologians, did not resonate with the newly arrived rural masses who initially opted for the more conservative "religious" discourse of the Protestant churches. The Protestant message and ethos helped the migrants construct their lives anew in view of the uncertainties of the urban context. The ecumenical movement of the fifties, for its part, stagnated among the theological *intelligentsia*.

Protestant theologians assumed a connection between liberal theology and the Theology of Liberation, the latter being conceived as neo-liberal, especially in regard to its ethical discourse, which seemed to clash with the cultural values of the people in the pews. This only increased the rejection of any theory or practice originating from Liberation Theology on the part of conservative Protestant leaders.

Another critique leveled by Protestant circles had to do with the way in which Liberation Theology approached the Bible. Liberation theologians proposed to read the Word of God through the lenses of the poor and the marginalized of Brazilian society, thus leaving aside the biblical-historical perspective that is central to conservative models of doing theology.

These background issues contributed to the Protestant rejection of Liberation Theology, which is found especially in seminaries and among church leaders. As a consequence, Liberation Theology has been identified with the Catholic Church, which made it even more unacceptable to conservative Protestants.

During the military government, the middle class, fearful of the increasing influence of Communism, of the loss of individual freedom and especially of loosing economic positions, supported the military coup. The fear of the coming of a regime with an ideology that was declaredly atheist (presumably as would communism) united the Protestants who were uneasy with any ideology that might sound suspicious to the political establishment. The strong emphasis on social issues as advocated by Liberation Theology was regarded by most Protestant Christians as political ideology rather than as biblical bases for doing theology. Such discussions were not to be found among the issues that regular Protestant theologians would discuss or even preach about. Such attitude evoked criticisms among the adherents of Liberation Theology who often opposed the Protestant conservative spirituality in a belligerent manner, which further complicated the relationship and dialogue between both sides of the theological spectrum.

CHAPTER 2

Towards a Theology of Wisdom

THE METHOD OF ELABORATION of the *curriculum* in theological education has to do with the relationship between three basic elements: the Scriptures and the tradition of faith, the world as it is experienced, and the practice of life.

Ross Kinsler states that experts on the Bible, history and systematic theology may be of interest to students in their areas because of their own skills and enthusiasm, however it is rare for the teachers or the students to make genuine, fundamental or urgent connections between these studies and the everyday experience and routine of the local or global church, or the local or global community.[32]

What we seek is a method of education that develops a dialectical form of theology. Clodovis and Leonardo Boff

---

[32] F. R. Kinsler, "Kairós en la educación teológica – Un cambio de perspectiva desde abajo" in: Vida y Pensamiento 8(2), 1988, 16-28.

propose that such a method will meet the following expectations: it will have faith as mediator of social analysis
(seeing), hermeneutics (interpreting) and pastoral practice (acting). Each aspect should be connected to the other
and one can start with any one of the elements or mediations. The integration should be steady and permanent.
This model known as critical mind offers very interesting
prospects for a new methodology of theological education
and should be applied to all levels of study in theology.

What has been considered is a new way of seeing or
perceiving both the Gospel as much as the world. The
tools for this new hermeneutic are coming in abundance
from those who are re-reading the Bible and history "from
the start." These re-readings have proved themselves to be
increasingly shocking and surprising, breaking hardened
minds and recovering insensitive hearts.

It is in the relationship between faith and life, between
academia and spirituality, between justification and justice, between theory and ethics that theological curricula
should be built around, in the city and in the countryside.
Theological education must be at the service of a specific
practice. Teaching theology in Latin American cities is to
discover ways in which to keep to the faith in times of violence and social exclusion.

A hermeneutic is proposed when in contact with the
oppressed. This is not a hermeneutics from a philosophical
reflection on language, on philosophical problems nor on
an internal theological concern. Another hermeneutic circle has started: a theology that is invited to give reasons
for its validity from the challenges posed by the economic
and social reality of Latin America.[33]

It is not enough just to speak about liberation, nor even
that this is its main content, allowing it to be a liberator. It

---

[33] M. Preiswerk, Educación Popular y Teologia de la Liberación, San José,
Costa Rica: Editorial DEI, 1994, 229.

is necessary to know how to articulate the Word of God in the perspective of social sciences and with the situation of oppression that affects significant sections of the Latin Americans in focus. The proposed practice of liberation theology can be summarized in this statement: for theology to become a liberator it has to participate in transforming the conditions of oppression.[34]

Towards a Theology of Wisdom

The growth of Pentecostalism emerged as a major social phenomenon at the end of the last century. Television networks, radio stations, newspapers and magazines, identifying themselves with the Protestant world, appear every day. Hospitals, schools and service organizations continue to be founded by the same fast-growing evangelical denominations.

Students taking theology courses usually come from Evangelical Churches with traditional spirituality both at Pentecostal level as much as the so called historical churches (Lutheran, Presbyterian, Baptist and Methodist).

Some seminaries point the way to a mature faith placing emphasis on the devotional ambit whilst others, influenced by a desire to break the dualism between the spiritual and secular, over-emphasize the social as an essential implication of spirituality.

Spiritual wisdom, in turn, wants to integrate the realities in pursuing the penetration of a distinct and profoundly biblical spirituality; a spirituality that reaches out to the poor and the weak in society, in whom, because of Jesus Christ, yearn for redemption and the anticipatory signs of hope for the Kingdom of God.

---

[34] Preiswerk, Educación Popular, 230.

Present day theology seeks a spirituality that arises from the challenges of our cities. It is a call to re-structure faith starting from spirituality as wisdom which is both reason as much as living the reality in hope. Theological education can be experienced as much personally as familiar and ecclesial, re-articulating theological thinking, the concepts of God, Christology, Ecclesiology and Eschatology as it does taking into account the practice of faith.

The student of theology needs, in this model to be motivated by the passion of Jesus Christ, the heart and engine of theology, and also by a passion for life, for the humanity that God created. This consistency is necessary for the student to form a spirituality that leverages the faith through a life of prayer and fellowship. "When faith appeals to reason, theology is born."[35] With this statement Clodovis Boff is in agreement with Thomas Aquinas: "In the fervor of his faith, the person who loves the truth that he believes in turns it over in his mind and embraces it, hoping to find reasons for his love."[36]

All these elements acquire a new meaning and direction with a new cultural dynamism, the prospect of creating an ethical and human being, in the stature expressed by Jesus Christ, faithful to the great challenges of our time. The aim is to lead students to a *ratio fide illustrata*: reason illuminated by faith. Therefore theology can be defined, according to Boff, as "an open-eyed faith"[37], a lucid, intelligent and critical faith.

Spirituality and the Academy, *Eruditio et Pietas* – under the power of this binomial lay should be the guiding values of a theology course. This is why it seeks to develop competencies and skills for the instruction of the faith of people not directly connected to the religious community

[35] C. Boff, Teoria do Método Teológico, Petrópolis: Vozes, 2007, 27.
[36] T. Aquino, Summa Theologica, II-II, q.2, q.10, c.
[37] C. Boff, Teoria do Método, 27.

with the intention of contributing to the welfare of human beings and citizenship, avoiding the religious proselytism and respecting the forms and systems of alternative faiths.

Theology on the Way

The model of theological education we are searching is *Theologia Viatorum*, Theology on the Way. Theology is a journey.

What can be seen today in contemporary society is a struggle for life, for justice and for better professional conditions with a quality of life is improving every day, in spite of a constant struggle against the narrow interests of political leaders, ego-centralized and corrupt. Theology is a way: going on, advancing and changing the way so as to enhance it and transform it.

It is the journey that encourages the people who live in troubled times of urban violence, that is always increasing, almost invincible. Theology of wisdom teaches that evil can never consume and weaken the cries for liberation, which come from the many different groups excluded from society. This has been the conviction of wise people from the dawn of theological and philosophical reflection. It is the teaching of both the book of Proverbs and Socrates, who said: "We cannot make evil disappear but we can prevent it from triumphing."[38]

Theology today is done in the context where church and society find themselves. Therefore, the previous model of a theology that was isolated from the world has no relevance to the challenges of the Christian faith in the present time. Present-day theology, as a result, must be fully contextual and fully engaged in the social issues affecting the church.

---

[38] E. Morin, O Método 6: Ética, Porto Alegre: Sulinas, 2005, 193.

Today, more than ever, history requires a theological education that goes the way of the people neither creating false expectations nor domesticating education which is usually the result of preachers who limit more than they liberate. They are experts in alien utopias, far away from the true hope of the Gospel, which announces the liberation project of the Kingdom of God with the coming justice. In the words of Luque Pascual's Latin American Biblical Seminary:

> *"It is among the people who live the revelation of God, it is the struggle of the people who live the mystery of God's presence that does not abandon us but that creates life and liberates us from sin and death." Continuing he concludes: "It is where we live the faith and we experience the presence and action of God in favor of life."*[39]

From the metaphor of the way we can think about and believe in new ways and directions for theological education starting from a correlation with the lives of the people. Theological education should be of a participatory and community nature, to flood the reality of daily life which grows into a kind of character that embodies the socio-cultural values of a people in their various styles. The theology of the way is that which claims and proclaims a new dawn full of hope derived from the expectation of the amazing day that was promised by God. Theology in these terms is a gift, a task and renewed hope.

The theology of the way of wisdom needs to learn to listen and not only to speak. The book of Job offers a great practical key to theological education as many times theological education seems too much like the friends of Job, Eliphaz, Bilbad, Zophar and the contradictory Elihu. How often, like them, theologians want to know more than

---

[39] P. Luque y R. C. Mamani, Identidad y Transformación, nuevos rumbos de educación teológica en Bolivia. Vida y Pensamiento 8 (2). 1988, 116.

God. Hans de Wit said, applying the experience of Job to the context of theological education: "There is only one time in all these 42 chapters when all these teachers are actually friends of Job. It is in the silence."[40] The text of Job, chapter 2 verses 11 to 13 says:

Now when Job's three friends heard of all this evil that had befallen him, they came each from his own place ... and agreed to go together to show him sympathy and comfort him. And when they saw him from a distance, they did not recognize him and they raised their voices and wept, and they tore their robes and sprinkled dust on their heads toward heaven. They sat down with him upon the ground seven days and seven nights, and none spake a word unto him, for they saw that his grief was very great.

Given the great urban challenges in our cities in the face of increasing symptoms of violence and death, of insecurity and the lack of wanting to live - theological education can contribute with wisdom for a new future. To be a theologian is more than manipulating techniques, using methods or discussing epistemologies. It is to be possessed by the passion "to be able to understand what [is] the breadth, length, height and depth" of the mystery of God (cf. Eph. 3:18). This is the secret and the soul of all theological work.[41]

For the builders of theological education in Latin America, some of the challenges continue to be urgent that were elaborated during the meeting between educational institutions and centers dedicated to ecumenical theological

---

[40] H. de Wit, "Muerte cotidiana y creación teológica en Chile" in: Vida y Pensamiento, Vol. 8, no. 2 [Universidad Bíblica Latinoamericana, San José, Costa Rica], December 1988, 123.

[41] C. Boff, Teoria, 17.

formation in Latin America, Mesoamerica and the Caribbean, in Managua between 14 and 18 July 1991.[42]

> - The acuteness of poverty, plagues, drug trafficking, alienation, depression and death which aggravate the differences within our society and reinforces the scheme center-explorer and periphery exploited just as that which culminated in the 500 years of conquest, colonization, exploitation and dehumanization.
>
> - We also recognize the ability of our people to resist and create signs of hope and solidarity which we interpret as signs and mediations of the Kingdom of God, in the tension between the "already and not yet."
>
> - This situation reinforces the urgency of questioning the models of education that we have inherited to seek a greater coordination of theological and educational resources.
>
> - This situation demands that we guide all to do theological-education in favor of a project for the life of our people and that we establish priorities among the marginalized sectors of society because of culture, race, class and gender.

What is observed is the proposal that encompasses anthropological reality, seeking to develop an ecclesial perspective that includes the recognition of the supremacy and popularity of Pentecostal churches. This needs to be recognized as an issue of the current theological education so it is necessary to expand the ecumenical vision as much as possible.

---

[42] R. Kinsler and I. M. del Campo (eds.), Educación Teológica en situaciones de sobrevivencia. [Consulta latinoamericana, 14-18th July 1991, Managua, Nicaragua.] San José: CMI-SBL, 9-10.

The impact on theological education, under the challenges of the last decades of the twentieth century, reaffirms the same factors mentioned in the same conference:[43]

- A permanent integration between theology and life. The theory and practice; the gospel and pastoral behavior.

- The passionate and disciplined circulation between a review of current reality, the confrontation of reading the Bible and facing this reality and the guidance of a pastoral practice consistent with both, from the perspective of the excluded.

- An epistemological break-alteration that results from this hermeneutic course and leads to an election, a theology and a pastoral vocation for life.

- The incarnation-contextualization of the Gospel of Jesus Christ and God himself in the sufferings and hopes of our people and communities of faith in their struggle for full liberation.

The pilgrimage of theological education in the Latin American way towards the Kingdom of God is to accompany people and to encourage them not to lose their dignity and hope while advancing in the practice of faith as the wisdom of God.

Theology as Wisdom

This research focuses on theology as wisdom, i.e., a living theology, in the understanding that this paradigm integrates both spirituality and life.[44] A theology of the way

---

[43] Kinsler and del Campo, Educacion Teológica, 11.

[44] Various metaphors have been proposed to refer to the kind of theology that is needed in the Latin American continent. Carlos Mesters writes about the "Flower without Defense" (Flor sem defesa, São Paulo: Vozes, 1983) and describes the "The Door to the Street of Life" (Por Trás das Palavras, São

and on the way — therefore, a theology in context — provokes and calls for a theological education leading to wisdom. The theologian is a pilgrim and as such, he or she needs to know the way while moving forward through the paths of the world. Knowing the way means knowing the *locus* of the city where theology as wisdom is situated. A theology of the way requires wise theologians.

Paulo: Vozes, 1974); Julio Santa Ana describes theology in "Trails of the World" (Pelas Trilhas do Mundo a Caminho do Reino de Deus, São Bernardo do Campo: Imprensa Metodista, 1975); John Mackay contrasts the theology of "the Balcony and of the Way" (El otro Cristo Español, 2ª. Ed. Buenos Aires: Aurora, 1988). These metaphors point to theologizing as an exercise in wisdom.

CHAPTER 3

What is Theology?

THE THEOLOGIAN ALWAYS plays his role within a context. In doing so we have to ask what theology is and what theology should be. There are many definitions of theology and many ways of doing it. It is impossible to answer the question about what theology should be without taking the context into account.

If we speak about doing theology it is in the perspective of scholarly training of students. It is about an academic curriculum that requires standards that fit in the ambiance of a university. Thus the question is: what should academic theology be?

In this chapter we will first deal with the question what theology in context should be and subsequently highlight its functions that follow from these reflections on the character of theology.

The Character of Theology

In its deeper sense, theology is a way of speaking-about-God, in His presence and for His glory. It is a reflection on the part of the faith community in connection with the reality of life. It is a reflection about the original and present

25

experience of the faith, in permanent renewal; it has to do with its origin in the divine purpose, its mission in the world and its destiny of hope in the promised Kingdom.

Religious Studies

In many universities theology is practiced as religious studies. The focus is on religious beliefs and practices of people. Theology of this kind is aimed to be merely descriptive. The researchers must leave out any normative aspect from their investigations and training. The question is only how to describe what people do and think with regard to religion.

For Christian studies this will imply that the sources of the tradition are investigated as documents of the past: What did people in Israel believe? What were the practices of early Christian communities? The question whether these beliefs and practices are right or not are left out and may not be answered. Whether they should be relevant for today is also excluded. The research is only interested in past religion.

Religious studies can also deal with present religion. It does so in the same descriptive way: what are beliefs and practices of religious people? What are their personal intentions and feelings? What does religion imply for building communities or for moral behavior? But again: any judgment about these intentions or behavior is not relevant for the research. Scholars may have their personal opinions and convictions, but these should not interfere with their academic work. One of the main purposes of scholarly training is to teach studies to precisely exclude their personal opinion and only describe what is going on.

Such a type of theology could be very interesting in the contemporary context. Understanding what is going on, why people believe as they believe, where there practices originate, would be highly interesting. Even more: it is needed to understand the context where theology is practiced, the people's beliefs, rituals, moral commands, etc. They are just as relevant as statistics about poverty and mortality. Thus, theology as religious studies is one option for doing theology and a necessary option.

The Community of Faith

However relevant are the religious studies for academic theology, they cannot be sufficient in themselves. The majority of students are not enrolled because of pure curiosity regarding religious beliefs and practices of people and communities. They enter the university in order to be trained as ministers for the church. They will work within the community of believers and not observe these from outside. Even more, they are expected to give guidance to these communities. They will be the people who give directions for life and faith. Being normative belongs to the very core of their future work. Therefore they should not only be trained to postpone their personal opinion but even more to develop normative insights and an attitude how to come to these normative insights.

In the contemporary's context, theological education cannot do without a normative training, so that the alumni of the academic institutions are equipped to inform people how to believe and act, and to lead the community wherein they work in the right direction. This will also have consequences for theological research. It is not sufficient to investigate what people believe and how they act. The university is challenged to not only train the leaders of religious communities but also to critically develop a theology that supports their work as normative leadership. A theological faculty or seminary that trains future ministers has to reflect in a scholarly manner on questions like, 'What are the right beliefs? What must be done? Which rituals are good?' Thus as necessary as religious studies are, theology cannot do without a normative discourse and thus produce theology as such.

Theology is about God

If we want to develop a normative discourse the question is: where do we find the norms? In a Christian context the simplest answer is: God is the norm. God's will, God's commandments, God's message and God's acting define how people must believe and live. They are the standards for a viable theological discourse. Therefore theology is theology in a proper sense indeed: speaking about God, as *theo-logos*. All theology is speech about God.[45]

The word theology is derived from Greek and means "Speech about God." The etymology of the term theology (*Theo* = God, *logos* = discourse, hence speech-discourse about God) is a connection between "God" and "language." Theology means that a language of God is possible. God is the subject in the mode of the Word as the basis for the many ways in which theology is made.[46]

As obvious as this answer is, that God is the evocative power for doing theology, it does evoke many questions. I will not deal now with the question whether it is possible to speak about God in a proper sense at all, at least in an academic setting. If theology is developed on behalf of and embedded in a Christian community, God's acting and Word are presupposed. God's revelation is the very presupposition of the church and thus axiomatic for her theological discourse. As such the question of the possibility

---

[45] J. Macquarrie, New Directions in Theology Today, Philadelphia: Westminster Press, 1952, 13.

[46] E. Vilanova, "Teologia" in: C. F. Samanes & J. T. Acosta (eds.), Dicionário de Conceitos Fundamentais do Cristianismo, São Paulo: Paulus, 1999, 793.

of God-talk may be interesting, it is not the most relevant question for theological education and research.

Theology is about God. But what does that mean? We do not have direct access to heaven. To talk about God is an almost unsurpassable challenge. This makes the actual theological reflection necessary an enterprise with a humble attitude, as it is a task that goes beyond our power. Augustine affirmed that theology "means reason or speech about divinity."[47]

John Macquarrie, in his book "God Talk",[48] emphasizes that theology is a strange form of language that differs strongly from other types of speech in general. It is not only strange, but it is also a struggle, due to its limitations of utilizing linguistics symbols. The main question regards how one can speak about God. What Macquarrie intends, is to challenge us to a new theological language. Although the time of the "theology of God's Death" has passed, it has left behind the question of speaking about God within life's contexts and pertinent language for the current time. Macquarrie quotes Paul von Buren, saying: "The matter now is that the word 'God' is dead, differing from the sorrowful screaming of Nietzsche who proclaimed the necessity of God's Death."[49] But if the theology of God's death had alerted us to the fact that a part of the theological language was really dead, meaning nothing to contemporary ears, we should accept with appreciation and gratitude that there is a possibility of speaking about God.

This possibility is not given by abstract speculations on a divine being. We can only investigate God's presence in and through His revelation. God communicates his actions

---

[47] Augustine, City of God, VIII, 1. http://www.logoslibrary.org/augustine/city/0801.html. Accessed on December 12, 2008.

[48] J. Macquarrie, God-Talk: El análisis del linguaje y la lógica de la teología, Salamanca: Sígueme, 1976.

[49] P. Van Buren, The Secular Meaning of the Gospel, New York: Macmillan, 1963.

and words. God speaks, elects, calls, enters human reality, acts, saves, heals, has compassion and loves. God expresses himself in categories of human comprehension. The human being is invited to reflect on this revelation given throughout history, and especially in the history of Israel, ending up in the light of Jesus Christ.

This implies that theology is the study of the Word as witness to and presence of his revelation. A solid Christian theology is based on study of Scripture. These are the canonical texts that the Christian community considers as the normative standards for theological research and for life and faith of the church.

Theological training educates students to elaborate *how* the canon is normative as God's Word. They must learn that they cannot just simply take any saying of the Bible and use it for their own situation. The whole hermeneutic process must be integrated in their theological consciousness.

Contextuality is a key issue precisely in a normative discourse. Both the writing of the Bible and present day Christians have their context and understanding implies understanding both. The Christian fathers, in the first centuries, said that theology has two perspectives, one forward and the other backward.[50] Looking backward, it sees the past from where the revealing, saving and restoring presence of God in concrete earthly history has historically begun. It looks to biblical texts and to the great texts of the councils of the church, which also were written in a historical situation.

Looking forward, theology perceives the present, detecting the challenges of the social-cultural reality, where it articulates the faith faithfully to God's purposes, expanding paths of hope.

---

[50] L. Boff, Fé na Periferia do Mundo, Petrópolis: Vozes, 1979, 4.

Theology in a proper sense is about God. It is about God who reveals himself. But precisely because it is about his revelation in history, theology cannot do with a simple quotation of a single verse as if it would be an article of a law. The theological task is a permanent search to connect the meaning of the biblical text to a concrete situation which lies among Christian communities. We must be aware that the meaning, adequacy and society are dynamic, so that interpretation is a permanent search, "submitted to the dynamic 'question and answer.'"[51] Hermeneutics is thus a key concept for theology. It is good to remember the statement of the Catholic theologian Claude Gefré: "Theology from the beginning to the end is hermeneutic."[52] We will come back to this more extensively.

Hermeneutics can also be purely descriptive as the scientific discipline that analyses what people do when reading a text. Hermeneutics should not be used for relativizing everything, by making the context absolutely normative. Hermeneutics is necessary, precisely in order to distinguish what is true and should be heard and done.

Tillich formulates hermeneutic in a slightly different perspective: not with reference to history and thus past, presence and future, but with regard to transcendence and immanence. According to him, theology moves "between two poles, the eternal truth of its foundation and the temporal situation in which the eternal truth must be received."[53]

These diverse aspects of hermeneutics make even more clear that the education of students to become trained in hermeneutics is a long and requiring way, but theology

---

[51] Lluis Duch. "Hermenêutica" in: J.-J.T. Floristán and C. Acosta (eds.), Dicionário de Conceitos Fundamentais, São Paulo: Paulus, 1999, 328.

[52] C. Geffré, The Risk of Interpretation, New York: Paulist Press, 1987, 6.

[53] Tillich, Systematic Theology, vol. I, 3.

cannot do without it. Theological research at the academic institutions is called to support them both in their education and during their ministry.

The situation of theology is even more complicated. That theology is embedded in the church as teaching about God characterizes the theological task, re-sounding the statements of Emil Brunner that theology itself is a "Church teaching function."[54] It is not merely an academic discipline. Theologians integrate academic reality and the reality of ecclesiastical spirituality and existential motivations, emotions and experiences. They execute the practice of the Old Testament theology *sapiential* tradition, sometimes found in theology as a statement of empiric wisdom. Theology is challenged to think about all aspects of life in the perspective of the relation with God as the church expresses in her faith. Karl Barth has affirmed that theology can only be summed up as an act of faith, and because of this, it is impossible to think of theology far from an intimate relationship with God.[55] In agreement, Helmut Thielicke has affirmed: "He who ceases to be a man of God would automatically be devoted to a false theology."[56]

Being *logos tou theou* (word of God) and having as its center God himself, theology can never be a neutral science. It is necessarily a practical science, circulating around its center, God. It is impossible to know God, without having entered into this orbit by the power of attraction of the same God. Without this previous condition God would be degraded to a simple object of study. Actually, He makes himself the object of theology, even being its generating center. Theology is not only speaking *about*

[54] Brunner, Dogmatics, vol. I, 4.

[55] E. Araya, Introducción a La Teología Sistemática, Santiago: CTEC, 1983, 7.

[56] H. Thielicke, A Little Exercise for Young Theologians, Grand Rapids: Eerdmans, 1999.

God, but before everything, it is speaking *with* God. A theology that is neither *doxologia* nor a *scientia eminens practica* (an eminent practical science) or not even *theologia regenitorum* would no longer deserve to be called theology. It would be a religious science.[57] Hence, theology is speaking about God and not speaking regarding God. In this act of contemplating and making theology, theologians cannot be situated in an objective investigation of the subject, as necessarily happens to other issues of human knowledge. Theology is, above all, a relationship with God and current life. For that, it is impossible to be placed apart from a relationship with God, and to emit general statements that are true, without considering the existential situation and the concrete and historical practice within social contexts, starting from the context of the one who speaks.

Paul Tillich gave a methodological contribution when he affirmed that theologians move in a theological circle. It means that they only state what their base was previously. If they are inside the circle, it would be because they have been making an existential decision. For being within a situation of faith, every theologian is committed and alienated; facing, at the same time, faith and doubt; they are in and out of the theological circle. We can only apply an approach here: a person could be a theologian as far as he would accept the theological circle content as its ultimate concern. "The object of theology is what concerns us ultimately."[58] Nevertheless, the scientific part of theology should not be sacrificed in favor of the existential one, like pietism did and keeps doing, a tendency that was also present in Barth's first theology, to which Harnack reacted

---

[57] Araya, Introducción, 8.
[58] Tillich, Systematic Theology, vol. I, 15.

and warned about the danger of an "uncontrolled enthusiasm" and a "gnostic occultism."[59] Such a theology could face the same mistake as a kind of theology that intends to be only scientific, without any existential relationship with the contextual reality. Faith and science are not mutually exclusive. Faith does not prohibit criticism, but faith challenges it to move forward critically and creatively. The church confesses that the world belongs to Jesus. As his world it is important in all its aspects. And as his world it no longer belongs to itself, but it belongs to Him who has called human beings in his infinite and loving grace (I Cor. 3; 21-23). Christians must look at the world critically (I Cor. 7:29ss) and creatively because it belongs to He who always renews all things.

Christian Theology is about God in Christ

God is known through the revelation as expressed in the history of Israel and, over all, through the manifestation of Jesus Christ. If theology means fundamentally speech about God, Christian theology is the Christian speech about God. To Christian faith, Jesus from Nazareth is the Mediator of this speech. His character, his preaching about God and his kingdom, his mission, death, resurrection and glorification, are the very heart of Christianity and thus of Christian theology.

From the beginning to the end, God in Jesus Christ is the main theme in Christian theology.[60] "What exactly does this mean?" Macquarrie asks.[61] Christian theology has confessed from its very beginning that God encounters us in Jesus Christ, in such a way that we see in Jesus who God actually is. Scriptures have affirmed that God was in Christ

---

[59] Araya, Introducción, 9.
[60] G. Gutierrez, La Verdad os Hará Libres, Lima: IBC-CEP, 1986, 15.
[61] Macquarrie, God-Talk, 11.

reconciling the Word to Him. All Christians say, one way or another, that Jesus is the revelation of God.[62] To speak about God is to speak about Jesus Christ, "the Christian faith stands or succumbs by it."[63] Hans Waldenfels has stated: "If we want to summarize in one phrase the peculiar in actual Christian theology we can formulate it like this: God has revealed himself to us in Jesus Christ."[64] It consists of a fundamental principle that centralizes Christian theology, according to Abraham van de Beek: Christology is the very heart of theology.

Christ, as the incarnate One, is present in concrete life. As Van de Beek has stressed, Christ truly participated in human history. He was present as material and bodily as human beings can be. God is not an abstract idea but is involved in real human history. A focus on Christology keeps theology to the earth.

Christian Theology is about God's Liberating Acts for Human Beings

God's revelation in Christ is not only an epistemological disclosure. It is God's liberating coming into the world. The incarnation doctrine is that the transcendent God has emptied and given himself to human beings in the human's own context. "God, who makes himself man in human beings expresses himself in what is *per excellence*, the human characteristic, love."[65] We must be aware that the message of the living God, who has revealed himself in Jesus Christ,

---

[62] A. van de Beek, Jesus Kyrios: Christology as Heart of Theology, Zoetermeer: Uitgeverij Meinema, 2002, 13.

[63] Van de Beek, *Jesus Kyrios*, 13.

[64] H. Waldenfells, Teología Fundamental Contextual (transl. from Kontextuelle Fundamentaltheologie), Salamanca: Sígueme, 1988, 30.

[65] J. Maraschin, Tendências da Teologia no Brasil, São Paulo: ASTE, 1977, 142.

is not to be proclaimed in a vacuum or historical abstraction. It is a message, and so it should be delivered, transmitted and lived in a social context. For it is given to human beings and regards concrete life situations.

We stated that theology is developed on behalf of the community of faith. In its proper meaning as a speech about God by listening to the message of the gospel it also is developed *within* the community of faith. Theology serves the life of this community, which lives from the liberating coming of God in Christ. Theology has an address. The *locus theologicus* is *the community of faith*. That is its appropriate place, its house.

Theology is reflection within this community and thus, even if practiced as an individual project, it is not individualistic. Mascall says that "a Christian theologian, no less than a Christian mystic or a common Christian, is a member of Christ's body and his theological research is the activity that takes place within this mystic body".[66] The theologian's common life is not any common person's life. It is a human being's life inserted into Christ's body. Theologians reflect on the way the church is the body of Christ and critically reflection thus is how she must teach and act according to Him who gave his body on behalf of other ones. Only the participation in this body enables theologians to speak theologically: in the perspective of Christ who loved the world so much that He gave his life. Theology is a service to the church to live this very identity as the body of Christ. According to Emil Brunner, theology is

---

[66] E. Mascall, Christ, the Christian and the Church: A Study of the Incarnation and its Consequences, London: Longmans, 1963, 228.

thought of as a service of faith. Over all, theology is a function of the Church.[67] "Essentially, dogmatics claims to be an academic study controlled by the Church."[68]

If we speak about the community of faith it is not only the present church. The body of Christ is the community of all places and of all times. Theological reflection, which takes place within the community of faith, inserts itself, for this reason, in the historical movement of this community. It goes back to its theological past tradition and relates itself to other theological and cultural dialogue results. It searches to become in agreement with past and present theologians as members of the same community of Christ. It also critically enters into a discussion with theologians of the past whether their theological designs contribute to the expression of the love of Christ. It quests that certain past convictions and established definitions should be rethought and translated in a liberating way into the actual condition of Church life and into the world. In this case, theologian takes their concern from past thinkers, fusing their thought with the new experiences in which they live.

The true theological attitude cherishes itself from the context, from the history of theological thought, and from theological thoughts in other contexts facing God's coming in Christ. The community of faith is essentially the base where theology operates and it is the environment in which people from different times and situations have sought and seek to reflect about their own experiences related to the world wherein God has come in his liberating revelation in Christ.

---

[67] E. Brunner, Dogmatics: The Christian Doctrine of God, vol. 1, Philadelphia: Westminster, 1950, 3.

[68] Brunner, Dogmatics, vol. 1, 5.

Thus we understand that contemporary theologians reflect on the same contents and seek within the same tradition the spiritual food they and the people they care for need. Beginning theologian, even having a great imagination and creative capacity, need to constantly return to the great classics of church theology and to integrate themselves to the theological community and also to develop the potential of the true theological work. "We expect that a theological system may meet two basic needs: the statement of the truth of the Christian message and the interpretation of this for every new generation."[69]

The Christian community is not an end in itself. It is directed to the world, participating in God's own movement to the world. That shapes the task of theology. The theological task within a given context will be action within the context of the Triune God's mission to the world. Theology is a task of the church that takes place within this mission. Theology reflects on the way this mission can be fulfilled. This reflection, that takes place within the community of faith related to the general community of human beings, has a purpose. The purpose is God's mission to the world, and the theological reflection seeks to serve this purpose. No reflection is just made for itself, no translation for self-complacence, no research for putting together data, but theological reflection inserts itself into a tradition that reveals itself as practical to new contexts in the wide community of human beings. Always faithful to its sources, it proceeds participating in the *missio Dei*, for the mission to which it was called to is not its own, but it is God's trinity mission to the world. The general pastoral constitution of Vatican II, *Gaudium et spes* expresses the relationship which we state here in the following terms:

---

[69] Tillich, Systematic Theology, Vol. I, 3.

To accomplish this mission, the church must permanently discern deeply the signs of the times and interpret them in the light of the gospel, and accommodating them to each generation the church could respond to the perennial human questions about the sense of the present and future life, and about the mutual relationship between them.[70]

Theologians, by being faithful to their theological task, need to be decisive and daring to interpret the current time in the light of the divine revelation registered in the Scriptures.[71] For this, theologians, aware of the gospel and responsible for their task, must be worthy of their time, seeking to give sense to their theological vocation in their mission, as followers of Jesus Christ, contributing to the context with transforming orientations of the gospel as God's wisdom to the world. Regarding this theological task, Karl Barth has affirmed: "Dogmatics is the science in with the Church, in accordance with the state of its knowledge at different times, takes account of the content of its proclamation critically, that is, by the standard of Holy Scripture and under the guidance of its Confessions."[72]

Barth let us by this definition see that theology is a function of the church and it is always at its service. On second thoughts though, he has stated that the most important church task is "to speak about God", and it must be understood within the mission context. Because the theological task is a *human* work entrusted by God's grace, it must be constantly open to scientific criticism. That means that observation of the world to which it is sent and listening to

---

[70] Gaudium et Spes, 4, in http://www.vatican.va/archive/hist_councils/ii_vatican_council/documents/vat-ii_cons_19651207_gaudium-et-spes_en.html. Accessed on December 10, 2009.

[71] This 'reading of the signs of time' is also dear to post second Vatican theologians, especially Liberation theologians.

[72] K. Barth, Dogmatics in Outline, New York: Harper & Row, 1959, 9.

those to whom the church speaks is essential. It must be emphasized that the church is church to the world. Its language is not pronounced for its own good and inner peace. It is an exercise that leads to self-criticism, self-correction in the light of the gospel, in order to accomplish its proclamation to the world efficiently and in an intelligible language as its aim.

When the Christian faith affirms that the church is for the world, it recognizes that the world is also for God. When we emphasize that theology takes place within the context of God's mission to the world, it enlarges the ecclesiastical concept of the mission. It values the world of human beings and things in the measure they are seen within the great divine plan and purpose.

The Scriptures tell about the God who creates the world, acts within human history and makes Himself into flesh to save the world. This is the reason that theology should observe that the great events told in the Scriptures are not ecclesiastical, but inserted socially and historically in the whole community of human beings and ultimately all creatures. God's interest is in the world and not only in the church. God is interested in the church in the measure that it is part of the world and it becomes a vehicle of his mission to this world as a good creation of his total project of salvation.

Theology, when inserted into the context of the world, takes place in a world seen as the object of God's love, in a world drawn by God to his glory, in the midst of rebellious contradictions. It is in this context of God's mission to the world that theological reflection happens, relating the experience of faith to the general community of human beings, and being an instrument of the comprehension of life and our destine before the Creator's purpose. It is only within this context that theologians can be a kind of excavators of big eternal truths, seeking to discover, underneath the earthly structures, those things that provide them with depth and foundation.

Schillebeeckx has written daringly: "Outside the world there is no salvation."[73] When theology emphasizes the *missio Dei*, it is inserted in a pastoral and practical territory, going beyond mere theoretical thinking, inserting itself within life and its implications. To Daniel Migliore, "Christian theology causes us to do more than think. Theology sings, confesses, rejoices, suffers and acts. When faith and theology are exhausted in thinking, they become utterly questionable. This is because of the understanding that illuminates life and practice."[74] As John Calvin has explained, "genuine knowledge of God is inseparable from worship and service."[75] Calvin has stated that the Gospel is not "a doctrine of the tongue, but of life."[76]

In Brazil, theology lives under the challenge that firstly comes from the exploited, from *"the non person"*, from those who are not recognized as people by the social economic order: the poor, the exploited, and the invisible to the global society, those systematically and absurdly deprived of human respect. Gutiérrez argues, "the non-person before everything, not our religious universe, but our economic, social, political, cultural world... the question will not be on speaking about God to an adult world but how to announce God as a Father to a non human world."[77] In other words, the question that theology, which intends to be Living Reformed Theology within the contemporary

---

[73] E. Schillebeeckx, Mensen als verhaal van God, Baarn: Uitgeverij H. Nelissen, 1989, 21.

[74] Migliore, Faith Seeking Understanding, 6.

[75] J. Calvin, Institutes of the Christian Religion, [1536] (transl. by Ford Lewis Battles), Grand Rapids: Eerdmans, 1986, I.2.1.

[76] J. Calvin, True Christian Life, Grand Rapids: Baker Book House, 1952, 17.

[77] Gutiérrez, La verdad os hará libres, 20.

context, must answer is: How can one speak about God in the light of the suffering of the socially excluded by the increasing world globalization? We must affirm that theological teaching, in the real world, must consider the unfair and excluding suffering of millions, seeking the path of wisdom to teach how to live in hope and transforming signs of God's kingdom, as a paradigm to new generations.

If theology is directed to God's movement in the world it is 'work in progress.' Theology must always comprehend itself as provisory in its answers. It consists of responding to new questions that arise from reality.

Theology will never achieve more than partial success in answering them. And, even though it is important to respect and learn from the answers given to these questions in the past, there is no guarantee that theology could simply be built upon past answers. For this reason, theology must always have the freedom and courage to "begin again at the beginning."[78] Since such freedom and courage are gifts of the Spirit of God, prayer is the inseparable companion of the theological enquiry: *Veni Creator Spiritus* (Come, Spirit, Creator).

Theology is Critical Reflection

Theology is *reflection* about the historical and contextual foundations of faith, from the past to the present, walking toward God's future kingdom. Reflection means: "Attentive consideration, serious meditation and thinking, application of knowledge and to ponder observation and commentary." The word *reflection* guides the existential experience of human beings because it says that every theological work has a personal character. Reflection and serious meditation is always something that takes place

---

[78] K. Barth, Evangelical Theology: An Introduction, Grand Rapids: Eerdmans, 2000, 146.

within a person. Without reflection it would not be possible to have any theological progress, for theology is a real and permanent reflection of faith, and the reflection of faith on a real contextual focus.

In addition to that, a contextual theology is impossible without the application of an *interpretative* reflection before the context. Theology must know and consider the context to understand the text. Hence, every theological task is a hermeneutic task. To move on, if seminaries train ministers, we can state that every sermon is a theological task, and thus a hermeneutic task.

True reflection is the one that ends up in understanding. There's no question that the strange ways of speaking about God which proceeded throughout the ages, need hermeneutics that not only please in translating phrases from other times, but also seek to express the reflected content as clearly as it can in connection with the present reality. Theology is the reflection that considers this second moment of its reflection, which is the exposure in and to the present.

"Translating" and "speaking clearly" are two important theological tasks that need to be taken seriously by our seminaries, theological universities, pulpits, and public services in our societies, because one of its theological angles is to become public theology. About this Macquarrie has stated:

Theology expresses the content of its particular faith 'in the clearest and most coherent language available.' Whereas faith is an attitude of the whole man and expresses itself in many fashions, notably in action and in a way of life. Theology, as the very name implies, is discourse, and although it is rooted in the total life of faith, it aims at verbal expression. In intending that language shall be the clearest and most coherent possible, theology shares the character of all intellectual enterprises, for they all aim at intelligibility and consistency. It may be that somewhere along the line, theology will come up against something that eludes or surpasses comprehension, but it can never relinquish its aim of attaining the highest possible degree of intelligibility."[79]

Barth has recognized that speaking about God is a dangerous thing inserted "within a difficult condition, full of temptations, and so, responsible." That is the condition in which the church speaks about God. It is important for the church not only to speak about God, but to make a pause in its speech and exercise some self-criticism. It may put its words under serious reflection and self-examination. We have two points here: the church that speaks about God, and the theologians that examines scientifically this speech and does this examination through the origin of its theology. The church needs permanent evaluation in the light of its mission in Christ and his Spirit.

Barth was correct when he defended that the theological exercise is part of the human effort for knowledge and, for that, requires intellectual faculties, attention and concentration, comprehension and judgment, decisions and good use of the same faculties, and its insertion through the human being in his speech.

Because of these dynamics, while theology participates in God's mission to the world, its essential theological characteristic would never be a definite work, but *in via*, being provisory, pointing to God's kingdom, like the Methodist Uruguaian theologian Julio de Santa Ana emphasized: "Through the world's paths serving God's kingdom."[80] Theology must always walk through a narrow path proceeding from faith to faith (Romans 1:17).

---

[79] J. Macquarrie, Principles of Christian Theology, New York: Charles, Scribner's Sons, 1966, 2-3.

[80] J. de Santa Ana, Pelas Trilhas do Mundo a Caminho do Reino, São Bernardo do Campo: Imprensa Metodista, 1984.

Theology is Systematic

The contextuality of theology does not mean that there is no coherence in it, as if in any situation at random can be said what people like. Theology as speech about the one God has unity as its very base. This is, however, not the unity of a linear argument. It is the unity of the living God who is the Father, the Son and the Spirit. It is a living and thus dynamic unity. The challenge for theologians is to express the coherence of this dynamics.

Coherence is not only required because of the doctrine of God, but also because theology is liberating. Liberating people does not mean that they are left to arbitrariness and their lives and communities are broken up into pieces, but precisely that their lives are healed and they are not excluded from society and thus live in a community that gives structure to their lives.

Coherence implies that theology is systematic. Christian theology, as proceeding from a coherent whole, is basically systematic. Although it is systematic, it does not stand imprisoned in a closed system. When I say that it has a systematic character, I mean that what is said about God the Father affects what we are to say about God's kingdom and history, and this happens to any theological topic. This is the reason why each theological fragment carries within itself a whole system.[81] Expanding on that, the notion of the system is found clearly visible within the traditional church creeds. The Nicene Creed is an illustration of this statement. What is more systematic than this creed, as fundamental to history and ecumenical to theology in its task? Christian theology is systematic by its nature with its historical heritage, and its practice of seeking doctrinal coherence and theoretical comprehension throughout the

---

[81] P. Tillich, Systematic Theology, Vol I, Chicago: University Chicago Press, 1951, 65.

ages. Even when recognizing the fragility and the limitation of the term systematic, it is most suitable to be used for a given rational structure. "Theology is *logos* and *logos* is systematic."[82]

One could disagree, arguing whether there still is a place for a renewed interest about the systematic character of theology. However, according to the practice of faith and theological work, the methodological elaboration of Christian doctrines is of vital importance to the life of the church and to Christian communities. The life of faith does not abstract reason for the Christian is a rational being who seeks to develop his intellect. Faith seeks comprehension and understanding, as Anselm used to say.[83] The Christian community life does not take place apart from basic principles of reason. The Church needs theological thought to rationally judge the many manifestations of its earthly existence. It is needed at personal level and for the community at devotional fields of ecclesiastic structure, and for personal and social ethics as well. Without the theoretical orientation of theology, results would be disorientation and an alienating fantasy causing highly destructive practices and also prejudice to Christian communities. Systematic theology seeks faithful comprehension (*intellectus fidei*) in any language and culture, and intellectual faith (*fides intellectus*) that acts within the history of the world.

'Systematic' is a word that comes from the Greek term *sustema* and it means a composition of different parts. It is possible to define systematic as a set of coordinated parts; coherent propositions; coordinated principles that form a rational whole and, the body of the doctrine. In the sense

---

[82] J. Maraschin, Sillabus in Teologia Sistemática, 1-9.

[83] M. OGILVIE, Faith Seeking Understanding, Milwaukee: Marquette University Press, 2001, 136.

of being coherent, every theology, in fact, is somehow systematic. To be systematic means to seek coherence and connection between the parts of the doctrine. For everything, it states, comes from a fundamental whole, even when this whole is not expressed methodologically.

Although we utilize the term systematic to qualify theology, we do not want to say that it does not have its own inconveniences as well. Every system is necessarily limited by the kind of problems it intends to deal with. Systems seem to be incapable of embracing every face of the truth. They cannot reach the totality of what is real. All of these limits are part of the nature of the theological work and it would also depend on the theologian's intellectual ability, because theologians display their material according to their own preferences.

We no longer live in the Middle Ages when the greatest aim was to make *Summae Theologiae*. *Summa* represents the intention of saying everything about everything. It was a noble effort that fit perfectly in the mind of that time. It is necessary to give the deserved credit to one of the greatest thinkers of church history, Thomas Aquinas, who has theologized this way. Nowadays nobody intends to elaborate a *Summa* about any topic, even less about theology. We are happy about having a theology being aware of its fundamental limitations and despite its increasing limits before the amplitude of knowledge that needs constant reformulation, creativeness, and autonomous reinterpretation. Pedro Meno says: "In that sense, the teacher's central and irreplaceable paper is not to give a class, but to make the student learn, with the supposition that the teacher is much more a specialist of learning than of teaching. Those who do not know how to learn do not know how to make the student to learn."[84]

---

[84] Pedro Demo, Metodologia do Conhecimento Científico. São Paulo: Atlas, 2000, 81.

The term *systematic theology* is normally used for a specific theological discipline in distinction to other ones, such as church history or biblical studies. In this sense it is also used within the reformed seminaries in my home country Brazil. Until not long ago "dogmatic" was used to define this discipline. For more than half a century and still today, the main reference text for Systematic Theology, to seminaries and Presbyterians, especially within the Independent Presbyterian Church, is one of the works of its founder, Alfredo Borges Teixeira, which in 1903 received the name *Evangelical Dogmatic*.[85] The word dogmatic, though, has fallen into discredit recently, for having the inconvenience of seeming to end up as the theological reflection in *dogmas* proclaimed by ecclesiastical authorities, however not always put into practice.[86]

After a severe crisis about how to name theology, "Systematic Theology" has prevailed in the *curriculum* of Brazilian seminaries, especially among the Reformed ones or, at least, among those that have had a Reformed origin or influence. It is the central part of the teaching of these theological schools.

When I say that theology should be systematic I do not refer to a specific discipline only. I mean that theology *as a whole* should be systematic. There is coherence in any field of theology and all the fields must be a coherent unity, as they all refer to the one God in his liberating acting and they all are about the whole of life of human beings. Life in freedom that is healed from exclusion and sin cannot be split up into pieces that are unrelated one to another, just like the members of the community cannot live unrelated next to each other. There is always an inner coherent *sustema*, a unity of people and subjects that are

---

[85] A. B. Teixeira, Dogmática Evangélica, São Paulo: Pendão Real, 1958.

[86] K. Barth has had no problem with this term. He used it in the title of the greatest theological work of the twentieth, Church Dogmatics.

brought together. Theology as discourse about the God who heals human lives and relations cannot be split up and thus is always systematic. By consequence the disciplines both in training and in research cannot develop separately.

The integration of theology as a coherent whole is also applicable to the relation of theory and praxis. This relation is emphasized by Latin American theology, especially by Clodovis Boff.[87] The distinction was present in the ecumenical movement of the World Council of Churches, from their very origins, in its separate organization of *Faith and Order* and *Life and Work*.[88] Other theologians make a similar distinction between reproductive and productive: the first directed to the content of the tradition, the latter to praxis and transformation. We agree with Eugenio Araya,[89] from the Comunidad Teológica Evangélica de Chile who, in his syllabus of systematic theology, emphasizes that theology will be productive and reproductive.

Though both are aspects of theology, the distinction easily leads to separate discourses and even to conflicts in seminaries and theological faculties, even entering into debates in books and newspapers throughout generations. In many seminaries and churches, a perennial fight has prevailed among the productive and reproductive functions of theology, theory and practice. In the twentieth century, a lot of energy was spent in this kind of debates,

---

[87] C. Boff, Teologia e Prática: teologia do político e suas mediações,Petrópolis: Vozes, 1978.

[88] W. A. Visser't Hooft, The Gospel for all Realms of Life, Geneva: WCC, 1975; Memoirs, London: SCM Press, 1973; Leon Howell, Fé en Acción, Geneve: CMI. 1982; M. Kinnamon and B. Cope, The Ecumenical Movement: An Anthology of Key Texts and Voices, Geneve: WCC, 1997; A. G. K. Bell, The Stockholm Conference 1925, London: Oxford University Press, 1926; Ans J. Van der Bent, Commitment to God's World: A Concise Critical Survey of Ecumenical Social Thought, Geneva: WCC, 1995; Ans Jan der Bent, Historical Dictionary of Ecumenical Christianity, Metuchen, N.J. & London: The Scarecrow Press, 1994.

[89] E. Araya, Introducción a la Teología Sistemática, Santiago: CTEC, 1983.

not directed to arrive to a consensus, but to combat the appearance of new proposals in theology, such as what happened to contextual theologies. It is especially in systematic theology where these internal tensions became problematic conflicts.

On one hand, there is the fear of the new, the fear of producing; on the other hand the fatigue of a theology that just reproduces concepts from other centuries and places, and answers questions from other contexts within strange categories. The new, in some places, is heard with suspicion, and in others, the old is seen with disdain. This can be accompanied by an aversion of rationality. There is also a crescent interest for practical theology in Latin American seminaries, which is not embedded in the whole of theology as a systematic unity, but is conceived as an alternative to study of the tradition and often even is opposed to it.

Also the ecumenical movement went through this conflict between doctrine and practice in the twentieth Century. In the Universal Conference on *Life and Work* in Stockholm in 1925, an intrinsic slogan marked the history of the ecumenical movement: "Doctrine divides and Service unites."[90] This dichotomy presented by Nathan Söderblom[91] has still prevailed in the common sense feeling of many church members in relation to theology. It has made the teaching of systematic theology even more difficult. Reducing the possibility of theology to be unilateral to one of its functions, whether practical or scientific, productive or reproductive, has reached a critical level. In the next chapter, when we think of theology as wisdom, we

---

[90] S. B. Dias, Doctrine Divides, Service Unites – The Universal Christian Conference on Life and Work, Stockholm, 1925. Masters thesis. Geneva: Unigeve, 2001.

[91] N. Söderblom was Archbishop of Uppsala, and a churchman at The Universal Christian Conference on Life and Work, Stockholm 1925.

come back to a different form of facing the subject methodologically, putting into focus the including character of the task and possibilities of theology, integrating it to all fields of human life. To think of theology as wisdom takes us to a point where all theological functions should be inter-dependent and necessary amongst themselves, while a reductionist inclination would harm the creative totality of the theological labor. Theology is to be developed as memory, reason, creativity and praxis. It needs to be at the same time, reproductive, rational, productive and pastoral.

The Functions of Theology

Only after we have stated that theology is a whole, we can distinguish functions of the theological task that flow from the aspects of the one hermeneutic way that theology goes. These are aspects, indeed, and therefore the functions can never be separated but must serve and support each other mutually.

We distinguish four functions on which we will focus more specifically: the anamnesis function as expression of the tradition wherein theology moves on; the rational - scientific function as expression of the coherence of the one theology in the one reality of life; the hermeneutic function as expression of the dynamics of history in which theology continuously moves into new contexts either in place or in time; the praxis function as expression of theology as a critical tool for transformation and peace.

a. The Anamnesis Function

The memory of faith is[92] essential to the theological enterprise. Almost all Christian thinkers have taken their immediate predecessors into account, whose works they have tried to deepen and improve. And all of them have reported themselves at least to one or other predecessor, to whom they felt indebted.[93] In spite of every evolution that theology has been facing, dialoging with several cultures and philosophies, the decisive criterion in order to have a theological reflection of quality, was always the revelation of God's mystery in the Scriptures and the great confessions of the councils. Theology should be understood as *anamnesis fidei*. In a more radical sense, we could say that a theology that does not open up for the memory of the historical faith through the Scriptures is not a Christian theology.

The Christian fathers have practiced theology with a clear concern of having the Scriptures as the constant source of their theology. This was the reason why the Reformers have insisted on coming back to the Scriptures and to the tradition of the Church Fathers, taking the Confessions seriously as an indispensable activity to build a clear theological position. The Scriptures and the confessions of the great Ecumenical Councils were the constant sources for the sixteenth century Reformers. Nothing characterizes the Reformers as much, regarding their theological method, as the Biblical concern of taking the

---

[92] For Johann Baptist Metz, the gospel is nothing other than the "dangerous memory" of the death and resurrection of Jesus Christ which has "interrupted" history, revealing the patterns of violence and injustice at work in the systems of our world and inspiring solidarity with the victims through the memory of their suffering toward a future of hope. Johann Baptist Metz, Faith in History and Society: Toward a Fundamental Practical Theology (New York: Seabury, 1980, 115.

[93] P. Boehner and E. Gilson, História da Filosofia Cristã, Petrópolis: Vozes, 2003, 11.

Scriptures as the *"norma normans"* of their theology in connection with the memory of faith. The primacy of the Scriptures is, for Reformed theology, the warranty of a correct theological method, coming as a formal and vital principle for theological labor. They have rediscovered that the theme and the content of theology are the revelation of God. That is not something isolated from present life, but the source for understanding it, as Calvin says: "It is evident that man never attains to a true self-knowledge until he has previously contemplated the face of God, and come down after such contemplation to look into himself."[94]

To speak about the historical memory of theology has been, from its very beginnings, not to speak about any tradition, but about the Apostolic Tradition. The ecumenical movement in the twentieth century has been pointing to the distinction between *Tradition* and *traditions*.[95] How differently formulated in the traditions of churches and denominations, in order to be Christian they must be rooted in the one Apostolic Tradition. Historical memory is the tradition through which the church transmits, from the Apostles, the mysteries of divine Revelation and the faith of the church throughout the ages.

The Reformed tradition has grown within history in search of the fullness of faith by stressing specific elements that they considered as important, such as the divine election and the work of the Holy Spirit who renews and strengthens the church, looking forward to the Kingdom of God. Faithful to the Scriptures and to the apostles' tradition, theology contributes to the dynamism through which the same Spirit of God always creates the church again in new situations. Only this way theology will serve

---

[94] Calvin, Institutes I, 1, 2.

[95] Kinnamon and Cope, The Ecumenical Movement. An Anthology, 139.

the church to become doxology and communion of life in the world.

It is within the Church and with its ecclesiastical and existential task that theology accomplishes its reproductive function in relation to its productive function. In other words, it coordinates the Biblical message and its interpretation in the past in an appropriate way to our era. That reproductive function was less emphasized by liberal and by liberation theologies. On the other hand, it is observed that most of the time it was excessively accentuated by fundamentalist and conservative theologies. Regarding theology teaching in my home country Brazil, many traditional Reformed seminaries have privileged the reproductive function of theology in detriment of the productive function. The result has been a fossilization of theology.

Reaffirming this point, it is opportune to stress both the productive and reproductive functions of theology. They do not exclude each other, but are mutually necessary, because theology is primarily the conscience of the liberation accomplished by Jesus Christ, which must update itself to each new generation and each new context. Likewise, theology loses its status when limiting its task to a productive and creative function. It should always keep itself alive, by speaking about the memory of liberation accomplished in the redemption as a memory of hope.

The memory of faith is an indispensable prerequisite for a new interpretation. Theology should not fight for alternatives: on the one hand the conservative, and on the other hand, the progressive one. But in a creative dialogue, it must continue to enrich itself dynamically. Therefore, it is important to notice that theology should neither hide nor deny the wealth of Christian theological memory, alleging prejudices or suspicion of scientificity. But it must explore humbly and courageously every possible subject about the history of Christian thought in a creative way.

Finally, it should be emphasized that the reproductive function of theology points to the Scriptures and to a living tradition of faith, keeping theology from being imprisoned by any new ideology.

This is one of the great challenges for the theological task: to cultivate the living memory of the church. In a confused culture and in a time of lack of life and liberation, it claims to rediscover hope as John Calvin affirmed: history is the schoolmistress of life.[96]

b. The Rational-Scientific Function

The rational or scientific function has always been a characterization of Christian theology, especially in a more accentuated way since the Enlightenment. Theology needs to appeal unavoidably to the availability of instruments that the world, with its knowledge and culture, gives to the theologian. By doing so theology will become an effective service to the world.[97]

This was the procedure of all great theologians in the history of the Church; all of them have made, somehow, use of conceptual and linguistic resources of their time to elaborate their theology. From the origin to current days no theology has been elaborated without a real contact with the context of each era. And it is in that dialogic contact with the reality that the rational character of theology can be seen, trying to make itself as close as possible to the scientific and philosophical rationality of that time. Theology cannot isolate itself from the cultural world without

---

[96] T. J. Gorringe, Karl Barth Against Hegemony, Oxford: Oxford University Press, 1999, 87.

[97] H. Rito, Introdução à Teologia, Petrópolis: Vozes, 1998, 99.

taking the risk of being a sterile theology, which would not produce fruits for the evangelization of the world.[98]

This dialogue with the reality of the surrounding culture can be done in different ways, which are sometimes labeled as inclusive and exclusive. The inclusive theology is opened up for human culture, looking for an inclusion not only in its language, but also in its theological content. The model of an exclusivist theology works within the limits of the sources given by faith and searches the confrontation with culture. From Justin the Martyr and Tertullian to the most recent theologians these approaches can be observed. Justin tried to interpret the culture in the perspective in its best representatives, calling Socrates a Christian as participant of the Word,[99] because he was passionate in search for truth and willing to give his life for it.[100] Tertullian confronted his context with his famous saying:

> *What then hath Athens in common with Jerusalem? What hath the Academy in common with the Church? What have heretics in common with Christians? Our principles are from the 'Porch' of Solomon, who himself handed down that the Lord must be sought in simplicity of heart. Away with those who bring forward a Stoic or Platonic or dialectic Christianity. We have no need of speculative inquiry after we have known Christ Jesus; nor of search for the Truth after we have received the Gospel. When we become believers, we have no desire to*

---

[98] Rito, Introdução, 100.

[99] Justin the Martyr, Apology I, 46, translated by Marcus Dods and George Reith, Ante-Nicene Fathers, Vol. 1, edited by Alexander Roberts, James Donaldson, and A. Cleveland Coxe, Buffalo, NY: Christian Literature Publishing Co., 1885.

[100] Justin the Martyr, Apology II, 10, translated by Marcus Dods and George Reith, Ante-Nicene Fathers, Vol. 1, edited by Alexander Roberts, James Donaldson, and A. Cleveland Coxe, Buffalo, NY: Christian Literature Publishing Co., 1885.

believe anything besides; for the first article of our belief is that there is nothing besides which we ought to believe.[101]

The rational function of theology along with the history of Christian thought can be understood under the optics of those two approaches. Nevertheless both are in relation with the rationality of their culture. However, a clear methodological understanding of these two models much facilitates the student's comprehension of the theological task and its functions in a didactic way.

Theology, as rational knowledge, should be in dialogue with culture and other human knowledge. That is where it should look for understanding and should want to contribute to the participation of the human being into the Kingdom of God, struggling in a liberating way for a fairer and more human world. And while it looks for that rational dialogue with human sciences, theology shows the recognition of its own limits. A self-sufficient theology would never be in dialogue with other sciences, but it would remain superb, boasting its own conquests. In time, it would become obsolete and die, condemned by its own temporary reality.

Theology, in its rational and scientific function, should be conscious that it will never be able to accomplish its task except inside its temporary and limited history. The theologian lives and accomplishes the theological labor within a set time although it may have an eternal sense. Theology represents a constant effort of the church in seeking to stay in contact with the reality of human beings, their problems, their doubts and their projects. It constitutes its continuous exchange among faith and reason, world and God, profane and sacred.[102] Under the reality of

---

[101] Tertullian, On the Testimony of the Soul and on the 'Prescription' of Heretics, translated into English by T. Herbert Bindley, London: SPCK, 1914, 45-46.

[102] R. Latourelle, Théologie Science du Salut, Paris: Cerf, 1968, 18.

the Word of God, it seeks to apprehend the insertion point in the world of each generation. The Brazilian theologian Honório Rito states clearly the place of reason in the theological task:

> *If theology is convinced that for Christians Revelation and faith means a light that is not just the light of reason but also the light of faith that enriches the reason, it has never the right to ignore the value of the scientific rationality for man's own salvation that is always historical and supra-historical, temporal and supra temporal, material and spiritual. A theology that is concerned in saving man as a whole could never neglect the rationality of human sciences on behalf of the supra-rationality of faith.[103]*

According to Paul Tillich systematic theology possesses a triple rationality:[104]

a. Semantic rationality. It refers to the task of clarifying concepts that have more than one sense. "There are words used as much in a philosophical and scientific language as in the popular use."

b. Logical rationality. "This principle refers above everything to the structures that determine every significant speech and that are formulated in logic discipline. Theology depends as much as any other science on formal logic."

c. Methodological rationality. It means that theology follows a method, a defined way of deducing and establishing its propositions. The character of that method depends on many non-rational factors. However, once established, we should follow it in a rational and coherent way. Hence, it means that theology has to follow a method because it is systematic.

---

[103] Rito, Introdução, 101-102.
[104] Tillich, Systematic Theology, Vol. I, 52-57.

c. The Hermeneutic Function

Hermeneutics has to do with the transposition of the Biblical message from its original context to the historical context of the modern interpreter. Without the hermeneutical function, theology would not be more than repetition of *formulae* built up in the past, incomprehensible to each later generation in history. It is the aim of theological interpretation that the text written in the past may have an impact on the present. It is for that reason that the strictly historical-critical approach has entered into bankruptcy, because it did not get, in its scriptural interpretation, the past to acquire life and illuminate the present.

Theology in its hermeneutic function exercises a critical approach in relation to the reductionism used by other approaches, which do not make justice either to the original or to current historical context, and their mutual correlation. In the first we see a premature adaptation to the contemporary needs, and in the other an attempt to fix in the past. But, the paradigm shift in modern hermeneutics consisted of the awareness that context plays a fundamental role in interpretation and that 'understanding' is not reproductive, but a new production of meaning. The new context makes the text 'grow' and enables the reader to discover meanings not even seen by its original author.

The message of the church needs to be as much biblical as contemporary. In the contextual hermeneutical approach both contexts are bound together. In other words, it is seeking in the current context what it has to do with the original context. Aware that the Biblical message can only be understood correctly in the light of its original context, the goal is to connect the horizon of the contemporary historical situation in a "fusion of horizons"[105] with

---

[105] H. G. Gadamer, Truth and Method, London: Sheed and Ward, 1979, 273.

the horizon of the text, so that the message proclaimed in the contemporary situation may have a dynamic equivalent to the message proclaimed in the original context.

Before modernity, it was thought that truth was fixed. It was a non-historical form of thinking, searching in a simplistic way to come to conclusions. Because of this, the conclusions were abstract, without any contact with historical reality. The doctrines were preached in the churches, but not explicitly elaborated in the context.[106]

The result of a hermeneutic that just takes into account only those dogmas that have been established in the past is only teaching reproductive theology, and never productive or creative ones. The discovery of the historical nature, the re-evaluation of cultures, the conscience of the ethnicity of people, the new economic and social conflicts have provoked the need of a new inclusive and contextualized hermeneutic. The Brazilian theologian João Batista Libânio states the hermeneutical issue thus:

> *The discovery of the value of cultures and their conditioning (positive and/or negative) to faith interpretation gives an enormous actualization to the hermeneutical task. Current Christianity results from several cultural processes and syncretism. Born in the midst of the oriental Mediterranean Semitic culture, it expands to the Occident. It transposes the Jewish horizon to the Hellenic one. Already in its beginning, it accomplishes multiple reinterpretations, as seen in the writings of the Alexandrian, Antioch and Cappadocia Schools. In the Middle Ages, it assimilated and promoted the new autochthonous cultures and the positive elements of the cultural pluralism of modern society, the reinterpretation of the faith data takes place and it is processed in new situations and contexts. It doesn't resign the nucleus of Christianity, to make it palatable and ready 'for the consumption' in the immense religious supermarket and pseudo mystic movements. On the contrary,*

---

[106] J. B. Libânio and A. Murad, Introdução à Teologia, São Paulo: Loyola, 1998, 336.

*it seeks faithfulness to the Gospel, maintaining its character
of Good News 'comprehensible, significant and interposing.'[107]*

As important as the relationship between theology and
tradition, is its relationship with real situations, as theology does not only intend to repeat the Biblical *kerygma,* or
just to make literary exegesis or to describe Church history, but it must reformulate all the aspects of this tradition process under the optics of the contextual situation.
The theological task is not being only a coordinator of tradition, but reformulating it permanently, because theology speaks about the living and active God in human
history.

Because hermeneutics speaks about and analyses what
happens between the old text and the current context,
both contexts are relevant and thus we can also argue the
other way around: from the present to the past. Latin-
American theology keeps to the already almost classic axiom: "The social place stipulates the hermeneutic place."[108]
This social hermeneutics of the present community, however, cannot lose its filial relationship with the memory of
faith, valuing the living spiritual and intellectual patri-
mony accumulated through the generations, while, at the
same time, hearing new voices and new understandings of
faith as it moves forward. Theologians throughout history
have, even if they thought they were proclaiming eternal
truth, practiced usually this kind of hermeneutics. Challenged by their own situation they interpreted Scripture
from their own perspective.

Both perspectives - from the past to the present context and from the present to the past context - are basic
for living critical theology. The progress of the Gospel in

[107] Libânio and Murad, Introdução, 337.
[108] Libânio and A. Murad, Introdução, 338.

time and space within Church history and its mission, demands that theology must reformulate the Christian truth contained in the old expressions, producing current interpretation. Theology not only orders the Biblical statements, as if they were small component stones of a mosaic, but it also developed a history of interpretation, accomplishing the hermeneutical function of theology.

This task has discernment as its prerequisite, purifying thoughts in the confrontation of the Christian faith and contextual ideologies. The testimony of theology consists of being a responsible and committed witness to the content expressed in the revelation of God's wisdom in Jesus Christ, which should be undertaken each time. Systematic theology, therefore, when deepened through God's Word, should be willing to acquire new experiences, or better, to facilitate a language that meets the reality of human beings wherever they exercise the faith.

Paul Tillich corrects Schleiermacher and states that "systematic theology is not a historical discipline, but is a constructive task. It does not tell what people thought to be the Christian message in the past or think it is in the presence. It tries to give us an interpretation of the Christian message that is relevant to the present situation."[109] For Tillich, systematic theology is a theology that answers the implicit situational questions with the force of the eternal message and with the means that the situation provides.[110] Consequently, Tillich applies the correlation method that relates the answers of the Christian message to questions of modern thought in both directions.[111] In addition, the adaptation of this correlation would enlarge, as

---

[109] Tillich, Systematic Theology, 52.

[110] Tillich, Systematic Theology, Vol. I, 14.

[111] "The method of correlation explains the contents of the Christian faith through existential questions and theological answers in mutual interdependence." Tillich, Systematic Theology, Vol. I, 68.

much as possible, the contact areas with contemporary thought. As legitimate *theologia viatorum*, it is always moving forward and seeking new contexts. Relating itself to a single effective philosophy would not satisfy it, rather it would seek a relationship with other human sciences, the natural sciences and also with intellectual life in general, such as poetry and contemporary literature. Of course, theology faces the danger of ignoring its limits when looking for such wide relationships in its productive function. The danger is falling into a faith of idealization, succumbing to its sources. The only way out is to remember its reproductive function, while exercising its productive function. During this passage, it should be remembered that the Gospel will always be a scandal to the world — *in the world,* but not *of the world.*

On the other hand, it would be a mistake to stamp theology as ideology only because it works with certain philosophical premises. Such premises are inevitable for any theology. Theologians, as any other Christian, possess preconceived ideas, derived from the sum of lived experiences that act as a selective knowledge filter.[112] Just in case a certain philosophy became the definitive answer to theology and theology were only a question, then one could speak about an idealized theology. The question-answer relationship between theology and philosophy is not interchangeable.

Correlation signifies matching the answers to the questions. Thus the productive function of theology is necessary to complete the reproductive function. Without this it would turn itself into a simple traditionalism, and without the existence of the reproductive function the productive function would be reduced to a simple modernism. Some evangelization methods and mission models have

---

[112] Libânio and Murad, Introdução, 337.

been made without taking into account the hermeneutical task. They have been generating a simplistic message for evangelism, and because of this, the Word of God ends up becoming *logos asarkos* (a word not made flesh), resulting in a fragile communication of the Gospel.

The Church should be a hermeneutical community and theology must serve her with regard to this. The goal of the theological task is to put each aspect of life and each aspect of the Church's mission under the Lord Jesus Christ's sovereignty in a concrete situation. By doing so theologians will be faithful to the vital traditions of the New Testament Church and to the sixteenth century Reformers.

In facing the challenge of relating the content of the faith to the historical contexts, Stephen Bevans, in *Models of Contextual Theology*, has emphasized five models that can be applied to the theological task. Bevan's clarity in presenting the models makes it indispensable to understand them in the context of teaching theology on the way to theology as wisdom. For this reason, a summary of their postulates is given:

The translation model. According to Bevans, the translation model departs from the assumption that the message of the Gospel is unchangeable and that culture and social patterns of change constitute "vehicles for this essential, unchanging deposit of truth."[113] The task of theology in this model is a translation of meanings from the Christian learning system into different contexts. In this model, we regard the essential message of Christianity as supra-cultural, that is, the message content is 'pure Gospel.'[114]

---

[113] S. Bevans, Models of Contextual Theology, New York: Orbis Books, 2002, 31.

[114] S. Bergmann, God in Context: A Survey of Contextual Theology, Aldershot, Hampshire: Ashgate Publishing, 2003, 88.

Bergmann states about this model that in spite of its aiming at interpreting the meeting between the Gospel and culture, it gives culture an inferior significance and raises the Gospel to be the norm of culture.[115]

The anthropological model. In the anthropological model, the human experience is placed at the center. The theologian makes use of social and cultural anthropological methods. The interpretation of life occurs in close connection with the symbolic conceptualization of the world view and religion of an ethnic group.[116]

In the anthropological model, according to Bevans, humankind is viewed as the place of the revelation and a source of theology.[117] Revelation occurs in the culture. A theologian working anthropologically treats the conditions of human life, questions and interests very seriously. Bevans criticizes this model for lack of critical thinking and for its tendency to stoop to 'cultural romanticism.'[118] He further asks if it is possible to find a situation where the origins of the Gospel depart from a particular culture.

Bergmann is more positive about this model: "The formation concept of inter-culture and contextualization grammatically constitute verb constructions. There is a deeper sense of expressing the contextual cause of theology, not through nouns or adjectives, but through verb constructions and prepositions. God acculturates Himself in a people's world: the Son and the Holy Spirit contextualize themselves and become flesh dwelling in different created beings in unique situations for the sake of the world. To contextual theology, God is God in function."[119]

---

[115] Bergmann, God in Context, 88.
[116] Bergmann, God in Context, 89.
[117] Bevans, Models, 26.
[118] Bevans, Models, 53.
[119] Bergmann, God in Context, 91.

The praxis model. The praxis model is central in western social theology. Within theology, this notion has been developed above all in Latin American liberation theology and in European political theology. Bevans emphasizes the theology of liberation as a meritorious interpretation of the revelation and he is of the view that this is in accordance with the approach of classical theology.[120]

About this model Bergmann remarks: "The propagation of Bible reading, the doctrine of salvation and the importance of the structure of the liberation theme, as well as the discussion on justice, the debates on and the relevance of theology might indicate this."[121]

The synthetic model. Bevans mentions a fourth model of contextual theology 'the synthetic model.' This model aims at balancing the insights of the past three models and trying to find a middle course. Bevans localizes the translation model on the side of the Gospel and the anthropological and praxis model on the side of culture. The synthetic model, logically, ends up midway between the two poles.[122]

We, too, plea for the need of a paradigm to embrace the totality of the values of these models of contextualization, if this implies on the one hand that they are not optional, so that one could choose one and neglect the other ones, and on the other hand that the synthesis is not a grey "in between" but a real synthesis of different aspects. Therefore I prefer to speak about *aspects* of the hermeneutical process to the concept of *models*, because the latter is easily seen as an independent approach.

Bevans distinguishes a fifth type: the transcendental model. This model is shaped within the frame of transcendental philosophy dating back to Immanuel Kant which,

---

[120] Bevans, Models, 92.
[121] Bergmann, God in Context, 92.
[122] Bevans, Models, 86.

since then, has constituted a leading theory for the view of knowledge in the west.

This model has four characteristics. Firstly, contextual theology, which uses this model is less interested in the question of how to shape a particular theology but is interested in the activity of producing theology. Secondly, transcendental theology is neither exclusively private nor subjective. A third characteristic concerns the revelation. Revelation in this model is not something which takes place 'out there', but it takes place in the subjective experience which a human being makes out of the world around him. Thereby theology only becomes possible for the person who converts and believes. A fourth trait in this model is the assumption that human reason in spite of all culturally and historically conditioned differences functions in a similar way with all issues at all times and in all places.

Actually this model has little to do with hermeneutics and contextualization because it is only interested in the knowing subject and neither in history as reality nor in the whole process of tradition. Actually it ends up the community of believers in time and space, because time and space are only categories of the human mind. A Christian hermeneutics that is interested in the communication of the members of the community cannot work with this model.

d. The Praxis Function

Theology is the ecclesiastical praxis theory. This function sends us to the ecclesiastical and pastoral realities of theology. Theological teaching is not viable without a perspective on praxis. Without action there is no Church, as there is no viable praxis without theological reflection.[123] The *doctrinal* is not opposed to *practical*, but both are essential and necessary.[124] Casiano Floristán[125] affirms that, "precisely for having separated the doctrinal function so much, we have been taken to a doctrinal function without pastoral nerves and to a pastoral action without theological work."[126] This interrelationship is not present in all theology, and it is very important to notice this. Floristán says:

> *Of course not everything that is given a theological stamp [of approval] is indeed theology. By introducing excessive or mistaken reason and philosophy, certain theologies have actually become religious metaphysics... the formulation of the message as doctrine can be so abstract that it serves no pastoral action.*[127]

There is no possibility of thinking *Faith and Order* without *Life and Work*. In the practical function of theology, Christians acquire consciousness of what they have been doing and what they need to do. In this function, affirms H. Denis, theology "accomplishes the maturation of the pastoral work at the Church."[128] With regard to this there is a statement of the Catholic theologian José Comblin that is very disturbing for Reformed theologians: "The Reformation has wanted to purify the Church from the sins of complicity with politics and all its corruption. It has rejected a Church of dirty hands, but it has made a Church

---

[123] Dias, Doctrine Divides, 80.

[124] C. Floristán, Teología Práctica: Teoria y Praxis de la Acción Pastoral, Salamanca: Sigueme, 1998, 149.

[125] Theologian from Spain (born 1926), priest in 1956 and doctor at the University of Tübingen (1959), was devoted to the teaching in the University of Salamanca especially in pastoral theology.

[126] Floristán, Teología Práctica, 149.

[127] Floristán, Teología Práctica, 149.

[128] Floristán, Teología Práctica, 150

without hands."[129] He accuses the Reformers of having preached an individualistic gospel and of suppressing solidarity among sinners and just people. "Unfortunately, Protestants have been preaching a message to individuals and not to people."[130] This voice that comes from a liberation theologian, rightly demands that systematic theology should commit itself in order to set theology free from an only speculative function, towards a Living Reformed Theology, involved in the life within the church and in the life of the church in the world.

Praxis (Greek for "acting" and "executing") has become a theological methodology in liberation theology Latin America, as a new theology paradigm. It develops a hermeneutic which takes the social context as its starting point. The situation wherein they live has taken their full attention indeed.

A theology without taking into account this reality is like the priest in the parable of the Good Samaritan. His theology cannot be a good theology, because it lacks the praxis of compassion. That liberations theologians are deeply touched by the social reality cannot be viewed as a mistake. It would only be a mistake if it would not be related to the source wherefrom the church lives. Theology should always take the tradition of the church serious, precisely because this functions as a critical instance to present reality. That is exactly what the best liberation theologians do. Facing classical theological tasks, Gustavo Gutiérrez has affirmed that they have a permanent value, in spite of all deformations that they have been suffering through the centuries. Gutiérrez proposes a critical reflection of the historical praxis under the light of the Word, not substituting the other functions of theology, but on the

---

[129] J. Comblin, O Tempo da Ação: O Espírito e a História, Petrópolis: Vozes, 1982, 176.

[130] Comblin, O Tempo da Ação, 177.

contrary, needing them. However he redefines the other functions, motivating them to have "the historical praxis more explicitly as a starting point and as a context."[131]

Theology claims that the Church is a sign of the Kingdom of God and the flag of this Kingdom that is to come. That implicates an ethical responsibility before God and before human society. The world should hear, but it should also see what is being proclaimed. Churches cannot change themselves into clubs of *self-satisfaction*, proclaimers of a *cheap grace*, as Dietrich Bonhoeffer has stated, and limit themselves to announcing a 'gospel' which gives everything without demanding anything.

A religion without responsibility is not restricted to systematic theologians. Jürgen Moltmann has pointed to a type of European Churches that preaches as if it was a supermarket, where low prices and all kinds of goods to be tasted are offered. Moltmann has accused the religious markets where people, instead of changing their lives, change their congregations, seeking the taste they like the most. In the competition of the religious market - 'the winner, as in any other market, is the one who offers to buyers the cheapest and most attractive price.'[132]

Unhappily, in Southern countries this reality is also visible and growing. This demands a profound answer from contemporary theological education as well as from ecclesiastical pulpits. It means that theological teaching should not compromise the commitment established by God's revelation in the Scriptures. In this situation the anamnesis function is highly relevant for the praxis function. Theology, according to a Reformed perspective, should constantly criticize contextualism - the danger of putting the needs as absolute preaching sources, turning theology

---

[131] Núñez, Teologia de la Liberación, 130-133.

[132] J. Moltmann, The Power of the Powerless, San Francisco: Harper & Row, 1983, 160-161.

into a function of human desires. There is a criterion for practice, which must be based on God's purpose revealed in Jesus Christ. The context is not the criteria of theology. It is necessary to touch life where it acts, but according to the revelation of God.

The conviction that the Gospel has two wings: revelation and ethics, theory and practice, life and action, spirituality and history, theology and culture, faith and rights, *eruditio et pietas* grows more and more in the conscience of Latin American theological education. The great danger of the theological task has been to fall into reductionism, privileging one function to the detriment of other essential ones. Eugenio Araya stresses the importance to keep them together:

> *Doesn't theology betray its rational function when it falls into sensationalism and marketing, when it doesn't use arguments, but only agitation, when it judges without a basis, when it thinks of alternatives as if they were white or black, and in already made sentences; when it delights itself with paradoxes and in arguing forms only seeking to cause surprising effects, when it parts from false previous judgments - damages and not from previous judgment of its content; when no longer it is interested in increasing its knowledge, but it simply recites its boasting?[133]*

On the other hand, doesn't theology forget its existential function when it falls in the displeased neutral style, in the dogmatism of the method, in a superstitious science and in rationalism, when it is made dependent on a scientific concept?[134]

Doesn't it forget its summons to an existential relationship with God in its function of ordering concepts, when it extracts some points from their group to study them

---

[133] Araya, Introducción, 18.
[134] Araya, Introducción, 19.

separately, when it deteriorates itself in a limiting special-ization and is rendered just to accentuate partial aspects of the Biblical message as fundamental theological begin-nings?[135]

If theology only has as truth, what people can experi-ence in real life, as to being profitable, practical, social and useful this method deteriorates into a consumptive theol-ogy. And on the other hand, if conservative theology did leave its productive function with its confessional doctri-nal romanticism, sometimes exaggeratedly sentimental, attaching to the inherited and criticized traditionalism, it unhappily converts the truth into an inheritance pre-served magically, without showing courage of being *sem-per reformanda*, while it purifies itself towards the Kingdom of God. Then theology hurt its task, maintaining an undecipherable theological language for contemporary people, answering questions that current human beings no longer even ask.

Unfortunately, theology has been, in many seminaries and universities, just the theology of professors of theol-ogy to theology teachers and not theology for the people of God. It usually speaks only about itself or its theological school, leaving aside its productive function, converting its work simply into a collection of quotations from the past. On the other hand, a theology that prioritizes the context without basing itself on the historical wealth of faith deteriorates into a socio-economic ideology and, even worse, in sectarian parties. This distortion has also been affecting theological education, and at the same time has been moving people away from theology, creating a ditch between theological education and people. This type of distrust of the theological activity is a product of a the-ology transformed into Religious Philosophy, Religious

---

[135] Araya, Introducción, 19.

Sociology or Religious Science[136] or simply economic liberation.

Theology must be traditional and contemporary at the same time; Christ centered and dialogic; theoretical, scientific and practical; pastoral, committed to memory, contemporary social company, and prophetic action. Theology would thus be both intellectual and servant, and at the same time, cognitive, constituent, and critic. It would always express a reminiscent perspective, a reflexive perspective, and a prospective perspective.

The theological task is, at the same time, faithful to its historical memory, faithful to its call in Jesus Christ and faithful to its hope. Reminding and proclaiming to Jesus Christ's Church, that it has a mission in the world and an eternal destiny, which is the reason that the theological task of the Lord's Church is a permanent challenge that needs to be answered with devotion, humility and faith.

Theology constitutes itself in a permanent task of the Christian Church, a hermeneutical community which has received as its responsibility a still expanding mission that should take place according to its postulates of faith.

The challenge of theology is how it should be practiced in such a way that it can serve this task best. We have argued that the functions of theology cannot be isolated and that not one of those can be practiced at the expense of the other ones. This requires a specific competence and attitude of theologians, especially in a time of social challenges that leaves people in deep uncertainties. That is the question we deal with in this research.

---

[136] Maraschin, Tendências, 149.

CHAPTER 4

Theology as Wisdom

THEOLOGICAL EDUCATION IS situated in the Christian
community as a critical discourse for human life, open to
the future. In the previous chapter we reflected on the
functions and aspects which such a theology implies. We
will now turn to the question how this theology should operate and how it must be practiced. By reflecting on this
question we will develop a perspective how theologians
should be trained for their task where with we will deal in
the next chapter.

We argued that theology has to do with the reality of
life in all its societal, psychological, economic, political aspects. It is a critical reflection on this reality from the perspective of the message of Christian faith. How is this
critical reflection executed? As we stated in our introduction one of the ways a critical theology can function is as a
prophetic discourse. Theology helps the church and individual Christians to raise a prophetic voice against injustice, exclusion and exploitation of human beings.
Certainly this support to the prophetic voice of the church
is an important task of theology. It cannot be, however, its
main paradigm.

As we argued, prophetic theology has become situated in a specific social and theological niche that makes it suspect for many people in the church and by consequence it cannot be effective. It has even become counter-productive because it makes people afraid of becoming involved in social transformation. It is also one sided because it is critical but does not take into account the whole of human life with its complexities and deeper layers that cannot be distinguished by sociological investigation and societal critique. What is necessary is a more comprehensive approach that takes into account all the aspects of life, including the ambiguities and atrocities, the irrational and meta-rational aspects that direct human life.

Such a comprehensive approach is found in theology as wisdom. Wisdom does not counter existing reality and does not confront it as prophecy does. Wisdom participates in the whole of life and tries to find ways for the future whereon people can go, taking into account who and where they are. Wisdom knows about the hidden sources wherefrom human actions and thought arise. Wisdom does not only call for societal reform but tries to shape human attitudes to a life that is viable for the future and thus transforms society from inside by being shaped by the inner wells of life.

Wisdom as a Comprehensive Approach

The central focus of this thesis constitutes a challenging personal involvement for theologians. There is a growing and surprising expectation of understanding theology as wisdom, which necessarily implies a transforming vocation regarding theological education, the rediscovering of the *habitus theologicus*, as theology is in its essence.

Theology, in the words of Justo González, should be understood in three dimensions: as knowledge, as discipline and as wisdom.[137] There is no doubt that theology involves knowledge. Even in its most rudimentary levels, it requires certain knowledge of the Bible, of the church, and of human reality. Certainly, we may increase our knowledge in any of these fields.

A growing knowledge of the Scriptures is necessary, starting from the original languages, knowledge of the historical development of Christian traditions, knowledge of the Church and of its path through history, knowledge of society, several cultures and their ethnicity, and also knowledge of parallel sciences and their perspectives and contemporary positions.

For all these reasons, theology requires knowledge; but it is more than that. It is important to underline this, precisely because modernity has so underscored the need of knowledge that it has lost sight of other dimensions of theology as discipline and as wisdom.[138]

Theology is also a discipline. As Justo González[139] states, the word may be used with two different meanings, and both are applicable to theology. On the one hand, a 'discipline' is a field of inquiry. Theology is a discipline in this sense, because it is a field of research with its own methodology. On the other hand, theology is a 'discipline' in a second sense, which is at least as important as the first. In this sense, discipline is a way of life to which we submit in order to reach a goal. This goes far beyond a program of study – although it certainly includes such a program. Theology is an entire process in which the theologian not only seeks to learn about Scripture and Christian doctrine, but also to be formed by Scripture and doctrine. It is not

---

[137] J. L. González and Z. Maldonado Pérez, An Introduction to Christian Theology, Nashville: Abingdon Press, 2002, 25.

[138] González and Maldonado Pérez, Introduction, 25.

[139] González and Maldonado Pérez, Introduction, 25.

merely a matter of reading the Bible, for instance, as someone seeking an answer to a puzzle, or a point of information; it is rather a matter of reading the Bible, seeking to have it give shape to both life and thought. So we come to what is meant by the claim that theology is also wisdom. There is a vast difference between knowledge and wisdom. Knowledge tells us how things are. Wisdom teaches us how to relate to them. Theology is much more than knowledge - that the ancients called *scientia,* but also wisdom – that the ancients[140] called *sapientia.*[141]

As a contemporaneous thinker, Edgar Morin, defends the idea of wisdom as a necessary proposal to life and society, the wisdom model implies complexity. To think in complex thought is to be capable of joining (*complexus*: what is weaved together) the fabric of reality as a whole,

---

[140] Gregory Nazianzen, in his Oratio XXVII, The First Theological Oration, A Preliminary Discourse against the Eunomians, part III, says: "Not to every one, my friends, does it belong to philosophize about God; not to every one; the Subject is not so cheap and low; and I will add, not before every audience, nor at all times, nor on all points; but on certain occasions, and before certain persons, and within certain limits. Not to all men, because it is permitted only to those who have been examined, and are passed masters in meditation, and who have been previously purified in soul and body, or at the very least are being purified. For the impure to touch the pure is, we may safely say, not safe, just as it is unsafe to fix weak eyes upon the sun's rays. And what is the permitted occasion? It is when we are free from all external defilement or disturbance, and when that which rules within us is not confused with vexatious or erring images; like persons mixing up good writing with bad, or filth with the sweet odors of unguents. For it is necessary to be truly at leisure to know God; and when we can get a convenient season, to discern the straight road of the things divine. And who are the permitted persons? They to whom the subject is of real concern, and not they who make it a matter of pleasant gossip, like any other thing, after the races, or the theatre, or a concert, or a dinner, or still lower employments. To such men as these, idle jests and pretty contradictions about these subjects are a part of their amusement." In: P. Schaff and H. Wace, eds., The Nicene and Post-Nicene Fathers, second series, Vol. VII: Cyril of Jerusalem, Gregory Nazianzen, Edinburgh, T&T Clark: 1867, 285.

[141] González and Maldonado Pérez, An Introduction, 26.

but at the same time able to recognize the unique, the concrete.[142] The first step to understand the purpose of this theory of complexity in Morin's words is trying to understand "the different avenues that lead to the 'complexity challenge'."[143] This idea of *challenge* is interesting: the complexity is not a theory that explains everything or anything, but it is an attitude of all scholars, the challenge of always seeking something that might have been missed in clearing any *phenomenon*. That is because one is convinced that nothing is quite simple. Everything is complex, and even to such an extent that reflection will never end, but goes on to challenge those who think about reality.

Such an attitude must always go through the different avenues that lead to the "complexity challenge:" "Watch out: go through different avenues because it is not enough to go along just one!" Only one or two would not be enough to solve complexity and perhaps not all of the ways that we can access. It is necessary to go forward and be always open to the new contexts of life. Morin's way of watching reality affirms a wisdom that integrates reason and effectiveness. We need rational intelligence but also, effectiveness, gentleness, and compassion.[144] To Morin, a purely rational life would be at the edge of life; the quality of life engulfs emotion, passion, joy.

Wisdom consists of the pertinence of overwhelming specialization and not shutting itself in it. It is the effort of joining the empiric and theoretic, the concrete and the abstract, the part and the whole, the phenomenon and the context. Wisdom allows us to break out the dogmatic par-

---

[142] E. Morin and J-L. Le Moigne, A inteligência da complexidade, São Paulo: Petrópolis, 2000, 207.

[143] E. Morin, Ciência com consciência, Rio de Janeiro: Bertrand Brasil, 1998, 177.

[144] Morin, Método, 135.

adigms that enslave in time and space for it knows theology just as any other science as an unfinished task and brings within it something undone.

Theology as wisdom is *habitus*.[145] Recent discussions about knowledge in theological education must be seen in a wider sense. Edward Farley says that wisdom is a new posture of the heart that comes with redemption; it is founded in God and is directed toward other human beings, the self, nature, and the world. It is a turning toward reality rather than a turning away from it by observing phenonema with an attitude of distance; it is oriented to truth rather than constructions and designs. Theology in the classical sense is not a technical discipline for scholars but "the wisdom proper to the life of the believer." As wisdom, theology is a kind of meta-thinking or *paideia* about a "mystery which resists partitioning" into scientific specializations.[146]

Farley criticizes the loss of theology as *habitus*[147] at the present time, which has gotten to walk alongside scientific

---

[145] "Habit, for Aristotle, is primarily an acquired propensity toward a determinate type of behavior. That is to say, ´habit´ refers a tendency that has received a specific direction and facility through the repetition of a certain type of action... In this way, Aristotle sets a precedent for giving 'habit' a double meaning – the specific meaning of an experientially acquired propensity and the more general meaning of all kinds of tendencies, whether acquired or innate" (Sang Hyun Lee: The Philosophical Theology of Jonathan Edwards, Princeton: University Press, 2000, 19.

[146] Farley, The Fragility of Knowledge, 87-88, 118.

[147] The concept of habitus is resumed by Jonathan Edwards in Reformed theology and more recently by the French Sociologist Pierre Bordieu, during the last quarter of the 20th Century. See Lee, The Philosophical Theology of Jonathan Edwards: "Habits, for Edwards, is also a relational principle – that is, a general law that governs the manner or character of actual actions and events", 7; "Broadly speaking, however, 'habit' refers to all qualities and abilities, acquired or innate", 23; "Again, habit is more than custom or the regular way something happens or is done. It is more than a summation of the character of some actual events. Habit actively brings about events of a particular sort. So habit is a purposive power that works with a design", 38; "Habit then governs the future actions and events as well as the past and present ones.

theology since the Middle Ages. Under the impact of the Enlightenment integration of life and research was broken and the consequence was a lexicalization and a departmentalization of theology, turned consequently hostage to scholastic rationalism. Farley affirms that it is necessary to overcome that dichotomy among theory and practices to rebuild a truly practicing theology. He emphasizes:

Theory meant that aspect of the habitus, or wisdom, in which the divine object evokes acknowledgment, belief. Practice meant that aspect of the habitus, or wisdom, in which the divine object sets requirements of obedience and life. Both reside in the single existential habitus called theology. Theory/practice is based here on what could be called a phenomenology of theology as a habitus.[148]

This *habitus* of theologians implies the totality of their being. Using J. B. Libânio's words: "Theology, as wisdom, concerns the person's totality... It values the dimension, the spiritual dimension open to the Mystery, involving the person's totality."[149] To affirm theology as wisdom implies that theology has to do with the human totality in their life relationships and in their whole context.

A theological *habitus* or attitude of wisdom implies spirituality, indeed. Theology does not only refer to the mind or its relation to praxis, but is rooted in the convictions and sources of the heart. One of the predominant forms of theology in Christianity has been theology as wisdom — *sapientia*. According to Libânio this *sapiential* dimension of theology would always have got its value, but its maximum peak was exercised at the patristic time,

---

Habit is a general law that governs all events of a particular class and is, therefore, more than the uniformity that obtains in the actually observed events of the past and the present", 40.

[148] E. Farley, Theology and Practice Outside the Clerical Paradigm. In Practical Theology, edited by Don S. Browning, San Francisco: Harper & Row, 1983, 25-28.

[149] Libanio and Murad, Introdução, 77.

when theology and mercy were similar realities. It contin-
ued in the theological tradition in the East up to the present time, with Augustinian heritage in the West, and with
the theology growing out of the spiritual and mystical traditions.[150] Theology experienced as wisdom was both in
the early church and in the Reformation a natural expression that tied heart and mind. It came from biblical reflection in connection to the life of people, which grew in the
depth of transformed reflection, coming back afterwards
to the intellectualized reflection, and moving forward in a
growing circular process, generating life by faith and
transforming communion.[151]

In the center of theology is Jesus Christ, the mystery
revealed as the Wisdom of God to the world. The Scriptures open up for human beings the possibility of understanding this revelation of God in Jesus Christ. According
to Libânio, during the patristic era, the authors were interested, above all, in the mediation of those texts as spiritual food for their mercy and Christian perfection.
Spiritual cultivation was made not as a source of estrange-
ment of the temporary realities of the world, but as its
wells to drink from.

Theology was crystallized as spiritual wisdom, using
platonic and neo-platonic categories.[152] This shape of theology is a reason to study the Church Fathers who filled
hearts with fervor and spiritual energy. Therefore this theology was fundamental for the reformers, and until now
it feeds the Church in its prayers and liturgy. Gustavo
Gutiérrez, quoting Y. M. Congar, affirms that "in the first

---

[150] R. J. Schreiter, Constructing Local Theologies, Maryknoll: Orbis Books, 1985, 85.

[151] Libanio and Murad, Introdução, 78

[152] Libânio and Murad, Introdução à Teologia, 76.

centuries of the Church, what now we denominate theology was narrowly linked to spiritual life".[153] In the first chapter of his book *A Theology of Liberation* Gutiérrez emphasizes theology as wisdom, where he concludes: "The spiritual function of theology, so important in the first centuries, later suspended, constitutes, however, the permanent dimension of theology".[154]

In the history of Christian thought, it is possible to verify that several of the great theologians, somehow, have always driven us to this model of theology as wisdom. An example was John Calvin, who has made in his theology a correlation between the knowledge of God and the knowledge of us, as an interlinked process in theological labor. The intrinsic understanding of the primary comprehension of what it is to be a theologian is also notable: "In Orthodox Christianity, the title 'theologian' has been reserved for those mystics who go most deeply into the wisdom of God".[155]

F. Honório Rito[156], when deepening the subject of theology as wisdom, has asked: What did, in fact, make theology not a pure scientific and neutral knowledge, but a knowledge of reality that has the anointing of a wisdom that is more than pure human wisdom, because it has been penetrated by the wisdom that is born in the Word of God and in faith? The spirituality that springs from the Word of God and from faith provides theology with a dimension, not just of rational knowledge, but one that always brings a nature of wisdom, that lights up and guides a person's faith for a lifetime, through world paths towards the Kingdom of God. Rito affirmed that "as wisdom, theology could

---

[153] Gutiérrez , A Theology of Liberation16.

[154] Gutiérrez, A Theology of Liberation, 17.

[155] Schreiter, Constructing, 86.

[156] Rito is a Professor at the Theological Institute of Salvador, Brazil, Catholic University of Salvador.

never be pure speculative knowledge; it is guided by its own nature to the spiritual practice of the man of faith."[157]

Theology, by its own nature, as well as faith, is more a lifestyle than knowledge of reality. Theology has a practical nature; therefore it approaches wisdom as much more than a speculative science. Theology wants to know not just for the sake of knowledge, but to live in a transforming way, practicing what it knows and believes. It has to recognize that the Church Fathers' way of making theology, as a deeply linked reflection into practice whether a spiritual or a pastoral practice, had something that should not be lost in the historical evolution of making theology. As wisdom that is inspired by the Wisdom of God revealed in the Scriptures, theology presupposes a serious academic work on the part of the theologians, although they always know that it is more than rational work. It is to serve the pastoral life in a real context of each generation, committed to God's mission to human history.

Unfortunately, the modern era has produced a rupture between theology and spirituality, generating a fragmentation that is harmful to pastoral formation.

Farley offers a brief history of the concept of theology as wisdom from the beginnings of Christian faith to the present. He uncovers two meanings of the term theology: it is an actual knowledge of God (theology as "wisdom"), and a discipline or "science," which uses appropriate methods and subjects in a body of teachings. While initially closely related, in the modern world these two meanings fall apart as the unitary discipline of theology evolved into a aggregate of special sciences (only one of which retained the name "Theology"), and even the aspect of theology offering wisdom was displaced by practical

---

[157] Rito, Introdução, 104.

know-how and ministerial skills, so that *theologia* lost it-self.[158]

Farley states that in our time:

> *Two genres of theology continue but undergo such radical transformation that the original sense of theology as knowledge (wisdom) and as discipline virtually disappear from theological schools. Theology as a personal quality continue (though not usually under the term theology), not as a salvation –disposed wisdom, but as the practical know-how necessary to ministerial work. Theology as discipline continue, not as the unitary enterprise of theological study, but as one technical and specialized scholarly undertaking among others; in other words, as systematic theology.[159]*

The bookstores are full of these Know-How books, which unhappily are put in general as adverse to theology as a discipline, and this is one of the biggest challenges to the task of theological education. Teachers need to show day by day the importance of theology as an academic and spiritual discipline. The solution would be to rediscover theologia as *habitus*, breaking this false dichotomy, which is a product of the encyclopedistic period. This is not only Farley's proposal, but also of other current theologians. They are concerned with theological education, and their group is growing.

We can affirm what Kelsey and Farley say: to understand God is to have a kind of wisdom or *sapientia;* this *wisdom* concerning God embraces contemplation, discursive reasoning, the affections, and the actions that comprise a Christian's life. It is under this focus that people can

---

[158] E. Farley, Theologia: The History of a Concept. In: Peter Hodgson & Robert King (eds.), Readings in Christian Theology, edited by, Minneapolis: Fortress Press, 1985, 29-48.

[159] Farley, Theologia, 39.

understand that the key to base the way of teaching theology as wisdom is Jesus Christ, in whom this integration of knowing God and the reality of life was integrated.

Theology as wisdom as a comprehensive discourse it not opposed to other models of theology. It is rather accepting them as aspects of the whole. They are only defective if they are considered as the only perspective wherein theology can be developed.

Wisdom includes the profane and the religious. Wisdom is, at the same time, the daily practice and the fear of God. It is a confessing knowledge about what we live. David Bosch has stated theology must have a head (*theoria*), a heart (*poiesis*) and hands (*praxis*).[160]

Theology and theological education, then involve a dynamic interplay and a creative tension between '*theoria, poiesis* and *praxis*', between head, heart and hand, between faith, hope and love, between the cognitive, the constitutive and the critical, between the intellectual, the relational and the intentional. It combines knowing, being and doing and seeks to communicate what is true, what is of God, and what is just.[161]

It is within these dimensions that theology teaching should be inserted with the purpose of accomplishing the challenges of its task, being faithful to its contents of faith and to the call of sharing a transforming message to current human history. On the remark of David Bosch theology and theological education involve the dynamic interplay and the creative tension between *theoria, poiesis* and *praxis*, between head, heart and hand, between faith, hope and love, between the cognitive, the constitutive and the critical, between the intellectual, the relational and the

---

[160] D. Bosch, The Nature of Theological Education. In: Theologica Evangelica 25 (1), 1992, 19.

[161] Bosch, The Nature, 20.

intentional.[162] Theology combines knowing, being and do-ing, and seeks to communicate what is true, what is about God, and what is just. What David Bosch has written is in agreement with David Tracy's contributions, affirming that the task of theology as a whole comes, in general, from within three public functions: academic, church, and soci-ety.[163] Bosch wrote: "In this, I wish to suggest that ideally, theological education should always be undertaken with respect to all three public functions: academic, church, and society."[164]

The issue of the relation of *theory* and *praxis* has been reflected upon since long time. Traditionally, and follow-ing the classical Greek and enlightened patterns of think-ing, theory has reigned supreme and has remained the focus of *academia*. Once the correct theory had been es-tablished, it could be applied in practice. Application, however, was the second and also secondary step. More recently, we have been made aware of deficiencies of this approach and the interdependence between theory and practice or, rather, *praxis*. This is, however, still not ade-quate. In addition to *theoria* and *praxis*, classical philoso-phy has contained the third, often neglected dimension, namely *poiesis*, which connects theory and *praxis* [165] We

---

[162] Bosch, The Nature, 20.

[163] D. Tracy, The Analogical Imagination: Christian Theology and the Cul-ture of Pluralism, New York: Crossroad, 1981, 3-46.

[164] Bosch, The Nature, 9.

[165] Stackhouse, Apologia, 84f. "Poiesis involves imaginative creation or representation of evocative images. It includes the kind of awareness and ori-entation to life that can be discovered by aesthetic and kinesthetic experience. Theoria involves observation, reporting, interpretation, and critical evalua-tion. It thus includes all that can be known by analysis, systematic study, re-flection, and contemplation. The central issues of theoria are less aesthetic or kinesthetic than ontological, metaphysical, and epistemic. In contrast to these, praxis involves intentional, practical engagement whereby people seek to do something for the common good. However, the kind of life and world orien-tation that derives from praxis is not unrelated to poiesis or theoria."

can say that *theoria* involves observation, reporting, interpretation, and critical evaluation. This dimension remains a *sine qua non* for theological education and constitutes the academic character of all authentic theology courses. The second dimension, *poiesis,* involves the imaginative creation or representation of evocative images, manifesting itself, in worship, liturgy, and confession. In our case, it gives expression to the ecclesiastical dimension of theology. It is in this mode of *poiesis* that theory finds its meaning and depth, wherein *praxis* is necessarily involved. *Praxis* means intentional, practical engagement whereby people seek to find expression of theological commitment, also for the sake of those who are not members of the church.[166]

When these dimensions are emphasized, the Church, as a community of faith, finds its necessary place within the theological task inserting itself within the interrelation between Christian and practical faith. It is at this point that theology becomes *poiesis,* an art rather than a science. As an art, theology breaks through the screen of objectivity and draws on our pre-conceptual capacities of contemplative vision. Theology is an indwelling rather than an intellectual affirmation. As a symbol, it not only touches the mind and evokes action but also compels the heart. Theology works primarily with symbols, and symbols are multileveled. They are not, and surely could not be reduced to either *theoria* or *orthopraxis,* although they may have an enormous significance. We rarely understand the full range of multiple meanings of symbols until they are theoretically sorted and practically applied to the wide range of social interaction.

To summarize: When proposing Systematic Theology as a discipline, it should be taught as the wisdom of God in

---

[166] Bosch, The Nature, 9.

order to meet human reality. It is necessary to integrate these three dimensions of theology: *theoria, poiesis* and *praxis*, not just to itself, but also to all theological education, which, unhappily, continues to be taught in a broken way within several disciplines, disputed mutually. It is right there that wisdom becomes an integrating principle. It is necessary to recognize, however, that the theological task is not an easy task.

David Bosch has placed these dimensions of doing and teaching theology as follows. He refers to three public theologies; the first has to do with *academic*, the second with *church*, and the third with *society*:

> *First, with respect to theology's first 'public', the academic: Traditionally, theological education has been predisposed toward an intellectual approach. Already in classical Greek philosophy, which constituted the matrix for Christian theology, the preference for theoria at the expense of poiesis and praxis was in evidence. From the point of view of the Enlightened world theoria was further abstracted from poiesis and praxis.[167]*

The second public theology has to do with church. It is closed and restricted in its relationship to the world. Its fundamental characteristic prioritizes the relational and the evocative, instead of the intellectual, prescriptive and definable.[168] It is the part of theological education that has to do with the heart, or poiesis.[169] Bosch has stated clearly:

---

[167] F. Young, The critic and the visionary. In: Scottish Journal of Theology , Volume 41(3), 1988, 311; Bosch, The Nature, 19-20.

[168] Stackhouse, Apologia, 104.

[169] "It does not only touch the mind and inspire to action, but also moves the heart. It gathers all of theoria and praxis 'into those symbolic forms that synthesize and evoke the integration of mind and will", Stackhouse, Apologia, 104.

We may, if we wish, interpret theological education as the grooming of candidates for a particular denomination and inculcate in them an attitude of dogmatic exclusivity. Otherwise we hardly take our students out of the world, teach them in the cloister-like environment, and prepare them for the ministry whose main concern is to help people distinguish between the sacred and the profane, the heavenly and the worldly. In neither case, however, would we be involved in theological education as poiesis.[170]

The third public theology has to do with *society*. It is a reaction against the simply epistemological and formal enlightenment method. It emphasizes practice, but at the same time, it clarifies that each practice has always something to do with theory. There is no good practice without good theory.[171] Bosch has emphasized theology and practice within society as follows: "Turning to theology's third 'public', society, or the praxis dimension of theological education, we have to recognize that there is no way of going back to the situation where theology exhausts itself in *theoria or poiesis*."[172]

In this perspective the prophetical aspect can have its full right. The Catholic theologian Bruno Forte calls this methodological procedure of *company, memory and prophecy*. The task of theology as wisdom should take into account some fundamental methodological procedures in theological labor such as the present as its social *locus* (company), and the past as its inspiring *memory* of the faith, while it is challenged to assume at the same time a new future perspective as its *prophetic sign* in permanent reform, purifying itself historically.

---

[170] Stackhouse, Apologia, 104.

[171] "It is becoming increasingly clear that every praxis is itself based on theoria, that stands in the need of theoria, and this not always only as the ʹsecond actʹ since, as it turns out, our praxis is only as good as our theoria (as, conversely our theoria will only be as good as our praxis)" (Bosch, The Nature, 20).

[172] Bosch, The Nature, 20.

In Latin American theology, integration of theory and praxis is considered a call to the theological task. Theology in Brazil, for instance, was petrified in traditionalism and did not penetrate in the challenges of societal, political and economic life. Therefore it had to be contextualized. In his explanatory book, *Constructing Local Theologies*, Robert Schreiter asks two questions regarding the relationship between *theologia* as wisdom and the construction of contextualized theologies. First he asks: *Can cultural conditions be indicated for a wisdom theology?* The second is more methodological: *What implications do these cultural conditions suggest for the development of local theologies?*

All answers to these questions lead us to the theme of this work, a contribution to the systematic theology teaching in the contemporary context, which is none other than a globalization atmosphere and growing social exclusion. In the midst of exploitation and exclusion we see the groan of crowds seeking a means to live by. Theology is called upon to give hope and answers that may make sense from the paradigm of Biblical revelation, in a new pastoral and relevant doxology as reformed claims to operate: dealing with the whole of human life and work for the glory of God.

Schreiter has answered some fundamental factors regarding cultural conditions in relation to *Theologia as wisdom*:

> *First, wisdom theology seems to predominate in those places where human life is seen as a unified cycle, marked by progressive development. Second, wisdom theology places great stock on being able to see the world, both the visible and the invisible, as a unified whole. The quest for wisdom carries with it a sense of being able to relate all the parts to the whole. Third, in cultures where human growth is not seen as personal achievement, but as discovering the underlying and unchanging patterns of the universe and coming into conformance with them, wisdom theology will find a ready home. Fourth, wisdom*

91

theology tends to prevail in cultures marked by a strong sense of interiority, by the pursuit of the psychological as the path to perfection. Fifth, cultures that adopt a two-level approach to ultimate reality, an exoteric and an esoteric one, are likely to follow the patterns of a wisdom theology.[173]

Schreiter has equally emphasized five necessary points to the task of rebuilding a local or contextual theology, according to a theology-as-wisdom perspective:

First, a wisdom theology will be a likely development in those cultures that have maintained their important rite of passage. It provides a way to bring together the wisdom of the ancestors with the wisdom of Christ, the first ancestor in faith. Second, only gradually Westerners discovered the deep interiority of many so-called primitive peoples, who often have an elaborate wisdom theology developed in their own tradition but keep it hidden from Westerners... Where people prize wisdom above learning and wealth, wisdom theology becomes the natural vehicle for their expression in faith. Third, cultures placing great value on a unified view of the world, often sacrificing many other things to maintain it, seek the way of wisdom. Fourth, wisdom-theology models have remained the most fruitful for catechesis. The development of the rite of Christian initiation for adults has utilized this form once again, and quite successfully. Fifth, wisdom theology functions best where a unity in world-view is possible. In strongly pluralist societies, where world-views compete, it is less successful.[174]

The importance of these observations is the fact that they challenge to search for a model for the teaching of systematic theology in seminaries. The need to assume a model according to the vision of theology as wisdom cannot be denied. This paradigm is the integrating factor of theological functions, accomplishing the task of theology.

Because theology was lost in an isolated discourse of the past, it must be broken open. Many people still identify the

---

[173] Schreiter, Constructing, 86, 89.
[174] Schreiter, Constructing, 89.

'academy' as a world apart, an ivory tower, in which not so practical figures use their time just to think, lucubrate, and speculate. A mere utilitarian approach is also inappropriate because it lacks theological critique. Both need one another, for if theory has nothing to do with practice, it is not a theory of anything, and if practice does not return to theory, it would never rejuvenate.[175]

A theological education as wisdom should look for the permanent correlation between *theoria* and *praxis*, which should not be separated, just as faith and love, root and fruit. In the conservative tradition of our seminaries it is necessary to read the Bible from a new social focus, from the reverse of history, from the place of the poor and the periphery of the world, from the socially excluded. It was under this focus that Carlos Mesters[176] proposed the hermeneutical path as a method of reading the Scriptures starting from the place of the people, where life takes place. This work proposes that theology needs again to rediscover its integrative function in a liberating practice.

Like the prophetical competence of theology, its rational meaning is of direct importance as well. It cannot be excluded either and if theology focuses only on the context it has to be turned upside down once again. Faith is clarified in knowledge and knowledge clarified in faith. Wisdom is faith that knows, and knowledge that believes. Theology is rational, because when using the intellect it honors the creator. John Calvin already reminded us in the sixteenth century that to respect the creativity of the human brain is to honor the Holy Spirit. Wisdom is to learn from the past as a historical treasure, but as well as this it is to understand the history of God's Salvation, to remind us that the revealed God is the God that makes history, to

---

[175] Demo, Metodologia, 20.
[176] Carlos Mesters is a Catholic theologian. See his: Por trás das Palavras.

take the memory of Christian thought seriously through-out the generations. Doubtless it is to honor the God of history. When proposing theology as wisdom, I do not re-fute rational and historical knowledge, I only make it a critical paradigm to the theological reductionism in many Christian sectors. Theology as wisdom is a proposal of driving systematic theology into a process of transforming action, wherein all aspects of life are integrated.

An isolated confession or an isolated event, a theologi-cal statement and an experience that are not related, are not legitimate and obsolete when we comprehend faith as wisdom. Wisdom will never be a neutral knowledge. For more than three centuries, western theology has been ob-sessed with the issues and matters postulated by moder-nity, in such a way that its ramifications became hostages of *Zeitgeist* or cultural *ethos*.[177] Theological education of our time is expecting a new paradigm or a new way of plac-ing theology, which offers a new unifying vision of Chris-tian theology that at the same time could be firmly based on the divine Revelation with a consistent regard to the great tradition of the Christian Church in its refreshing spirituality.[178]

Jesus, the Wisdom of God

Paul the apostle makes a connection between Jesus Christ and the Wisdom of God and also the power of God (see I Cor. 1:24, 31). For the Christian faith Jesus Christ is the incarnation of the Wisdom of God. The Wisdom of God hidden through the centuries became flesh inhabited among us, and in him we saw the glory of God.

---

[177] R. Olson, The story of Christian Theology, Downers Grove: Inter Var-sity Press, 1999, 631.

[178] Olson, The story, 630.

To speak about Christ as the Wisdom of God made flesh, implies speaking about God who was made human; about the Rich who was made poor; about the Lord who was made a servant and about the Righteous who was made sin. Christian theology can only be a theology of Wisdom in the perspective of an incarnational Christology and it is precisely this theology that brings liberating transformation.

To understand the real presence of the incarnated wisdom of God in Jesus Christ, it is necessary to bear in mind that in contemporary Judaism there were several illustrations that personified the power of the presence of God in the world e.g. Wisdom, Word and Spirit. When Jesus is called the Wisdom of God we must keep in mind the whole tradition of Wisdom as it is developed in the Old Testament and Judaism. Looking at Christ as wisdom of God, we must keep in mind that wisdom plays the role of being the divine light, revelation of God, divine teacher and prophet of God. Proverbs 1-9 sketches wisdom as a person who is proclaiming, evoking and summoning an alliance with the will of God, it calls on streets and at doors, that means: it speaks to the context of human history and in its existential paths. Wisdom becomes here a celebration of life because God celebrates the life of his creation to take it to the full. Theology as wisdom has to do with life in all its areas of action.

Wisdom calls people to follow the way to life. Elisabeth Schüssler Fiorenza emphasizes what the way of Wisdom implies.[179] Wisdom searches the streets for people, invites them to her table, and offers life, knowledge, rest, salvation to all who will accept her. Initially she resides in Israel, her very special people, but the later apocalyptic Wisdom theology suggests that she has not found a place

---

[179] E. Schüssler Fiorenza, Wisdom Ways: Introducing Feminist Biblical Interpretation, Maryknoll: Orbis Books, 2001.

and has returned to heaven, where she dwells with God and is the glory of God, a collaborator in God's work, a pure effervescence of the divine light.[180] In wisdom literature however she is pervading the world so that it may share fullness of life.

Casting herself as sister, mother, female beloved, chief and hostess, preacher, judge, liberator, establisher of justice, and a myriad of other female roles wherein she symbolizes transcendent power orientating and delighting the world. She pervades the world, both nature and the human being, interacting with them all to lure them along the right path to life.[181]

From this point of view theology has to do with infusing the Creator's wise purpose in the human mind, renewing and always moving forward in order to benefit the creation. It must, therefore, be guided to practice the principles of liberation and integration of human beings as a divine councilor, and not just as abstract knowledge. Theology is a reflection on the true light of God revealed to the world, it is a walk in fear and expectation before the mirror of the glory of God.

The Bible affirms that manifestations of the *Shekinah*, the habitation or the presence of the divine glory present in Hebrew tradition, dwell on earth, such as Wisdom, the Name, the Spirit. As Wisdom this manifestation is again present in Jesus of Nazareth.

The wisdom of God is the new logic, the logic of grace and freedom in which the *basileia* overturns the oppressive logic of the world and it is the spiritual power that shapes Jesus into becoming the proclaimed and bearer of the *basileia*. The logic and the power of divine Wisdom

---

[180] E. Schüssler Fiorenza, Jesus: Miriam's Child, Sophia's Prophet: Critical Issues in Feminist Christology, New York: Continuum Publishing Co, 1994, 133.

[181] E. A. Johnson, She Who Is: The Mystery of God in Feminist Theological Discourse, New York: Crossroad, 1992, 87.

are, in a single expression, "communicative freedom." Understood in this way, Wisdom encompasses yet transcends both *logos* and *Spirit*. Jesus is the Word of God and the Spirit of God because he is the Wisdom of God, the incarnation of God's caring, truthful, communicative *Sophia*, who sets us free from the lying, foolishness, and boasting of the world.[182]

This means that Jesus Christ is not only a teacher and a prophet of wisdom, but he must be understood as the bearer of Wisdom. Jesus is prophet and teacher because Wisdom is *incarnate* in him. The person and the work of Christ are inseparable. He teaches the truth about the world and human life, he embodies a way of living that coheres with the truth, and he empowers life by his sacrifice and example. Jesus Christ, the *Kurios* is himself the Wisdom of God.

As Wisdom he firstly teaches. He teaches a way of salvation. His knowledge is much more practical than theoretical, and his teaching is followed by his actions. "Jesus teaches not in a narrow doctrinal sense; rather, he teaches 'the truth about history' as God's governance and the truth about the world as the realm of God's grace. He teaches the value of love, humility, care, non-violence, trust, loyalty, self-denial. By his teaching and deed, he imparts the saving power of God, the power of conversion and transformation, the power of the cross to turn and to renew life."[183]

In Jesus' teaching the truth of the will of God for humanity is revealed, allowing human beings to discover the purpose of the Creator in such a way as to apply it to life in a transformative and practical way.

Jesus is however more than a teacher of Wisdom. As the Wisdom incarnate his life and death themselves are

---

[182] Hodgson, God's Wisdom, 97.
[183] Hodgson, God's Wisdom, 100.

Wisdom. Since he *is* the Wisdom, a theology of Wisdom cannot but be Christ centered. Especially the Reformers focused on the Christ centric character of faith and theology in an emphatic way. For them Jesus Christ is without any doubt the very heart of Theology.[184] Shirley Guthrie emphasizes this Christ centrality to the Reformed Tradition[185]:

The name Christ is by definition the clue to what Christian faith is. If you want to know what God is like, Christian theology says – look at Christ. If you want to know what real humanity is and how you can live a genuinely human life – look at Christ. If you want to know what God is doing in the world and in individual lives – look at Christ. For Christian theology, the person and work of Christ is the key to all truth about God, ourselves, and the world we live in."[186]

The core of theology as wisdom is to affirm wisdom as an expression of the glory of Jesus Christ. He is the Lord who brings people in the freedom of the fullness of life. With regard to this Hendrikus Berkhof writes:

Immediately connected with this ministry is the freedom to which he calls the people, a freedom which is in the first place the ambient in which he himself lives. It is not something which needs to be captured from the people and the circumstances, but which he, from the outset, possesses relative to them on account of his fellowship with the Father.[187]

---

[184] T. H. L. Parker, Calvin: An Introduction to His Thought, London: Continuum, 2002, 79-80: "The object of faith is Christ, we said. But, more precisely, it is Christ 'clothed with his Gospel'" (ii.6, 13-16).

[185] "Reformed is a theological, not a denominational, title. [It] is a doctrinal-theological description that cuts across all linguistic, national, racial, class, political, and cultural distinctions ... The Reformed perspective aims not at setting up but at breaking down between Christians." S. C. Guthrie, Jr., Christian Doctrine, Louisville: Westminster John Knox Press, 1994, 17.

[186] Guthrie, *Christian Doctrine,*10.

[187] H. Berkhof, Christian Faith, Grand Rapids, Eerdmans: 1986, 302.

The life of freedom in Jesus Christ is a life of total dependence on the Father in full solidarity with the people on earth.

To speak of theology as wisdom only makes sense for theological education if it comes from the revelation of God in the person of Jesus Christ, as this is the only way to avoid the risk of speaking about abstract theories and not about the real life of the Christian faith that was delivered to human beings as good news of redemption. Christian faith stems from Christ and thus he is the fundamental center of all theology and constitutes all manners of a relationship, a communion of the creature with the Creator. Theology is, above all, a relationship with Jesus Christ.

What this implies can be understood if we compare the relation of God and human being with a relation of loving people. To speak about love only makes sense if, instead of speaking about love as a philosophy, we speak about the person who is loved. When speaking about love, it should be spoken of as an attitude and action, while speaking about love as an abstract reality is radically a tiresome activity. To speak about love is to speak about wisdom with taste, a transforming and encouraging taste; it is the speech of a person we love. This changes the discourse completely, that a simple word becomes living passion, a feeling of presence. God's coming in Christ changes the theological discourse from an abstract discourse on the Absolute to the presence of Love in a living Person, related to human beings in compassion.

This is the reason why theology is a discourse about God from the moment of revelation that he himself has given from his own self. It is a discourse which originates from God who came as Jesus Christ in human life in all its needs and weaknesses. It is for this reason that the apostle, when describing the coming of Christ, counters with theology as a communication of the law. "The law was given by Moses, grace and truth came by Jesus Christ" (John 1:17). Note the words "was given" and "came." God did not want to give anything abstract to be virtualized in the human mind and life through time, but he came in a historically event in the form of grace and truth. Therefore, theology is wisdom and as wisdom it is a relationship with God. To speak theologically is to speak in his presence and for his Glory; this is the heart of theology: God relates himself to us in Jesus Christ.

By affirming that Jesus Christ is the manifestation of the glory of God, we are already methodically declaring that Jesus is the hermeneutic key to theology. We can also express this in a more academic way: every science has its own method; each discipline has its own method depending on the object that is being investigated. For theology, the focus is defined by the way God makes himself present in our lives as a living God: his action and his presence is manifested in the man of Galilee as registered by the Gospels. When any theologian assumes another method, for example a Marxist ideology, or the application of human sentiments on religion, many things can be arrived at, but never at the nucleus on which Christian theology is addressed. Christian theology is not the sum of concepts but the affirmation of a person as the revelation of God.

Accepting theology methodologically as wisdom should start with the experience of God confessed by the Christian Faith: in the person of Jesus Christ, wisdom of God. This means theology begins with Christology. Christology is the main axle of the method of all theology: the heart of theology. The greatest expression of the heart of God and the most determined factor of dynamics of God's people, redeemed by the Spirit of Grace. For the Christian faith, Jesus Christ since the time of the first Christians is with whom we know who God is. "No one has ever seen

God but he who was born God, who is in the bosom of the Father, has made him known to us" (John 1:18).

In Cana of Galilee he comes with his mother and his disciples to a wedding where he performs his first miraculous sign (John 2:11). It is at this wedding, as symbol of life and love, that John describes Jesus Christ as the centre of attraction, using some of the most profound theological affirmations registered in the Scriptures. "He manifested here his Glory and many believed in him" (John 2:11). These words we see as the objective of his life and his mission on earth. He is in his being, the manifestation of the Glory of God. And for God to properly manifest his Glory in him, he begins his mission on earth to save the fullness of life from disaster and to seek that which had been lost.

a. The Incarnation as the Way of Theology

The most ancient Christology is known as high Christology, also called a Christology from above. This paradigm of theology tends to emphasize the divinity of Christ while a Christology known as theology from below, accentuates the humanity of Jesus Christ. Unfortunately this dichotomy creates a false ambiguity and theology does not need this polarization as if they were antagonistic. There is a Christology that emphasizes at the same time divinity as much as humanity: the true God is really human, by sharing the sufferings, the guilt and the death of humanity.

Christian theology affirms that God was made flesh (John 1.14). The eternal God invaded human history and through Jesus showed his glory, his grace, his light and his truth in the man who died on the cross. He is the bearer of loving action from God towards the lost world. He is the God that was made human, the Lord who was made the servant. In the incarnation the glory of God is revealed. In the letter to the Philippians, Paul affirms his incarnational mission. In contrast to Adam, who wanted to be as God, Jesus being God wanted to be human, and so he was. From the perspective of the Philippians he got the ladder not to go up but to go down: "and deprived himself, taking the form of a servant" (Phil. 2:5-6). However, not only was he made human but he humbled himself and became obedient unto death, even the death on the cross (Phil. 2:8), and so the incarnation should be seen biblically from the perspective of the cross. Thus according to the apostle Paul in Philippians 2:6, the being of Christ is that he is God, — not that He *was,* but *that He is.* He is so in his death on the cross and *therefore* the name above all name is given to him.

By affirming that all knees will bow and that all tongues will confess that He is the Lord, it is finally affirmed that by being the Lord he is the exact expression of the glory of God. He is the glorious wisdom radiant from Trinity. This affirmation is courageously made about Jesus. Observe that Paul does not use the word "Christ" or "Jesus Christ", but "Jesus", a real earthly person that God made human in whom we see the glory of the Father.

When Paul calls Jesus the Wisdom of God he does not refer to Jesus teaching as a wise religious leader, but to the cross. The foolishness of the crucified Jesus is God's wisdom (I Cor. 1:23-25). This Jesus is the wisdom of the glory of God, who does not share His glory with anyone else but grants his glory to Jesus.

On the road from Damascus Jesus revealed his glory to Saul and this manifestation created a theological impact of the glory of God. This would be the central theology of Paul in all places until the end of his life: "I determined not to know anything among you save Jesus Christ and him crucified" (I Cor. 2:2; 1:23).

From its very beginning the life of Jesus was the paradigm of true human life. His communion with the Father was a way of living. An intimate relationship with God as the Father was central to him. H. Berkhof wrote: "The first and central element of Jesus' life on earth is his love for the Father. This filled his whole life, to the farthest corners. There was between them a relationship of mutual intimacy of all temptations (the temptation in the wilderness) and all threats (Gethsemane) where he suffered a shipwreck."[188]

His life of prayer was an example and it was intense. It did not only call God *Abba* but lived in a relationship with Him in a unique and special manner. He left us with his way of living as an example of the secret intimacy with the author of Life. "No one knows the Son except the Father, and no one knows the Father except the Son and anyone to whom the Son chooses to reveal him" (Mt. 11:27).

The consequence of this radical love is the no less radical obedience to the Father. Jesus is not will-less with respect to God. He has a passionate will, whose driving force is to have his own will nothing else than what God wills. "My food is to do the will of him who sent me, and to accomplish his work" (John 4:34).[189]

On the life and work of Jesus, Hendrikus Berkhof affirms:

> *This element includes the fact that Jesus represents the people before God, because his actions that are in complete solidarity with the Father are an analogy and an instrument of God's purposes and deeds. And they glorified God, saying: 'A great prophet has arisen among us!' and 'God has visited his people!' (Luke 7:16).*[190]

---

[188] H. Berkhof, Christian Faith, 300.

[189] H. Berkhof, Christian Faith, 301.

[190] H. Berkhof, Christian Faith, 301.

b. The Incarnation as a Paradigm of Victory against Violence

The Scriptures and the Christian tradition unanimously affirm that the death of Jesus was "for us", "for our sins," "for many," "for the world." "Christ died for our sins in accordance with the Scriptures" (1 Cor. 15:3). Orlando Costas, a Latin American theologian affirmed that "the incarnation looks to the cross for its accomplishment."[191] For Paul the cross is the power of God (I Cor. 1:18). For the Jews the confession that Jesus is God is blasphemy. For the Greeks this was foolishness (I Cor. 1:23). For Christians, however, it is the source of salvation and the power of life.

In classical theology the cross has at least four dimensions: in the first place it is redemption and in this dimension it is presented as freeing human beings. The cross is also a substitute offer (Isaiah 53). It is the Lamb of God that takes away the sins of the world (John 1:29). In a third dimension the cross is reconciliation. And as such it is the gesture of the love of God to restore everything in Jesus Christ. It is the fundamental paradigm that puts an end to the antagonism that has separated human beings. Finally the cross is a symbol of victory. It is victory over the power of evil, victory over the threat of human life and over the empire of death.[192] Migliore identifies others aspects of the death of Jesus for us in his theology:

Christ died for us in order to expose our world of violence for what it is — a world that stands under God's judgment, a world based on coercion and leading us to death.

Christ died for us in order to enter into utmost solidarity with us as victims of violence and to mediate God's forgiveness to us as perpetrator of violence.

---

[191] O. Costas, Hacia una Teología de La Evangelizacíon, Buenos Aires, Aurora: 1973, 118.

[192] Costas, Hacia una Teología, 119.

Christ died for us in order to open a new future for a new humanity in the midst of our violent world.

Seen in the light of the resurrection, the cross is the indelible promise of the victory of the nonviolent love of God.

There is good news in the message of the cross that becomes radiantly clear in God's resurrection of the crucified.[193]

By means of the death of Jesus on the cross we are invited to perceive the magnitude of the weight of our sins and the cost of our pardon. That which really affects us and could affect us, was really taken away from us in the death of Christ. It is for this that there is in a Christian theology a limitless sense for the affirmation of the indelible divine Grace in the words of Christ on the cross. "Everything is consummated" (John 19:30). It is a testimony that nothing hangs over us and we were absolved thanks to the wonderful grace of Christ. He is the wisdom of God for us.

c. The Resurrection as Fullness

The mystery of incarnation unfolds itself between the cross of Jesus and his resurrection. The cross reaches its fullness in his rising. In Jesus, God was humbled and humanity was exalted. With his rising again it is clear that the word "humbleness" gained its real meaning from the divine action. He was made sin for us so that we were made the justice of God. He drank the cup of sin so that we could drink the cup of deserved forgiveness. He was in darkness at mid-day so that we could be as human beings to inhabit his eternal light. He assumed our eternal alienation so that we could live his eternal communion. In his rising from

---

[193] Migliore, Faith Seeking Understanding, 160.

the dead the human being is exalted and raised to that position conquered by Jesus Christ at his crucifixion. In Jesus Christ God accomplished everything for us. He is the righteous person who was made sin so that we were made the justice of God. How is this possible? Faith answers with a triumphant conviction: "Everything is by the life and work of Jesus Christ, in whom God entered our lost existence."

Theology was born as proclaimed at Pentecost as a power of the Spirit of the risen Christ. The first lesson of theology took place soon after his resurrection. This lesson is recorded in the New Testament and was ministered by Christ himself on the road to Emmaus (Luke 24). The core theme of the primitive church liturgy was that the humbled Christ was rising again and that God gave him the Name above all names on earth and in heaven. We can without doubt admirably affirm: The first lesson of theology in the Christian era was Christological and the theme was the resurrection of the Crucified. The basic generator of Christian theology in its work and content has been the resurrection.

The determining factor of a new era was the personal revelation of the resurrection by Jesus. Concepts about the resurrection were not capable of making an impact on the two disciples at Emmaus but the revelation of the glory of the resurrected, after exposing the matter, changed the night at Emmaus into a radiant resurrection morning. The night was no longer, the glorious day had begun. The weariness of a long journey gave way to strength for new journeys. They returned happily and enthusiastically to Jerusalem full of the power of the resurrection. From where did they get such force and motivation? It was from the meeting with him who had risen from the dead and was revealed during the breaking of bread. A window opens on the land of memories generating thoughts and emotions that emanate from decisions that alter their destiny forever. They are testing the power and the force of the resurrection. Everything is made new.

For theology as a manifestation of the wisdom of God, the resurrection is a source from where the power of the redeemer and conciliator of the cross comes. It is the heart of all Christian theology teaching activity. Abraham van de Beek, on emphasizing the meaning of the resurrection of Jesus Christ for the Christian faith, points in the following direction:

> *At first blush, the meaning of resurrection is that death is not always victorious... The meaning of the resurrection is complementary to Jesus' person and work. We saw earlier that this death can be interpreted as the death of a righteous one. His resurrection is a confirmation of that, for the righteous shall live by faith. His being raised from the dead is a confirmation by God of this life. And when Jesus has prayed for the perpetration it is the confirmation that his death is accepted as reconciliation.[194]*

The resurrection is not only the dynamics that make the Gospels the Power of God for salvation but it is also the event from which theological education owes its existence. The order to teach all God's councilors present at the Great Commission was authorized by the Risen One.

Paraphrasing Costas, we can affirm that the resurrection is the means through which theology and theological education exists, in its service to human beings and to its obedience on the command of Christ, just as the grain of wheat that falls on the ground and dies in order to gather more fruit for the power of resurrection.[195] With Christ's resurrection, theology can be living theology in that it does not speak of happenings in the past as a simple past but as historical happenings that are represented in the

---

[194] Van de Beek, Jesus Kyrios, 182.
[195] Costas, Hacia una Teología, 121.

power of the Holy Spirit while this same spirit inaugurates the glorious future of the sons of God.

Christian theology bases its foundation on Jesus Christ, its motivation and dynamics on the Holy Spirit and its future on reality, a splendid and festive reality of the new creation of all things for the glory of God. As Moltmann says: "In this spirit of resurrection, I can live fully, love fully and die fully as I am sure that I will be fully resuscitated."[196]

d. The Ascent as Glory

Christian faith believes that Christ descended to the deepest parts of the earth, rose up to heaven and sat on the right hand of the Father. According to the author of Hebrews, seven glories have been manifested in Christ (Heb. 1:2-3). Jesus is He who shines in full glory from the creation to the ascent to the right-hand of the father. According to this text:

Jesus Christ is the heir of all things.

He made the universe.

He is the radiance of the glory of God.

He is the exact expression (representation) of the being of God.

He sustains the universe.

It is He who purifies us from sin, and

He sat at the right hand of the Majesty on high.

The importance of the ascent of Christ has far-reaching implications. In the first place it has to do with the infinity

---

[196] J. Moltmann, Jesus Christ for Today's World, Minneapolis: Fortress Press, 1995, 89.

of resources that are liberated for the accomplishment of the great commission given to the people of God according to the Ephesians 4:10-14. This is the reason why according to the gospel the disciples did not see the ascent as a sad happening, but as something triumphant and festive (Mk. 16:20). Secondly, the ascent is a mark of the moment in which Jesus assumes supreme and glorious authority. He is revealed as He who sustains all things by the word of his power (Heb. 1:3). In it all things exist. (Col. 1:17). He reveals himself from then on as the Lord, not only of the Church but of all creation.

As the humiliated Lord his activity is directed *toward God*. He represents us, wandering and failing, suffering and showing guilt, before God. He is the guarantee that our covenant bond with God is not being broken. As the exalted Lord his activity is also directed *toward the world*. Not as if he would possess a separate ruling power over our province beside God; rather, God's rule over the world is exerted by the risen Christ. As the exalted Lord his activity is also directed *toward his community*.

We do not now refer to the fact that by his Spirit he works in the community, but as our representative he is the guarantee that the movement he established through his resurrection will not stop, but will always carry on, in whatever form, against all the forces that aim to undermine or destroy it.[197]

From the Christological vision as the center of theology, Christology is and should be the perspective on life in all its questions. Theology should revolve round the Lord that has been incarnated, was crucified, resuscitated and glorified. This same victorious Lord will come as the King in Glory. Today the Church announces and proclaims Jesus Christ as the Lord, but also believes and announces

---

[197] H. Berkhof, Christian Faith, 321.

that his Lord comes in glory when all tongues confess that Jesus Christ is Lord to the glory of God the Father (Philippians 2:10-11)

Genuine Latin American theology should be built on — and continue to be so — a single center, which is Christology, placed at the very heart of the American Latin theology. The interpretations made from the reversal of history, as Gustavo Gutiérrez proposes, privilege the historical presence of Jesus with an emphasis on the incarnation that becomes the paradigm for the mission and for the Latin American method of theology. It is in this perspective that Reformed theology, in order to be alive at the present time cannot stop considering the context of social life as the paradigm of understanding true wisdom: the wisdom of the cross.

This wisdom is not mere knowledge of the head, it includes compassion of the heart and acting according to this compassionate love. Jesus takes his disciples to the basic principles of an alternative practice that criticizes the current system, and he does so from the perspective of the Kingdom of God and the real life of the *ecclesia* — the community of faith.

The Roman Catholic theologian, Hugo Echegaray describes the practice of Jesus[198] on three levels: economy, politics and society, that correspond to the three very human gestures: the gesture of the hands, the gesture of the feet and the gesture of the eyes. It is possible to agree with this perspective that in the inclination of theology as wisdom, the practice of the hands has to do with love, where one can see the economic dimension of theology; the practice of the feet has to do with hope, the political dimension of the theology is recognized here; and finally the political practice of the eyes and of the ears that has to do with

---

[198] H. Echegaray, A Prática de Jesus, Petrópolis: Vozes, 1984.

faith, the dimension of the ideas and purposes. Everything has to do with the practical involving character that means *wisdom*.

Jesus reveals that theology should take human dignity seriously. Even so serious that he himself became the most indignant of human beings (Is. 53:3), in order to restore their dignity. This is as concrete as the right distribution of resources, the solidarity with the poor and oppressed, the respect regarding the freedom of others, the disposition to serve, the capacity to support conflicts and a universal love that overcomes all human differences. As emphasized by Casiano Floristán, a Catholic theologian of Salamanca: "In the face of fear, Jesus exalts freedom; in the face of fear, trust; and in the face of selfishness, generosity. The Church is the community of believers in Jesus and his Gospel."[199]

e. His Coming to Judge

"From where he will come to judge the living and the dead."
Though this statement of the Apostles' Creed has received little emphasis in most systematic theologies, is belongs to the basics of Christian faith. The creed proclaims the central mystery of Christ eternally begotten of the Father, his living in human history, passing victoriously through the cross and resurrection to this supreme declaration of his return. With these words the creed points to the grand finale: "He will come again in glory to judge the living and the dead."

Barth says about it: "After many verbs in the perfect and in the present, a future tense follows: 'He will return.' We can parse the entire second article (creed), [to the effect

---

[199] Floristán, Teología práctica, 37.

that] He came, He is seated at the right hand of God and He will come again."[200]

This faith has influenced the Christians' walk since the early days of the faith. Benedict XVI, in *Spe Salvi*, says the following:

> At the conclusion of the central section of the Church's great Credo—the part that recounts the mystery of Christ, from his eternal birth of the Father and his temporal birth of the Virgin Mary, through his Cross and Resurrection to the second coming—we find the phrase: 'he will come again in glory to judge the living and the dead.' From the earliest times, the prospect of the Judgment has influenced Christians in their daily living as a criterion by which to order their present life, as a summons to their conscience, and at the same time as hope in God's justice. Faith in Christ has never looked merely backwards or merely upwards, but always also forwards to the hour of justice that the Lord repeatedly proclaimed. This looking ahead has given Christianity its importance for the present moment. In the arrangement of Christian sacred buildings, which were intended to make visible the historic and cosmic breadth of faith in Christ, it became customary to depict the Lord returning as a king—the symbol of hope—at the east end; while the west wall normally portrayed the Last Judgment as a symbol of our responsibility for our lives—a scene which followed and accompanied the faithful as they went out to resume their daily routine. As the iconography of the Last Judgment developed, however, more and more prominence was given to its ominous and frightening aspects, which obviously held more fascination for artists than the splendor of hope, often all too well concealed beneath the horrors.[201]

The future, which will the Lord bring in judgment and justice, gives theology the character of the wisdom of God,

---

[200] K. Barth, Esboços de uma Dogmática, São Paulo: Fonte Editorial, 2006, 185.

[201] Benedict XVI, Spe Salvi, III:41. http://www.vatican.va/holy_father/benedict_xvi/encyclicals/documents/ hf_ben-xvi_enc_20071130_spe-salvi_en.html. Accessed on March 21, 2013.

and gives Jesus Christ, the fullness of divine wisdom revealed, its eschatological meaning. Theology as wisdom brings in its essence the sense of urgency of Christ's return and his judgment on the world.

The people of God is characterized by hope. Christ is hope. They hope in Christ, who in turn waits on them. He is not only the One Who was, but also the One who will come (Rev. 1:4). A. van de Beek, in analyzing the words of the Creed, says:

> However, without eschatology, everything else loses its meaning. To New Testament authors it is unthinkable to speak of an atoning death, resurrection, or pouring out of the Spirit, without the eschatological context. For all of those aspects have to do with the Day of the Lord. The entire New Testament is eschatology.[202]

Only in this context it is meaningful to speak of theology as wisdom. The expectation of the Day of the Lord is the foundation of the Christian faith that has crossed the centuries.

Truly, as Benedict XVI says,[203] the thought of Judgement has been diluted. In contemporary thought, the ideal of progress and eternal youth obstructs the thought of judgment. However, the pain and violence against the excluded, against life and nature on our planet, are crying for justice. Not to affirm the judgment of God who is coming with justice is to allow the killer to prevail over his victim and violence to triumph over peace. God will bring judgment: He is the God of Justice. His righteousness is his faithfulness to his covenant with creation.

In the Old Testament we find that the experience of Israel relies on this justice that liberates, saves and installs the right of the oppressed of the world. The promised

---

[202] Van de Beek, Jesus Kyrios, 187.
[203] Benedict XVI, Spe Salvi, III:42.

Messiah "will judge the poor with justice, and decide with equity in favor of the meek of the earth" (Is. 11:4). "He will declare righteousness to the Gentiles" (Is. 42:1). The prophet Malachi calls God the "Sun of Righteousness" (Mal. 4:2).

What should be said from the perspective of Scripture is that with the coming of God, the world of evil will be overcome, the realm of death and hell will be annihilated and destroyed. "His judgment is an annihilating 'no' all the forces that oppose Him and a radiant 'yes' to all his creatures."[204] Jesus Christ is the one who makes all things new. We can thus say that faith in the final judgment is first and foremost hope — the hope that He is the Omega, He will have the last word. It is noticeable the revival of this theme in theology, as confirmed by A. van de Beek who declares:

> *Then all things shall be made right on earth. Is will not be through a velvet revolution but with cosmic violence. The established structures of heaven and hell will collapse. The oppressor will be crushed and the righteous shall be liberated. That day will bring forgiveness of sins for those who waited on the Lord. Those who died hoping in the Lord will be raised in glory and those who dismissed the Lord's righteousness will receive their punishment, whether their live or died a long time ago.*[205]

What leads us to move forward with confidence can be summed up in the following: what remains for us even with fear and hope in the face of judgment is decidedly to blindly throw ourselves into the arms of the Lord, who knows us and loves us.[206] We are certain that in the last judgment, the books are opened (Rev. 20:12). But, at the moment that everything seems to have come to an end,

---

[204] J. Moltmann, Vida, Esperança e Justiça, um testamento teológico para a América Latina, São Bernardo do Campo: Editeo, 2008, 81.

[205] Van de Beek, Jesus Kyrios, 187.

[206] Hans Urs Von Balthasar, Meditaciones sobre El Credo Apostólico, Salamanca: Sigueme, 1997, 65.

one more book is brought in: the book of life (Rev. 20:11-15). "This book of grace is worn and abused a thousand times. But if it were not present, all would be lost."[207]

Living in the wisdom of Christ is to know that "it certainly gives no small security, that we shall be sisted at no other tribunal than that of our Redeemer, from whom salvation is to be expected."[208] The Creator of the world, the Redeemer and Savior, in His justice will prevail against injustice, love will conquer hate, peace will overcome hostility, humanity will overcome inhumanity, the Kingdom of God will extinguish the rule of evil. Therefore, in the biblical view, the judgment will not come primarily to reward some and punish others, but to create order and re-establish the eternal purpose of God. The final judgment shall not come against life but in favor of it.

Theology as the Way of Christ

The community of the faithful in Christ knows and understands that with the incarnation God was made human, the Lord became Servant and thus God showed his glory, his grace, love, truth, forgiveness and purpose. He showed not only his divine self but how to act. It is easy to agree with José Maria Abreu: "Every Christian mission has to be incarnated just as the life of Christ has been. A sweet Christian mission, impersonal, is the greatest Christian heresy in the existential expression of church life."[209]

Paul, in the same letter wherein he Christ calls the Wisdom of God, expresses the life of Christians by three words: faith, hope, and love (I Cor. 13:13). If theology is about the Wisdom of God it is about this life. Theology as wisdom is not only *speaking* about faith, hope and love; it

---

[207] Van de Beek, Jesus Kyrios, 193.
[208] Calvin, Institutes II, 16,18.
[209] J. M. Abreu, quoted by Costas, Hacia una teología, 122.

is rather an *expression* of these as it is an expression of the totality of life. It is this life in a specific way: as critical discourse in an academic setting. It is learning and teaching and therefore we can see it as learned faith, hope, and love: *docta fides*, *docta spes*, and *docta caritas*.

Theology is *docta fides*, where it will deepen the concept of the memory of faith that emphasizes that there is a way that can be summarized in one word: conviction. And it is under this conviction that the context is affirmed as a fundamental space where the great theological concepts lie, built in historical tradition.

It is here where the ideologies are judged. These are the ideologies that are usually turned axes in the calendars of theological education. It can be said that theology finds in *docta fides* a way that frees it from becoming hostage to dominant ideologies.

There has always been a unity since the origins of the Church between faith and Christian existence. Faith in Jesus, 'Lord and Christ' implied conversion, the beginning of a new life and its permanence in it. In Paul's writings the term 'faith' designated the totality of the human being's existence under Christ's grace.[210]

Then, we will be facing the task of theological teaching from an expectant perspective, that is to say, theology as *docta spes*. It is here where we found the task of theological labor, in a permanent and enriching dialectics, between the past and the future, between fides *et spes*, that we will be challenged towards the third concept, to face the challenges of the present, starting from understanding a provocative context of theological actions, that is to say, theology as *docta caritas*. However, it does not mean to practice charitable activities, but to assume the reality of agape.

---

[210] J. Alfaro, Revelacíon cristiana: fe y teologia, Salamanca: Sigueme, 1985, 89.

In Moltmann's words: theology works within three transitions, which are necessary for theological education; these are the theoretical reason of faith, the historical reason of hope and the practical reason of both: *intellectus amoris.*[211]

When understanding theology as *docta fides, docta spes* and *docta caritas*, the intention here is to aim the existent methodological relationship regarding the inseparable connection between faith, hope and love. So, Christian faith is a way and transition from hoping to seeing, and from loving to understanding.[212] Daniel Migliore writes that "faith, love, and hope are thus the expression of a new human freedom in relationship, a new way of being human in solidarity with others, made possible by the grace of God in Jesus Christ."[213] Theological education should act according to a basic presupposition, to understand itself as *docta fides*, which implies in the perspective of the crucified and risen Christ *docta spes* and *docta caritas*. Understanding is the objective of this faith.[214]

a. Theology as Docta Fides

Theology as wisdom operates on the foundation of faith, and this means it is primarily a reflection of faith, by faith and about faith. Theology presupposes for Christian faith the intellectual understanding of the truth of God in which we believe, and for this reason an agreement is made between the hearts and the minds of those who believe and know and the One who is believed and known.

---

[211] J. Moltmann, Experiences in Theology, London: SCM Press, 2000, 38.

[212] Moltmann, Experiences, 45.

[213] Migliore, Faith Seeking Understanding, 138.

[214] K. Barth, Fides Quaerens Intellectum: Anselms Beweis der Existenz Gottes (1931), Zurich, 1958.

When human beings know him in whom they believe, this is knowledge of God himself. To put it in Moltmann's words: "That is the theological concurrence between the 'object' and the perception of it (the *adaequatio rei et intellectus*). Truth is always accord, correspondence and harmony. Those who are in accord with God and who "correspond to him in thinking, feeling and acting are possessed by an infinite happiness, for they come to themselves and become what as human beings they are intended and destined to be: God's image on this earth."[215] To see with the eyes of the faithful is equal to a conversion and change of values. The conscience of the present links itself to the memory of the normative past as a source of faith, transmitted within the living tradition of the church, mainly in its confessions.

However, some arguments are necessary to clarify this topic: why is this memory necessary? This question constitutes an interrogation concerning *the sense, the position* and *the form* of theological memory; the answer to this question places all theological activity under the focus of theology as *docta fides*. Faith as lived, thought and communicated to guide life and history starting from the event of God in Jesus Christ, has been registered in the Scriptures and became effective with the Holy Spirit. For this reason faith is an answer to the voice of God in Jesus Christ, that pawns definitely the human being's freedom in his eternal destiny.[216] Even with its eyes focused on the future encounter with Christ, it still has eyes for the past from where its sense emanates.

---

[215] Moltmann, Experiences, 49.
[216] Alfaro, Revelación, 95.

a.1 The Sense of the Past for the Theological Task

One may ask what is the *sense of the critical memory of faith* that is exercised in theology? Are the consciousness of the present and the openness to the future not enough?

John Calvin, quoting Cicero, says, "History is the mistress of life."[217] Any theology without the memory of the divine acts in favor of human beings cannot fulfill its task of discernment and judgment of the present towards the future, because it would lack the decisive base of its task. It does not refer to the only one capable of making sense and measuring of things in a truer way, illuminating and transforming them, by establishing the core of redemption and reconciliation. Without referring to God's disclosure of new life, history would offer itself to the closed circle of the eternal return of identical things, a sad repetition of what had already been given, without novelty and surprise, because it is the fruit of things already available and programmable.

A theology without this past is, "human, too much human", and precisely therefore it will be shown in fact as the enemy of the human being as it would leave human beings in the narrow horizon of human's current or remote possibilities, without a true future or hope. A theology without the memory of the past cannot be a theology of hope.

Theology as *docta fides* constantly lies on the *anamnesis* of Christ's redeeming work that penetrates human existence and transforms it continually. "*Anamnesis* is not a simple intellectual function; it is an action."[218] The memory of faith recapitulates and becomes aware of the economy of God in Jesus Christ by the work of the Holy Spirit which

---

[217] Gorringe, Karl Barth, 87.

[218] D. Plou, Juntos en el Camino, Informe oficial de la Octava Asamblea el Consejo Mundial de Iglesias, Geneva: WCC Publications, 1999, 31.

renews all things, bringing light from the incarnation, crucifixion, resurrection and glorification of Christ. The community of faith experiences these events and shares them, not by its own force and ability, but by the grace of the Holy Spirit. In this perspective, Archbishop Anastasio affirmed during the eighth Assembly of the World Council of Churches, in Harare:

> *For the power of God anamnesis is an incessant dynamic movement, for which we come back to God, the source of our being; we are united with Christ and we received the Holy Spirit; it is an orientation that gives sense to our life and our march through space and time. By the renewal of anamnesis the Church maintains its vitality and its truth.*[219]

By practicing its task of memory of faith, theology recapitulates the center of its source, Jesus Christ; it makes a true thanksgiving doxology for all the wonderful actions of God in human history. The memory of faith lights that challenge up in such a way that it calls for an authentic love and respect before all people. This memory gives force and sense to the present and committed hope to the future, challenging the community of faith to face the new challenges of the present.

Theology as faith is born listening (cf. Rom. 10, 17): it is neither invented nor produced only by human forces; it is received and, at the same time, it is an answered word. "Theology depends completely on the word that precedes it and for which it is created, vivified and turned necessary. Thinking and speaking to human beings would be empty, saying nothing, being sterile, and if it were intended to be something more, something less or anything different, then an answer to that word."[220] "Any right

---

[219] Plou, Juntos, 34.
[220] Forte, Companhia, 162.

knowledge of God is born from obedience"[221]: a theology that does not obey the revelation testified in the Word, can speak about many things, but not about God, whose acting is the only novelty and hope of the world.

Within memory the conscience of the present is built; from memory the prophecy is born, for this, the memory of faith is alive. It is not just listening to the Word of Life as revealed in the past, but it is also moved by the expectation of the living, stimulated and cherished by the vital interest of the present. "The remembrance makes the hope present, makes it certain; and the hope keeps what is past present."[222]

a.2 The Places of Faith According to the Past

The relationship between faith and the past raises the issue about the sources, the places where God is known according to the past. There are, two fundamental sources that faith must observe: the Scriptures and the historical tradition of faith. On one hand, we have the Scriptures, the essential foundation of Christian faith, which drives us to Jesus Christ, the definitive foundation of faith. "Take away the Word and there is no faith left."[223]

The disclosure of God's divine presence is registered definitely and forever in history in the Scriptures, the "home" of the true theological word, where it inhabits the words of human beings expressed by the newborn church by the action of the Holy Spirit through the inspired authors. Theology must always go to the Scriptures as its source to cherish its faith and its thoughts of faith, to let itself be accomplished and be contaminated by the power of the foundational event, Jesus Christ.

---

[221] Calvin, Institutes I,6,2.
[222] Moltmann, Experiences, 56.
[223] Calvin quoted by Parker, Calvin: An Introduction, 81.

In the Scriptures, theology as memory of faith, will not only find its foundation and approach, but equally receive from it the strength to walk and in a creative way to move forward within human history along the paths of life, and in the abandoned territories of the human soul. By the life spilled by Christ and the renovating act of the Holy Spirit, the Scriptures can continue to be young forever, therefore, capable of speaking to all generations of human beings, in different contexts, satiating lives without life, thirsty for the Word of the Highest, which provides living water and feeds the hungry. For that, theologians will need the exegesis that gives the faithful a contact with the text and the message of the Scriptures; and, equally, those who make the exegesis must be theologians, who think of the biblical testimony organically and tell it in a significant and faithful way in the language of their own time.

On the other hand, the Word, consigned in the Scriptures, is vitally in the tradition and faith of the people of God. Theology in its task needs tradition, it will always read the Scriptures, but at the same time it will hear the voices of the acts of God within the history of the Church, respecting the Christians and their writing and honoring the Holy Spirit that liberated its talents throughout history.[224]

The ecumenical movement brought a great contribution with regard to tradition that opened new perspectives to Protestants who used to be always suspicious towards tradition. In the Report of Section II: Scripture, Tradition[225] and Traditions, of the Fourth World Conference on Faith and Order, Montreal, 1963 is recorded:

---

[224] Calvin, Institutes III, 2, 6.

[225] "In our report we have distinguished a number of different meanings of the word tradition. We speak of the Tradition (with capital T), tradition (with a small t) and traditions. By the Tradition is meant the Gospel itself, transmitted from generation to generation in and by the Church, Christ him-

By tradition we do not mean traditionalism. The Tradition of the Church is not an object which we possess, but a reality by which we are possessed. The life of the Church has its source in God's act of revelation in Jesus Christ, and in the gift of the Holy Spirit to his people and his work in their history. Through the action of the Holy Spirit, a new community, the Church, is constituted and commissioned, so that the revelation and the life which are in Jesus Christ may be transmitted to the ends of the earth and to the end of time. Tradition in its content not only looks backward to its origin in the past but also forward to the fullness which shall be revealed.[226]

The concept of tradition cannot be confused with traditionalism. Jarolasv Pelikan opposes these two concepts with a good contrast: "Tradition is the living faith of those already dead – traditionalism is the dead faith of those now alive."[227]

Through tradition memory becomes presence and an up-to-date experience. It is the event that happened once and forever in Jesus Christ, turning itself contemporary, presenting action by the force of the Holy Spirit. In this sense, it can be affirmed that Tradition is the history of the Spirit within the history of his Church. "As Christians we all acknowledge with thankfulness that God has revealed himself in the history of the people of God in the Old Testament and in Christ Jesus, his Son, the mediator between God and man. God's mercy and God's glory are the begin-

---

self present in the life of the Church. By tradition is meant the traditional process. The term traditions issue in two senses, to indicate both the diversity of forms of expression and also what we call confessional traditions, for instance the Lutheran tradition or the Reformed tradition." Kinnamon and Cope, The Ecumenical Movement, An Anthology of Key texts and Voices 139

[226] Kinnamon and Cope, The Ecumenical Movement: An Anthology of Key texts and Voices, 142.

[227] J. Pelikan, The Emergence of the Catholic Tradition (100-600), vol. 1 of The Christian Tradition: The Development of Doctrine, Chicago: University of Chicago Press, 1971, 9.

ning and end of our own history. The testimony of prophets and apostles inaugurated the Tradition of his revelation."[228]

Theology must dialogue permanently with all traditions of the history of the Church in its expressions and diversity of voices of the one Tradition. There is a place for all the great classic texts, from the apostolic fathers, the mystics of the Middle Ages, to the Reformers. Theology is made within that historical path. The history of the faith of the believing community is the homeland of theological articulation. The Report of the Fourth World Conference on Faith and Order, Montreal, 1963, stresses:

The life of the Church is lived in the continuous recalling, appropriation and transmission of the once-and-for-all event of Christ's coming in the flesh, and in the eager expectation of his coming in glory. All this finds expression in the Word and in the Sacraments in which 'we proclaim the Lord's death till he come again' (I Cor. 11.26).[229]

Looking at the old Christian writers known as the apostolic fathers, we learn two inseparable dimensions about the theological labor that emphasize the character of the wisdom. Every reflection and all action are characterized by fidelity, in testifying the Word both with words and with life. The fathers of the church have an expressive place in theological labor – they occupy a privileged place in the memory of faith. Their characteristic was the fact that they "didn't seek to exercise their own mental ability, but serving, they sought to express, to defend and to illustrate faith in a common way in an intimacy with Christ. That is the reason why they are called 'fathers,' as if the

[228] Kinnamon and Cope, The Ecumenical Movement: An Anthology of Key texts and Voices, 1997, 139.

[229] Kinnamon and Cope, The Ecumenical Movement: An Anthology of Key texts and Voices, 1997, 142.

Church were indebted to them, more than to the individual mind or to their group as such."[230]

From them theology learns to love the Scriptures, the sense of totality that she embraces, the unitary horizon in which life should be lived under the light of the Word of God and the symbols of faith, which are fruits of centuries of the pilgrims' mission, everything connected with the eternal Mystery revealed in the Son of God, by which the community of faith is called to receive, to celebrate and to communicate it to the world as divine wisdom.

Another place where the tradition of faith is explicitly notable are the Reformed Fathers. We are indebted to Luther and Calvin for the testimonies of their thoughts. They stressed the importance of faith as base for life, not only as knowledge but as a lived reality of freedom. From the Reformers the Church receives non-negotiable emphases for the reconstruction of the theological labor. For example, the teacher of theology learns the superiority of the Word of God over every human word; the Sovereignty of God renews and judges the powers of institutions and destructive, oppressive and exclusive empires.

A theology that operates in a rupture with that past or is unable to heal the harmful separation that was introduced between intellectual knowledge of the past and spirituality in its several and multiple expressions, not only will become poor in memory, but will also become weak and ineffective to the present conscience or to a future that seeks to be significant in facing the new and surprising challenges that are presented to the Church in a society where globalization reigns and where people have lost reference points and existent values that maintained the foundations of civilization through the centuries. In the disposable and superfluous society, which is illusory

---

[230] Y. M. Congar, La Tradizione e la Vita della Chiesa, Roma: Paoline, 1983, 143.

and wherein human beings are just passengers, theology with an eternal message that invaded time needs to adapt its language connecting its source as a place of faith to contemporary time. Adaptation to the present does not mean forgetting the past, but precisely bringing in the past as healing tradition that refers to the healing deeds of God.

Finally, the task of theology does not consist in new building, but in reconstructing the places of faith. That makes theology debtor to history and the whole life of the Church and the history of the community. It is the tradition that a countless line of witnesses has lived and still lives. Theology does not invent the truth; it can only find a possible place of resonance and presence of the great event of the past, for today and for each new generation.

For this, theological educatory must know how to make and how to teach theology and thus how to bring in the tradition. It does not only consist in pointing out the faith registered in the sacred texts and in the statements of the confessions and in the great classic of the history of Christian thought. It brings in tradition as a living stream wherein people must be involved. Moltmann, in his introduction to theology, affirms:

> *Christian theology presupposes the Christian creed — belief in certain objective truths, the fides quae creditur — and unfolds the inward reasonableness of faith, the intellectus fides, within the orbit of the church. Anselm does not yet have modern subjectivity of faith in mind, the so-called fides qua creditur — faith as intimate personal conviction. But according to his program for theology the path runs in a single direction, from faith to understanding — credo ut intelligam. It does not run in the reverse direction either, from understanding to faith — intelligo ut credam, I understanding so that I may believe.*[231]

---

[231] Moltmann, Experiences, 47.

Moltmann opposes the traditional position of faith to understanding and defends the dialectic complementation: I understand in order to believe.[232] Actually both are entwined. John Calvin binds faith and knowledge firmly together. Faith is sited not in ignorance, but in knowledge, and that not only of God but also of his Divine will.[233] Similarly Clement of Alexandria says: 'Now neither is knowledge without faith nor faith without knowledge',[234] and Cyril of Jerusalem: 'Faith is an eye which enlightens every conscience and imparts understanding'[235]; and Augustine: 'We believed that we might know; for if we wished first to know and then to believe, we should not be able either to know or to believe.'[236]

Calvin was concerned to show that faith was not only subjective or mainly subjective but thoroughly objective as well; not simply an inward state of mind or heart but a relationship, and that the special relationship with God for us is Christ.[237] In this relation the life of Christians and the work and the life of Christ, his death and resurrection are connected by an inseparable unity by the work of the Holy Spirit.

It can be said that the dynamics of faith is the understanding that it is from memory to memory, from faith to faith that the Word comes to inhabit several generations

---

[232] Moltmann, Experiences, 47.

[233] Calvin, Institutes I, 2, 10-13

[234] Clement of Alexandria, Stromata V,1, transl. William Wilson. From Ante-Nicene Fathers, Vol. 2. Edited by Alexander Roberts, James Donaldson, and A. Cleveland Coxe. Buffalo, NY: Christian Literature Publishing Co., 1885.

[235] Cyril of Jerusalem, Catechetical Lecture 5,4, transl. Edwin Hamilton Gifford. Nicene and Post-Nicene Fathers, Second Series, Vol. 7. Edited by Philip Schaff and Henry Wace. Buffalo, NY: Christian Literature Publishing Co., 1894.

[236] Augustine, Homily in John 27,9, Homilies on the Gospel according to John and his first letter, transl. H. Brown, A Library of the Fathers of the Holy Catholic Church Anterior to the Division of the East and the West, Oxford: Parker/ London: F. and J. Rivington, 1848.

[237] Parker, Calvin, 80.

through the eras, opening every wonderful renewed novelty by the Spirit in the Word of Revelation. It is only in this hermeneutic, fed and vivified by the transformative experience of the Holy Spirit that the reality of the "already now" and the expectation of the "not yet" find convergence. "Tradition, far away from being a longing for and missing the past, it is the permanent "today of God" within the "today" of men; memory is the presence of the Eternal and anticipation of the promised future."[238]

a.3 Faith in Progress: From Assensus to Fiducia

Theological orthodoxy differentiates three stages of faith corresponding to the three traditional concepts of faith in God: *notitia*, which is 'knowing.' Starting from this concept we can speak about *"credere Deum"* (to believe that God exists). A second concept is the *'assensus'*, which is 'recognition', when we speak about *'credere Deo'* (to believe in God); as a third concept of faith we have *'fiducia'*, which is 'trust', when we can speak about *'credere in Deum'* (to believe trusting God).[239]

These three concepts can be understood in connection with the two dimensions whereto is referred in the above quote from Moltmann. On the one hand we have the *fides objectiva* or the *fides quae creditur* (the objective faith or the belief in which one puts faith, faith as content); on the other hand we have the *fides subjectiva* or *the fides qua creditur* (the personal faith or the belief that produces the faith or the faith that has to do with the believing person, faith as an act of believing, trusting). *Faith as fides quae* feeds the faithful theological memory and nourishes the

---

[238] Forte, A Teologia, 173.
[239] Araya, Introducción, 64.

living faith, the act of believing and abandoning itself to God, the *fides qua creditur.*[240]

Traditionally this subjective faith (fides qua) was seen as identical to faith understood as fiducia (trust), while the objective faith (fides quae) was understood as the one that embraced the stages notitia (to know) and assensus (to recognize). The cognitive dimension of fides quae makes possible and justifies the decisional-practical dimension of fides qua, which acts and informs the content and the motivation of fides quae itself.[241]

In a wise understanding of theology, none of the stages can be left out from the progress of theology as the dynamics of the Christian faith. For it will be impossible to recognize God *(assensus)* without knowing him *(notitia).* And it will be impossible to trust God *(fiducia)* without recognizing him *(assensus).* This theological reflection according to a living theology could be reconstructed as follows: trusting in God *(fiducia)* has as a requirement to appreciate *(assensus),* and this appreciation has another requirement that is listening *(notitia).* All these aspects belong to the dynamics of faith.

Theology as wisdom seeking a *fides qua* that comes without the *fides quae* is insufficient while it is without any base; it results in superficiality of an uncontrolled subjectivism, but it may also not deal with a *fides quae* that comes without the *fides qua,* which results in a deteriorating faith in beliefs or in a dead orthodoxy. Nowadays many Latin American 'evangelical spiritualist' movements have been privileging the *fides qua,* falling into a mystic pragmatism, while not only the formalistic orthodoxy but even more

---

[240] "The term faith indicates at the same time a decisive act and a continuing attitude of believing (fides qua creditur) as well as a set of beliefs and convictions (fides quae creditur). This fides qua can never be without or separated from the content of faith (fides quae)." N. Lossky and others, Dictionary of the Ecumenical Movement, Geneva: WCC Publications, 1991, 407.

[241] Alfaro, Revelación, 120.

neo-liberal Protestantism privileges theology as study of the faith as *fides quae*, falling into an excess of intellectual encyclopedism. This polarization has been showing itself harmful to the theological task, creating a non-transposing ditch between Churches and theological Seminaries, between orthodox and charismatic, between liberals and evangelicals.

A *fides quae* that does not want to be at the same time *fides qua*, degenerates itself in a faith in superficial beliefs without transformation and human liberation; and also, *a fides qua* that does not want to be at the same time *fides quae* degenerates itself in a fanatic and limitless enthusiasm or subjectivism.[242] In this direction, the Roman Catholic theologian Alfaro wrote:

Only in the vital unit of *orthodoxy* and *orthopraxis* could the total verification of Christian faith be based. Each one of them is as indispensable as insufficient for this verification: orthodoxy, as a human expression (concepts, symbols, language) of the reality of our salvation already accomplished in Christ; *orthopraxis*, as a receptive appropriation of this salvation. They are insufficient (each one by itself), because they need one another; Christian *orthopraxis* should be guided by the orthodoxy, and the last one, taking its turn, would not have authenticity unless it is within Christian *praxis*.[243]

It is under this conviction that I propose in this study that theology is to be understood as wisdom. Wisdom integrates faith as theoretical reason, hope as historical reason and love as practical reason.[244] Faith as trust

---

[242] Araya, Introducción, 67.

[243] Alfaro, Revelación, 120.

[244] Moltmann, Experiences, chapter 5, where the chapter on theological reason is divided into these three points: faith as a theoretic reason, hope as a historic reason and love as a practical reason.

overcomes the old concept of being a jump in the darkness, a jump into the unknown. Faith is like a jump into the love of God, a jump into the arms of the living and merciful God, whom we know through Jesus Christ and by the whole tradition of the church.

Practical theology has been affirming more and more that faith is only real if it is related to practical life and not just with believing in doctrines. It seeks to overcome the old concept emphasized by Catholic and Protestant theologians that the believer's *praxis* was only the result and expression of faith, and that it was not a constituent dimension of faith itself.[245] We fully agree with these considerations, but we will not oppose them to historical research, as history cannot be opposed to sociological research. A living faith with critical research into the past tradition and present society is the aim of theology as *docta fides*. It affirms a faith that finds its credentials in the expressed Revelation of God in the history of Israel and, above all, in Jesus Christ, but it does not come without the reflection and thought built through the centuries up to now, achieved by Christian thought and human sciences.

Theology as wisdom of faith wants to be a public declaration that faith is dynamic and alive, and as it is life, it modernizes its content through each generation, because faith is not and it cannot be frozen in cans. It is not a treasure inside a coffer locked by a thousand keys, but it is an ocean to be navigated and explored in depth.

Faith is the "memorial" of the Lord faithfully transmitted through the succession of the generations of Abraham's children: "This day will be for you as a memorial, and you will celebrate it as Jehovah's party; in your generation you will celebrate it; it is a perpetual ordinance" (Ex.

---

[245] Alfaro, Revelación, 118.

12:14). In this ceremony, the great event of liberation becomes present to the faith that celebrates: each one should know that the Lord also drove them out of Egypt to him. The current *"here"* enters in the great *"honor"* of the experience and brought to the memory of the people that walked with the Exodus to the promises of those who chose and were summoned.

Theology as wisdom of faith is not imposed on from outside the community of believers and their relation to God. It is fully embedded in God's merciful coming to human beings. Faith is *theonomous*, which means faith in God, in the presence of God and for the glory of God, who is present in the world in the living Spirit as he was present in the human Christ. It is to believe in Christ as *fiducia* and not in human petrified traditions that seek to impose themselves by force, either by the power of any rationalism that seeks to manipulate, or in emotions that want to dominate magically. "As trust in Jesus' faith is a gift, it is not a product, it is Gospel and it is not law."[246]

Theology as *docta fides* affirms the necessary unit of *fides qua creditur* and *fides quae creditur*. Wisdom *(sapientia)* is the mediator and integrative concept of these poles of faith. Wisdom is the daily practical experience and fear of the Lord at the same time. Therefore, if we understand theology as *docta fides*, it is clear that the alternative between faith and reason is surpassed. Theology from this perspective is never neutral knowledge, but it is an admitted understanding, and it is a living confession, and as it lives it expresses its foundation, trust.[247]

---

[246] Araya, Introducción, 71.

[247] "Confession, Barth defines the necessary implications of acknowledgment and recognition as a standing to one's faith, or to its object. The Christian makes confession, not just by what he says and does, but what he is – the little light reflecting the big light form which derives and in which is has its being" (Geoffrey William Bromiley, Introduction to the Theology of Karl Barth, Grand Rapids: Eerdmans, 1979, 196).

Finally, theology is the reflexive conscience of faith as trust, it is the powerful memory of God's acts in the history of humanity, from where it departs and under such a perspective it acts and moves forward, believing, adoring and testifying while it seeks signs of transformation. Without the confident and transformative existence, the theological form of memory would be an ineffective revisitation of the old, unable to say and to raise new things that come from the living Word of God.

Without *docta fides*, theology would be an empty dispute or longing voice or just a cheap speech full of an incomprehensible silence of God, as human talk; but, for the sake of *fiducia*, it is a living word, witness of the event and anticipation of the promised future. In *docta fides* theology does not capture the object of its memory, but it makes itself humble due to the wonders of God, thoughts of admiration and celebration before the aesthetics of Christ's Gospel that saves the world; in *docta fides* theology is no longer a hypothesis of an isolated subject, but it is the language of a chosen people by the election of grace, turned into critical memory according to the redeemed community; in *docta fides*, raised and fed by the provocative and reminiscent memory, and summoning of the Word, theology as wisdom of faith does not betray the deepest expectations of the people of God as a community in exodus, but it offers them the water of life in historical deserts, unique and capable of satisfying the thirsty contemporary hearts in its longings in a society that has been forgetting the art of being truly human.

Theology as *docta fides* seeks to be a liberating act. Being wise, faith will try to be a warrant of freedom and of the liberating force in its reflexive thought and in teaching theology; as theology of wisdom it will manifest itself as the updated memory of history for human beings[248] in search of a planetary identity, while at the same time, it will contemplate its purpose in the presence of the creator in his creation.

Theological education in the 21th century could be or become, as wisdom of faith, a critical conscience within history, an interpreter of the signs of time, maker of bridges between the Revelation and the existential situation, while it is at the same time a homelike community including the social victims excluded by economic and technological tensions. Faith has been and is the source, the driving force and the common goal of theological education.

b. Theology as Docta Spes

Now we come to the second aspect of theology: *docta spes*. Theology is a contribution to transformation. As *docta spes* wisdom will not strife for unrealistic goals. That would only lead to frustration and thus be the end of hope. Wise hope is aware of the stubbornness of human society. But wise hope also knows that realistic hope is really hope: things can change and there is transformation. The church does not need to preach an illusion that will change the world, which is beyond its mission and beyond its forces, but can and should express itself as the salt of the earth and light of the world, both calling and capable to work in the perspective of Christ who is the Light of the world.

It is in this context that the prophetic task of theology as a critical reflection on the prophetic voice of the church has its place. By theological prophecy, the Word of salvation is faithful to its origin: it is the task of theology as a

---

[248] Barth wrote: "In face of the world the individual believer has to be, 'very humbly but very courageously, a confessing Christian in the confessing community." Cited by Bromiley, Introduction,198.

prophecy to be described as responsible for speaking about the God of the *event* in a variety of human situations. Theology as a proclamation takes into account the challenges of social and cultural contexts, as well as the interrogations of human existence and of the experience of believing, in order to significantly share the message with them, pointing to its comprehensibility, its practical effectiveness, its historical-critic relevance, its capacity to offer a global horizon of sense to the senseless shouting of "ultra modernity".[249]

Theology must be open to the signs of the time, distinguishing what is going on and in this context proclaim the message of hope. In this perspective the message of the eighth Assembly of the World Council of Churches (WCC) held in Harare, Zimbabwe, 1998 should be noted:

> We live in such a destroyed world, so smashed by violence! The whole inhabited world (oikoumene) is full of the hopelessly poor and children dying of hunger, excluded people and innocent victims of war and ethnic conflicts. The eminence of a nuclear apocalypse continues to gravitate as a cloud on our horizon, and our planet shakes among the claws of an ecological crisis.[250]

As *docta spes* theology supports the prophetic task of the church. Students must be trained to raise their voice in order to combat exploitation, oppression and other forms of injustice. In a theology of wisdom the prophetic voice is not violent. Wisdom knows that violence evokes new violence. Wisdom does not want to destroy structures by revolution. Those who violently combat violence

---

[249] This ultra modern concept appeared in the current debates opposing the little understood idea of the so-called post-modernity published in IHU Unisinos Magazine, number 126, December 2004.

[250] D. Plou, Together in the Way:Official Report of Eighth Assembly of the World, WCC Publications, 1999, 40.

become violent themselves and build on the vicious spirals of death.

Wisdom works in a different way for transformation, working from within the existing structures and changing them by convincing and luring. First of all it teaches people to find ways for changing their fate. There is always a risk that those who intercede on behalf of others make these other ones dependent on them and thus leads them in new relations of dependency. This is even more the case because it is attractive to have people dependent on you. It is an aspect of docta spes to be aware of this and to be self-critical. Liberating hope frees people from dependency and makes them free to serve freely other people. Therefore the praxis of hope only secondarily is undertaking action on behalf of those who are not able to do so themselves. Empowerment has priority and only where no power is left the ministry of the church takes over responsibility by finding access to those who are in power where no access is for the powerless.

Here we come to the next aspect of the praxis of hope: luring the powerful to transformation. It is an eminent task of theologians to inspire those who are in a situation where they can practice influence to envisage a better hope than material gain. A vision of hope that opens new ways will change society in a better way than conflicts and violence.

Theological hope is *docta* spes. It is critical, not only self critical but also critical to the other ones. Sometimes this critique must be expressed severely. It is however the challenge for theologians to learn how this critique is most effective, depending on the person involved and the situation wherein it is applied. An ideology is easily proclaimed, but solid critique that can be heard and people gives the opportunity for change is a subtle task. If anything, than critique is a matter of wisdom: not to oppose in such a way that conflicts are deepened, but even less in such a way that one is actually silent and does not contribute anything to transformation of the *status quo.*

Critique is needed to those who oppress, both from the security complexes of the wealthy people and in the slums of the poor who exploit the other poor. Critique is however also needed to those who are oppressed and have become blunt for any transformation. To those people the hopeful voice of the prophet Isaiah must be heard: "As the heavens are higher than the earth, so are my ways higher than you ways and my thoughts than your thoughts... You will go out in joy and be led forth in peace" (Is. 55:9, 12). God is a God of hope, of new times and new ways that his people never expected.

Thus we come to the third aspect: *docta spes* is always related to *docta fides.* The *anamnesis* is a memory of hope. Faith reminds the stories of liberation of the past. It recalls the liberation of the people of Israel from the oppressive power of Egypt that was so much stronger than they were. It commemorates the story of David and Goliath. The reason of faith argues by all those stories wherein the liberating deeds of God are recorded by his people. By faith hope becomes well-founded hope and thus *docta spes.*

Above all the reason of hope is founded on the anamnesis of the resurrection of Jesus. He overcame the powers of death. He who was rejected by the political and religious leaders was raised by the power of God and made the King of kings. Faith as the memory of Jesus is the solid ground of hope (Heb. 11:1).

Nowadays, the cities in Brazil are in a crisis and also that theological education in Brazil is in a crisis. A solution to this problem cannot be found without knowing the true character of the problem. The problem is of theological order. In Brazil, theological education has lacked a solid theological fundament in the traditions of faith and in the

Scriptures. The result is that the theological centers produce fragile pulpits with a superficial message. This result is a growing number of Christians without a corresponding quality in the content of faith and the due Christian ethics. Theological seminaries produced a theology that is contingent to what the customer desires.

I understand a solid theology to be that which bases its fundaments on the Scriptures, on the fundaments of theological tradition and history, in the confessions, the fathers of the church, the reformers considered under the light of the problems at the time as is reflected and found in the context. Theology should first of all focus on the content of faith for, as Orlando Costas said, methodology is subordinate to theology instead of the inverse.[251]

Jesus Christ is, thus, the center, the heart of theological education. Without him there will neither be Christian theology nor theological education as wisdom because he is the content, the wisdom of God and the central nucleus of theological teaching. From that said it can be concluded that all theology as divine wisdom should be Christ-centric. And all action for teaching theology should also be Christ-centric; otherwise it will lose its authority, effectiveness and relevance in context, and thus lose its character as *docta spes*, because it does not evoke any hope.

A theological education pertinent to reality should be with wisdom and discerningly take seriously the Lordship of Jesus Christ, the holy love of God, human sinfulness, the sovereignty of the Holy Spirit, the place of the church, the transforming power of *kerygma* and the place of faith, always bearing in mind the reality of the Kingdom of God.

Theological teaching is not only indispensable to Christianity but essential. Christianity is existentially a religion of the Word of God. A church exists for preaching and

---

[251] Costas, Hacia, 263.

teaching the Word of God and it is on this basis that the church either sustains itself or falls. To save a true place for theological teaching in the world needs to be the greatest concern of the church.

We live in an interval of time with a society in transition of paradigms. It is a time of confusion and a lack of seriousness of values. Ethics are in a substantial crisis. The great sources of traditions of the people have been eliminated. There is an uninstalled certainty in the world of today and we live seeking an island of certainty in a sea of uncertainties. It is in this context that theological education seeks a meaning of reference in the middle of the confusion of voices.

This is the objective of theology as wisdom, to place itself on the way to public theology in the middle of the uncertainties of human life. The fact is that theology cannot renounce either its source or its cultural context for that which should communicate the content of faith. It should, with insistence, work for the Kingdom of God and for the world in the Kingdom of God.

The church needs to understand its message to be able to be truly a church. The understanding of this message is the task necessary for theology. That is to say, theology is connected to the message of the Gospel that is an expression of the relationship between God and his world and the nature of God that is expressed in this relationship. Only by understanding the nature of God and his relationship with the world can the church keep its identity.

Opposing an attitude of indifference to teaching brings theology down to its place on the backbone of Christian faith, and, as we have already affirmed, theology has to do with the Gospel that is not an abstract concept but a dynamic way that changes until an end and for a specific purpose. Thus as theology seeks to understand a message from the Gospel, so the activity of theological teaching gives a finality to the labor of theologians and consequently gives to them the purpose and the meaning of fidelity to theology as wisdom of God to the encounter of human reality.

The cities in the contemporary world need a theological education full of hope that leads to resuscitation. The resurrection is a great theological avenue for a living theology, wisdom of the manifestation of the glory of the Lamb of God. He is the savior, and salvation is not only to be saved from sin but from all that has broken intimacy with God the Father. He has saved us from the world of sin and condemnation and still more he has saved us from ourselves. As affirmed by Moltmann:

> *In the Christian faith, affliction is not separate from God, but on the contrary, it takes us to an ever deeper communion with God. Christian faith in God is essentially a communion with Christ and a communion with Christ is essentially communion with an injured Christ, sufferer and abandoned. In his afflictions the human being shares the afflictions of Christ as Christ in his pain withstood the afflictions that befell human beings.*[252]

The path to the resurrection points to a glorious victory of life over death and because of this the Christological character of theology is important for theological education; there can neither be Christian faith nor Christian theology without the resurrection. Without the resurrection Jesus simply becomes reduced to an historic personality, and theology will be delving each day further into the past and not dealing with the Christ living by his Spirit. Any theology without this motivating process of Christ is just a step away from any religious paganism, in a relativity that obstructs the glory of the Son of God. "God yes, Jesus

---

[252] Moltmann, Jesus Christ for Today's World, 22.

no" is definitely not the way for Christian theological education. To be snatched by the Spirit of resurrection means to be put in a new dimension of life, the life of God.

In 1969 the Evangelical Association of Theological Seminaries (ASTE) promoted a seminary to try to identify the faces of Jesus in the modern world. Under the title "Who is Jesus Christ in Brazil?" the event counted on the participation of important theologians and scholars from that period such as Leonardo Boff, Hubert Lepargneur and João Dias de Araújo.[253] During the seminary was argued that the Christ that emerges from popular religion is a "dead Christ." He was fixed to the cross and unable to react, the result of years of the use of the crucifix of a distant and artificial faith. João Dias de Araújo, a Presbyterian theologian wrote: "We can affirm that in Brazil we have, thinking about the majority of religious people, a Christianity that emphasizes passion and the suffering and death of Christ rather than to his victory over death and to his ascent and to his office as mediator and priest, our advocate, the Living Christ that is spoken about in the New Testament."[254]

From this perspective a "distant Christ" emerges and in this sense an image like that of Christ the Redeemer positioned on the top of the Corcovado hill in Rio de Janeiro makes complete sense. "He is a distant God that is always there above" – say the people. According to Araujo "the person of Christ does not occupy the central place in the spirituality of the majority of people; it is not a figure of having arrived and being intimate with devotional life."[255] This distancing ends up producing other "helpers" who

---

[253] J. C. Maraschin, Quem é Jesus Cristo no Brasil, Aste: São Paulo, 1974.

[254] J. D. de Araujo, Imagens de Jesus Cristo na cultura do povo brasileiro. In: J. Maraschin, Quem é Jesus Cristo no Brasil, São Paulo: ASTE, 1974, 45.

[255] Araujo, Imagens, 46.

take the place of the Messiah in everyday life. "Christ always stays away from the devotional life of the people because he is substituted by others considered to be possessed of divine powers thus dispensing the presence of Christ."[256] Mainly among the poorer levels of society, the figures of saints such as Maria and even those who are not even saints such as Padre Cícero perform more miracles and are more present than "Christ without power."[257] The sources of the Christian message do not proclaim a distant Christ, but Christ incarnate and risen from death in order to give new life to human beings.

As *docta fides* the reason of faith is critical and so the source of *docta spes*: critical hope. It knows that the road to victory is a narrow way. The resurrection of Jesus was preceded by his crucifixion. The Christian message tells about sacrifices and seemingly deadlocks.

It is also a message that prepares for patience. The stories of liberation are embedded in stories of long lasting suffering. The gracious prophecy of Deutero-Isaiah is in the face of seventy years of exile and Moses was called after 430 years in Egypt. The way to the Promised Land was a forty years journey through the desert. So, as critical hope, theology must train people for perseverance in the hard contexts of social and political oppression and exclusion. This training is not directed to resignation but to perseverance on the long way to liberation.

This perseverance is even more required because the liberation in Christ is eschatological. The final freedom will not be attained in this world. Freedom in this world will always be limited, not full freedom and also limited in time. The moments of freedom are signs of a greater future that is given in the resurrection of the dead. Therefore the reason of faith is also the reason of hope for those who

---

[256] Araujo, Imagens, 48.
[257] Araujo, Imagens, 48.

were the victims of history. Those who died are not lost, but we expect the resurrection of the dead in the eternal kingdom of God. While a political ideology is only hope for those who survive and overcome, the message of faith is hope for those who are killed by the powers of history but will be set free by him who will judge history in the final judgment that will set things right.

Finally, the anamnesis of faith is the anamnesis of the crucifixion of Jesus as the one who gave his life on our behalf and to rescue us from our sinful nature. In the anamnesis we cannot leave out human sin. That means two things: (1) human reality will not change easily because (2) human beings are inclined to evil. The message of hope will be contested by the world. Sin is so strong that it brought the death of the cross. We cannot exclude our own sin. Christ died on behalf of us and thus we are sinners. That prevents Christian theologians from boasting on their own righteousness. The gospel calls first and for all themselves to conversion. We have to take into account our own resistance to freedom and hope.

As Christ gave himself for the sins of humanity in a world of sin because of love, then the Church and the individual Christians should also love the world to which they are sent. They should not look at people who are outside the Church with suspicion or belligerence forcing them to repent or desiring to control them. It must be made clear that you will not go to the world as a conqueror but as an agent of reconciliation, not with hostility to the non-Christian sinners but with the same compassion with which Jesus looked at those prisoners of inhumanity, alienated from God, from others, from themselves and from nature. Theologians are not in a position to judge sinners since they themselves also need to be forgiven for their own sins. Each teacher of theology is not a savior of the world but is dependent on the Salvation of God just as any other person..

Christians will not resolve the problems of injustice and suffering in the world as, in truth, they are part of the problem. The danger is the approximation of the people with an attitude that reveals arrogance so that he or she approaches the fellow beings as a strong person against a weak one; a just one against an unjust; a superior one against an inferior one. Christians, being sent to the world on their mission, should be conscious of never pointing to themselves, not even for his moral and spiritual accomplishments.

Christ died for sinners because he loved the world. That implies that Christians cannot refute the world. They are called to love a sinful world, not by affirming its sin, but by loving it and thus taking away sin's sting. Maybe here faith as *docta fides* gets its deepest meaning: in the *anamnesis* Christians are prevented from fighting against other people and called to lure them to the love of Christ. That is the wisdom of God as the wisdom of the cross. And so finally the *docta fides* turns to the *docta caritas*.

Theological education must train students on this threefold way of *docta caritas*, *docta spes* and *docta fides* as the one way of Christ As argued before it is education into a *habitus*. Wisdom is not isolated knowledge but an attitude of life, nourished and shaped by love, hope and faith.

This has great consequences for the way the program is shaped. Certainly there must be sound knowledge. Students must be well informed and well trained in critical thought. It requires also a deep involvement in society, so that love is not abstract but has the face of human beings on the streets and in the houses of Londrina. Study is also sound case study, not in order to objectify a person to a case, but bringing in her or his case as a critical question in the theological discourse. That does not mean that cases are the only entry in training as a problem directed education. The entries of wisdom are manifold. It means that cases, *anamnesis*, statistics, consistency must be brought in and meet each other in the one theological course.

This has also consequences for the different disciplines of the theological study. The classic encyclopedic separation of disciplines cannot serve the development of a theology as wisdom. Exegesis, history, sociology, psychology and all other fields must be intertwined in the one hermeneutic network of theology. Certainly one person can be more trained in a specific field and another in another field, but they cannot operate separately as if the other field does not influence their own work. After the encyclopedic separation since the Enlightenment a new type of theology must be developed where a theologian is not firstly a representative of a specific department, but an all round theologian and subsequently has his or her own focus, but this always as a contribution to the whole. That should not be at the cost of scholarly standards but, on the contrary, a challenge for higher standards and for both more relevant and more academic theology, because relevant and academic are no opposition in wisdom but one and the same.

Theology not only looks to the past, in a faith that is founded on God's acting in Christ. It also looks to the present and to the future. The church is sent by Christ to proclaim the Gospel to all human beings; and the task of teaching theology consists of bringing the revelation of God's action within the history of his people and the fullness revealed in Jesus Christ, and at the same time, seeing the victorious consummation of the Lord at the very end.[258]

---

[258] Kinnamon and Cope, The Ecumenical Movement: An Anthology of Key texts and Voices, 143.

Faith points to the promises of God and Christian hope contemplates their fulfillment. Therefore, theology should be understood as *docta spes*, wisdom of the hope.[259] Theology as wisdom emphasizes a transformative truth that nurturing in the hope on God's promises encourages self-criticism and thus restores the force for committed action and clarifies both the promises and the situation so that nobody is historically excused. Jürgen Moltmann emphasizes:

> *"Hope is not something which is added to faith, or tags on to it. It is the other side of faith itself, if faith sees itself as a Christian faith. Christian faith is the power through which men and women are born again to a living hope."*[260]

The modern world and the desires of the human soul demand a message of hope. Theology as *docta spes* is an answer to the cry from a society that has been losing its own center of reference, or in the words of the French psychoanalyst Charles Mellman: a man without gravity.[261]

Theology as wisdom of hope is a prophetic action as well, while it brings the thought of the present communion under the light that comes from the living memory of the Word of God. It has an impact that opens up a new future in every "today" of the human community where it is inserted socially. Theology as *docta spes* is the decided denial of the negative aspect of the present; it is an anticipation of the positive Kingdom of God. Jürgen Moltmann states:

The resolute negation of the negative cannot exist in isolation. It is dependent on the anticipation of the positive. But the anticipation of the positive leads to powerless

---

[259] E. Bloch already detected this from Columbus's journals. Cf. Das Prinzip Hoffnung, Frankfurt: Suhrkamp, 1959, 873; The Principle of Hope, Cambridge, MA: MIT Press, 1986.

[260] Moltmann, Experiences, 52.

[261] C. Melman, L'homme sans gravité, Paris: Donoel, 2002.

dreams unless it is bound with every breath to the negation of the negative. It is only through the wise conjunction of the two that hope becomes wise – *docta spes* – comes into being.[262]

With the same clarity, Forte affirms:

> *If the believing reflection were memory without the present, it would be sterile nostalgia, dead memory; if it were present conscience without memory, it would be arrogant ideology or pure sociology; while it is at the same time memory and presence it is also commitment and a prophetic action, transformative for the world today.*[263]

The biblical witness is a book of hope. From Abraham and Sarah to the present day, the people of Israel have placed their hope on the promises of God who has entered into a covenant with them. "The theology of the people of God, wandering in the faith of Abraham and Sarah, is a theology of the way — *theologia viae* — not yet a theology of the home country, *theologia patriae.*"[264]

The prophets envision a time of universal accord when the Lord shall be glorified on Earth. The New Testament, too, is saturated with the spirit of expectation. Jesus proclaims the coming reign of God in word and in action. In his ministry of forgiveness and healing, and above all in his resurrection from the dead, the beginning of God's victory over all the forces of sin and death in the world is declared (I Cor. 15:57).[265] In the knowledge of God's final victory Christians can persevere and serve society.

The problem was that, when expanding and when adapting to each culture, both the Church and Theology lost the eschatological character of their messages. Initially they became a state religion after Theodosius in

---

[262] Moltmann, Experiences, 57.

[263] Forte, Teologia, 176.

[264] Moltmann, Experiences, 50.

[265] Migliore, Faith Seeking, 232.

380[266]; it was the very moment when the theme of the eschatological hope was marginalized, due to the implementation of the institutional ecclesiastical triumphalism. The doctrine of Christian hope or the *eschaton* had got a secondary theme in theology manuals or simple appendixes. Eschatology became, Karl Barth said, the "harmless little chapter at the conclusion of Christian Dogmatics."[267]

However, in American Latin theology a new reading of Christian hope arose during the last fifty years as, especially influenced by the *Theology of Hope* by Jürgen Moltmann. The most focused theme in Latin American Theology has been, since then, the prophetic liberating action. It is already an established contribution in the theological world. In the beginning it was mainly sociologically founded but later it got a spiritual bedding. From the theme of the Kingdom of God in an including way, we hear voices that speak as much about the spiritual as about the social, and the economic and the political role that includes individuals, social and ethnic groups and all creation.

For Hugo Echegaray[268] Christian hope brings signs of the Kingdom of God as a transformative practice. So hope is a habit of the feet, that is to say, to follow Jesus Christ has implications of walking in the direction to those who are in need in this world, there is no place for *apathies*, but for a committed historical answer in favor of the excluded by unjust systems.

Christian hope necessarily summons human alterability. The Gospel narrates Jesus' activity through a wonderful itinerary, in a form of ascent, from Galilee to Jerusalem

---

[266] "On February 27, 380, he declared 'Catholic Christianity' the only legitimate imperial religion" (C. J. Klein, Curso de História da Igreja, São Paulo: Fonte Editorial, 2007, 81).

[267] K. Barth, The Epistle to the Romans, London: Oxford University Press, 1933, 500.

[268] Echegaray, A Prática de Jesus, 131.

in compassion to people. Through the perspective of the Kingdom of God, Jesus proposes that his disciples do not act as the chiefs of nations that dominate and impose, but only as servants, capable of giving their lives to serve in hope and love. This is the action that integrates, cures, and encourages for life.

His way of hope evokes a committed diaconal action on the part of the ecclesial community among people, as a service that fights in favor of equality and respect to fundamental human dignity among all human beings. The opposite of this solidarity practice in hope is power as a domain that alienates and oppresses. Theology as hope through a transformative perspective in Jesus is a proclamation of the direct reign of God in favor of the socially excluded.[269] Jesus Christ's Church is a community of servants, therefore, in its essence it is diaconal and its hope should bring signs of visibility to the invisible ones that the world has been eliminating.

As a diaconal and eschatological community the Church is a sign and anticipation of Christ's Kingdom, and it is from this inclination that theology should reflect on its teaching. As *docta spes*: anticipating thought, knowledge rooted in and fed by hope.

c. Theology as Docta Caritas

Theology as wisdom of hope is a promise. It is the promise that the Kingdom of God approaches in grace. But it is not just a promise, for hope invades the present with ethical commitment. "Hope is a history of burning love."[270] In their mutual interconnectedness faith, hope, and charity are aspects of a single fundamental attitude, rooted in

---

[269] C. Bravo, Jesus, Hombre en Conflicto, México: CRT, 1988, 261.
[270] Plou, Together, 41.

love, which is the highest of all. Believing, waiting, and loving are trust, self-abandonment, and self-giving to the grace of self-communication with God in Christ. Faith already sees the reality executed in the event of Christ; hope sees the fullness of the coming salvation; the very aspect of charity is the gift of communion with God, which is expressed in truly loving the neighbor.[271]

"We have talked about the theoretical reasonableness of faith and the historical reasonableness of hope up to now. Let us now turn to the practical reasonableness of them both."[272] With these words Moltmann introduces the theme of theology as *intellectus amoris*, the reason of love, a borrowed concept of liberating theology, especially of Jon Sobrino. In Latin America, this theological concept as a practice of love implies reading the reality according to "historic reversal."[273] This means: reading according to the socially excluded. It is in this context that a Christian must understand that he does not live for himself, but for the one who died for him and is resurrected (I Cor. 5:15). Under the light of this text the believer is chosen to live by the new life, by which he was transformed as an agent of reconciliation.

Christian life is a commitment of diaconal loving; it is a liturgy of the celebration of life in love; and at the same time it is sign anticipating the Kingdom of God. There would not be a Christian life without the concept of the other one. In the words of Luther: "We conclude therefore that a Christian man does not live in himself, but in Christ, and in his neighbor, or else is no Christian; in Christ by faith, in his neighbor by love."[274]

---

[271] Alfaro, Revelación, 116.

[272] Moltmann, Experiences, 57.

[273] G. Gutierrez, A Força Histórica dos Pobres, Petrópolis: Vozes, 1982.

[274] M. Luther, First Principles of the Reformation or the Ninety-five Theses and the Three Primary Works, London: John Murray, 1883, 131.

Theology as wisdom of love has to do with the practice of hands. In Jesus' ministry he touched the sick, distributed bread to those who were hungry, helped people with their basic needs. Many people asked: "What virtue is this that comes from his hands?" (Mark 6.2). For Hugo Echegaray, that level of Jesus' practice was called a "practice in the concrete level of life, the economic level, the production level, and the circulation of goods."[275]

Jesus educated his disciples to an attitude of giving with a committed love. For example, the rich man accomplishes the demands of the Kingdom of God when he distributes his goods to the poor and he accomplishes the practice of solidarity that places him in suspicion of the social systems. Precisely as *docta* caritas, love as wisdom is not a romantic field of emotions, but has to do with very concrete societal and economic issues, that are critically assessed in light of the gospel. Theology as wisdom is solidarity in an individualistic society, as servant of the living Church, the community that welcomes and shares in Christ and because of Christ.

Theology as wisdom of love has to do with the practice of the eyes. We should remember that hope has its roots in the one which "we have seen with our eyes, which we have looked upon, and our hands have handled" (I John 1:1). Only what is visible is practiced with love, because what is visible is the brother, what is visible is the socially excluded from wild capitalism, what is visible is the poverty in which millions of children live. What is visible is racism. What are visible are the machine guns on the violent streets at war. What are visible are the terrorist attacks and the attacks against innocent people by the retainers of evil political powers. What are visible are the

---

[275] Echegaray, La práctica de Jesús, 183.

starving and explored bodies, starved of food, health, affection and human dignity. What is visible is the growing ditch that separates rich and poor. What are visible are the exploited children sold for lust and pleasure. What is visible is the exploitation of women.[276]

Therefore, the answer of the church is that as a community of believers they should also be visible. The grace of love and the commitment with the Kingdom of God cannot act invisibly. The Gospel insists on the visibility of the testimony of faith. Religions seem to exalt the invisible, but only the Gospel of "hearing, seeing and touching" can share the hope that does not disappoint.[277] Love as theological wisdom is the practice of the Kingdom of God and its justice in human society.

Theology is a passion for life. To speak of passion for life includes the socially excluded, those distressed by the social systems and the overloaded ones, humiliated and offended by the retainers of power and human pride. The love of God, source of acts of solidarity of the Christian Church should be creative love, which has its greatest moment in openly forgiving the enemy, and thus opening the future by liberating it from being captive of the past. The creativity of that love demands reaching all fields of human life, the political, economic or social sphere in their many forms and systems. Theology as wisdom of love takes the form of liberation, which integrates the weak and voiceless in a love that goes beyond the oppression, and strength of the powerful. Its strength is a greater power: the power of the love in Christ.

Moltmann states:

> *This creative love stirs up understanding and all the senses, so that they can perceive the misery, and in order to pierce*

---

[276] Plou, Together, 42.
[277] Plou, Together, 42.

through our own blindness or the indifference born to famili-
arity: 'we have got used to it.' In order to understand misery
we must understand the reasons for it, and analyze the system
of violence. Without political, economic and sociological criti-
cism we cannot understand the world of growing inequalities
and deadly injustices.[278]

A Christian from Latin America has been learning according to his faith that it is not necessary to be a Marxist
to either understand the inhuman violence of wild capitalism or capitalist to notice the socialist oppressive dictatorships. Each human being in Latin America experienced
scorn for political dictatorships, daughters of the doctrine
of *'national safety'* or on behalf of the revolution, fruits still
harvested today.

Theology will only be effective if it understands that
only starting from faith in human dignity, as was the creator's vital project, it will be possible to combat the marks
of death and lack of solidarity among people. In this
thought about Christian solidarity and the loss of humane
conditions, theology can be conceived as "wisdom of the
love", i.e., *docta caritas.*

The work of theology as *docta caritas* is to open up the
eyes to possible liberation, for this theology as wisdom of
love is transformative. Theology is a critical conscience of
the ecclesial *praxis* under the light of the Word of God
born within history, being placed towards listening to discern before the complexity, the wealth, and the matters
that are its own.

A living theology must always remember the theological thought of Calvin, which has rejected a kind of faith
that was not the result of love:

Moreover, the faith envisaged, with or without love, was a fides
acquisitia, largely an ascent to reveal truth in Scripture and

---

[278] Moltmann, Experiences, 58.

tradition. Thus there was a possibility of a faith existing without love, a poor, weak faith, needing to be filled with acts of love, but still faith... Faith is the act of the whole man. Faith and love are inseparable. Take away love and what is left is not faith at all.[279]

c.1 The Place of Theology

Theology as wisdom of love is always contextual, determined by the *kairos* and related to the community. Moltmann states:

> *"The forms of theological thinking, theological language and theological metaphors are contextual, always and everywhere. They are determined by their situation and are guided by particular interests."*[280]

I agree with him when he argues that this is not only visible in the new theologies of liberation, but was already present in early church theology, in medieval theology, in modern theology, including European, African, and Asian ones. Any historical analysis of theological texts can check this fact.[281]

The *locus theologicus* of theology as wisdom of love is where it inhabits the context of injustice that lowers and exploits human beings in their dignity, as the place where God in Jesus Christ became the most indignant among human beings, because he valued their dignity higher than his own divine dignity. This world is "the place of the Gospel". If it were not like this, the thought of the company of life would be profanation, losing the sense of the mystery in order to go after that human wisdom, which is "madness before God" (1 Cor 3.19). God's wisdom and the place

---

[279] Parker, Calvin, 81.

[280] Moltmann, Experiences, 60

[281] Moltmann, Experiences, 60.

where it is present is in the foolishness of the cross and the cross bearers. Theology is listening to this wisdom.

Listening can in fact be interpreted in two ways: according to history that rises up for the evangelical word or as a discovery in the present according to the Gospel. In the first case, one looks at the human situation simply as the addressee of a message; in the second case, one makes an effort to notice the presence, with a mysterious and hidden certainty of its own message in the face of the gospel. The first attitude is concerned, above all, to accept and to defend the truth itself, in order to proclaim it later to the world: it is more attentive in defining the truth than to evidence the sense of the concrete historical situation for humans, in which the theological act places itself.

God is the God of history. For this the early church confesses that creation happened not only by Christ, but also in view of him, which recapitulates everything created: "Everything was created by him and for him" (Col. 1.16). The whole cosmos is embraced by the love of God that is revealed in Christ. This understanding of human history implies that human culture itself comes laden with the creative touch of the Holy Spirit. Everything that human beings are able to do is involved in the grace of God to restore life. As Calvin, with a surprising opening that includes and values human sciences, says:

Without a doubt, we should not forget that all these things are excellent gifts of the Holy Spirit, released to those who want, for the good of mankind. God doesn't stop filling, vivifying and moving all his creatures with the virtue of this same Spirit according the nature given when he created them.[282]

Everything created is, therefore, an intrinsic reference to the Creator, which for the Christian faith has to do with

---

[282] Calvin, Institutes II, 2,16.

Christ: nothing of everything that is human and historical is strange to the God in whom Christians believe. In all things, therefore, it is possible to discern the deep echo of the eternal Word that tuned the life of the Nazarene. The cosmic value of the incarnation is saying, therefore, that the Word assumed human nature, embracing in a certain way the whole universe, in order to redeem everything and to give everything to the Father in glorious adoration one day (cf. 1 Cor. 15.28). If *what was not assumed was not saved*", according to the patristic axiom, and everything is recapitulated in Christ (cf. Eph. 1.10), the paschal reconciliation extends to embrace all reality of present history: "For it pleased the Father that in him should all fullness dwell; and, having made peace through the blood of his cross, by him to reconcile all things unto himself; by him, I say, whether they be things on earth, or things in heaven" (Col 1.19-20).

That is the reason why the voices of time contain themselves inseparably "wailings of the Spirit" (Rom. 8:22): they appeal to Christ and from him they receive the tension towards the promised future reconciliation. Listening to them theologians drive themselves following the footprints of their Living Master.

Finally, besides the theological and Christological motivation, another pneumatological motivation emerges inextricably united with them: it is the Spirit that "modernizes the new, which came with Jesus Christ. He operates this way: the continuous passage from the letter to the spirit, from the spirit to freedom. He himself is the historical dimension. He grants it to the Church."[283]

The presence of God in his creation always takes the form of concrete creatures in a specific time and at a specific place. Theologians should not ignore but listen to the

---

[283] Forte, Teologia, 152.

pure voice of the Gospel: everything can hide a sign from the Spirit, fruit of the absolute grace and freedom of the divine gift. Also in this sense, to recognize in the world a "place of the Gospel" is not to betray the event, but to make an effort to obey it with full conscience, responsibility and decision, before the new surprise, that the *paracletus* is raising in human history.[284]

If the world is the place of the Word, it can be said that all history and every human being is involved in the mystery of Christ's reconciliatory grace, as if it were and still is inside the mystery of sin. Any rupture between the Gospel and history contrasts with the theological, Christological and pneumatological depth that unites them. The task of theological education is, therefore, knowing how to read, in everything that is human and historical, signs to discern what should be done. A critical conscience of the *praxis* of the people of God's theology should stimulate the Church to become a believable sign of reconciled existence helping to observe real problems and to seek concrete answers. "Many times we answer questions that nobody asked and we don't know how to answer the questions that were asked."[285] Theologians should be trained to listen to the voices that express the crucified Christ and ask for signs of hope.

Theology is not producing at random statements on everything. If it is about signs and answers in history we must discern *which* signs and answers to *which* questions are in *this* place and time relevant. In Latin America, the *locus theologicus* is understood to be a place of social exclusion. Therefore, the task of theology is more than a dialogue with other theologies, philosophies or cultural

---

[284] Forte, Teologia, 152.
[285] Dias, Doctrine divides, 70.

movements; it is the encounter with the Latin-American reality of oppression and underdevelopment itself.[286]

The theological task in this contact with reality, should develop a real commitment of love committed to the transformative liberation of human beings. Theology as *docta caritas,* cannot only justify the need of commitment to reality, but it must insert itself in this reality with a critical action promoting hope. In Jon Sobrino's words: "It is not with such movements as liberalism, freemasonry and theosophy questions are raised for Latin American theology today, it is the whole problem of reality and concrete life itself, of the second stage of the Enlightenment that now holds the center stage. The problem of the believer, who may now find it hard to see the importance or truth of faith, has taken a back seat. And the sinfulness of the situation is not something just to be explained; it must be concretely transformed."[287]

In fact, Sobrino states that the theological task in Latin America should overcome the speculative character of traditional theological problems when seeking important themes for the current situation and not to despise the old theological problems but move forward to prioritize what is more committed to current life in the concrete existential context. Theology cannot be alienating, but it must face the real problems of humanity. It doesn't intend to be theoretical, but praxiological; it does not intend to reconcile God and poverty in thought, but to reconcile reality with the Kingdom of God.[288]

Theology is not *docta* as a critical discourse because of abstract speculations and academic subtleties. It is critical in a practical way. Jesus Christ, when coming to the world as the wisdom of God, condemned the powerful ones that

---

[286] Sobrino, Christology, 33.

[287] Sobrino, Christology, 34.

[288] Sobrino, Christology, 36.

were using their power to oppress others. Sobrino emphasizes this practical character of the wisdom expressed in Christ:

Jesus hurls anathemas at the Pharisees because they pay no attention to justice; at the legal experts because they impose intolerable burdens on people and have expropriated the keys to knowledge for their own use; at the rich because they refuse to share their wealth with the poor; at the priests that impose restrictions on people's freedom; and at the rulers of the world because they govern despotically.[289]

These condemnations of Jesus are the expressions of the wisdom of God, which prioritizes the grace that includes the marginalized. Sobrino states: "Religious oppression exists because the Pharisees imposed intolerable burdens on people. Ignorance exists because the Levites expropriated the keys to knowledge. Poverty exists because the rich will not share their wealth."[290] He further says:

Jesus relates the essence of sin to the essence of power. Only one kind of power is proper if one seeks to anticipate the kingdom of God. It is the power of love, of sacrifice, of service, of truth. Every other kind power, far from being neutral, is historically sinful. To the extent that it is not power dedicated to service, it is sin.[291]

c.2 In Space it Discerns the Times

How to hear the present in order to satisfy the demand of recognizing the signs of the presence of Christ and to help the church to grow in communion and in charitable dialogue with the community of human beings?

---

[289] Sobrino, Christology, 53.
[290] Sobrino, Christology, 54.
[291] Sobrino, Christology, 55.

Along its historical path discerning the signs of each era is not only given to God's people. Regarding this the Roman Catholic Church expressed in one of its most challenging documents of last century, *Gaudium et Spes*:

> *All people of God, above all the ministers and theologians, with the help of the Holy Spirit, must hear sincerely, discern, interpret the several manners of speaking of our time, and know how to judge them under the light of the Word of God, in such a way that the revealed truth would always be more deeply comprehended, it would be better understood and could be presented in an adapted way.[292]*

Reading the signs increases the dynamic and provisory character of the theological task, because as wisdom, theology and expression of the love of God revealed in Jesus Christ by the power of the Holy Spirit can never be static, for the Holy Spirit always modernizes again the Word given once in the past, turning into the present to transformative power. The *Gaudium et Spes* text states:

> *It is a permanent obligation of the Church, to seek the signs of the times and to interpret them under the light of the Gospel, in an appropriate way for each generation; it can answer to man's perennial interrogations about the sense of the present and future life, and about its reciprocal relationship. It is necessary, in fact, to know and to understand the world where we live, as well as its expectations, its aspirations, and its frequently dramatic nature.[293]*

It is here that the theologian, through the results of historical knowledge, psychology, sociology, anthropology, literature, hermeneutics, philosophy, and all other human sciences, can be supplied with a wider and more articulated knowledge of the world and its languages. As already Calvin argued:

---

[292] Gaudium et Spes, 44. In http://www.newadvent.org/library/docs_ec21gs.htm. Accessed on September 4, 2006.
[293] Gaudium et Spes, 44.

If God wanted to use the unfaithful to help us to understand physics, dialectics, mathematics and other sciences, we served ourselves with this, fearing that our negligence may be punished if we depreciate the gifts of God wherever they are offered.[294]

Theologians do not have to do all the work themselves. There are many fields whereon they are laypersons and they should recognize that.

[The theologian] won't presume to replace himself by the experts in several fields, but he won't hesitate to let himself be provoked by them, by their readings and interpretations, evaluating their proposals and capturing the disturbing weight of their questions. Far from being enclosed in a calm castle of easy certainties, theology, critical conscience of the Church determined as a whole to distinguish the signs of the times should live in the breach of history, dialogue, and demand the fruitful company of men, which constitutes the real situation where it is inserted.[295]

We must agree with Karl Barth, who says that: "The theologian is the one who has the Bible in one hand and a newspaper in the other,"[296] and with Shirley Guthrie that Christian hope is a critical view of the historical optimism regarding human potential, as if justice, freedom and peace would come as a simple human effort, but that Christian hope is also a critical view of the pessimism of the ones who have no hope.

Christian hope is faith in the triune God. "Hope in the triune God means that we will expect and work for preliminary sings of the new humanity and new world that we

---

[294] Calvin, Institutes II, 2,16.

[295] Forte, Teologia, 157.

[296] Forte, Teologia, 157.

know are surely coming."[297] Love is not only wisdom but the maximum expression of wisdom.

c.3. Love is the Best Wisdom

Theology as *docta caritas* expressed by the power of love that comes from God impels the Christian community to be in deep solidarity with other human beings. It is a pulse at service of the cause of promotion of people in fullness, while the liberation of everything that offends their dignity and mortifies their freedom as creatures of God.

Docta caritas is love shaped by thought so that human life is more and more evaluated, guided, and realized: here it is theology listening to and discerning the complexity of life. "Love is solidarity, love is patient, love is helpful" (I Cor.13.4), or in Wanda Deifelt's words in her message about the theme of the eighth WCC Assembly, in Harare:

> *We see the world through our tears. To see with tears is to recognize that our glance cannot be less than partial, that we are beside the ones who suffer. To look with the eyes stained by tears is not to be absent from the world as Maria Magdalena said, crying at the closed sepulcher: her tears identified her with the one who had been persecuted and with the one who had died on the cross. To cry for and with the ones who suffer it is to be beside them and to suffer the consequences of our option. It is to announce with Paul that it is not the death that prevails, but the integrity of the creation of God, because of the resurrection.*[298]

As *docta caritas* theology is not an empty intellectual curiosity, nor abstract ideology nor indiscreet presumption of reason; as *docta caritas,* it is a service of love and knowledge; it possesses an operative character, while

---

[297] Guthrie, Christian Doctrine, 375.
[298] Plou, Together, 38.

Christian faith takes in the commitment for the demands of *praxis*.[299]

Theological work without love would be a fire of straw and a castle of cards, but as an anticipation of the Kingdom of God, as an appetizer of the party that is to come, it will exhort the people of God to seek God with the happiness of hope, witnessing here and now that the signs of the Kingdom of God are already present.[300] As *docta caritas* theology takes place in the dynamics of the provisory, therefore, it is on its way – it is *theologia viatorum* and not *theologia in patria* yet.[301]

Theologia Viatorum

Theology as wisdom is a *theologia viatorum* because contexts continuously change in the course of time. Wisdom is open to the whole experience of life in all its aspects and life is not a fixed body. It is an ongoing way through history, continuously changing and finding new tracks that are opened to the future. Therefore a theology of wisdom can never be finished. A *Summa theologiae* is impossible. As wisdom of hope it knows about new perspectives, as wisdom of faith it knows itself rooted in the past when people different from our own society lived and loved, and as wisdom of love it is open for new experiences, new challenges to overcome the sufferings of human beings due to sin and the limitations of created beings.

Theology as wisdom moves on a way through history, not as a unchangeable entity but by fully participating in the dynamics of history and being part of these. That is not

---

[299] Alfaro, Revelación, 122.
[300] Plou, Together, 38.
[301] Moltmann, Experiences, 50.

detrimental to theology. It is the only way it can be practiced, precisely as God-talk, because God himself is involved in history. The Word is incarnate and the Spirit dwells in the history of life. God has revealed himself not by a book with absolute rules but in historical disclosure, by calling human beings in a disclosure of his presence in the concrete twists of history.

God's revelation in Abraham's life is a signal that He comes toward a context, raises a response and calls for a following in the History of his Grace. God's election is the response God gives to the confusion and God's judgment that fell upon humankind at the tower of Babel. Babel is the symbol of human ideology and of the glorification of the creature over the Creator. It is the portrait of the egocentrism and of the narcissism of humanity. While in Babel, men state: "Let us make us a name, lest we be scattered abroad upon the face of the whole earth" (Gen. 11:4), God states about Abraham, "I will make thy name great" (Gen. 12:2). One is the way of man, another, the way of God; one is the religion of human deeds, another, the undeserved grace. Theological education shall always need to discern between those two poles in order to avoid building new Babel towers in the ideological market.

Grace is God coming to a couple that has no future because they have no children. God opens his purpose for a new future and gives them the promise of a child and a piece of land. If Babel is the fruit of human *hubris* that ends up as a curse, God's call to Abraham in *sola gratia* points to a blessing to all nations and it is a call on the way of realization.

Theology, because of the God of all Grace, cannot be but a *theologia viatorum*, of people living from the grace of faith, the trust of the hope for the future and receiving love rather that already being perfect in it. That's why it has no right to pride but humbly understands the provisory character of its task in each context.

Likewise in Moses, God's call had the purpose of turning Israel into a model nation to be the sign of God's Mastership over the world, Israel should, in its historical journey display its devotion to God as a testimony of God's action. The final goal was not the national grandness but to express a life of service to the glory of God. So, when God calls Moses and sent him to liberate the people from slavery in Egypt to serve him, He said: "Let my people go, that they may serve me" (Ex. 8:1). That is why Israel is called for obedience in its walk: "Then ye shall be a peculiar treasure unto me above all people" (Ex. 19:5). Israel was elected to be an example amongst the nations. This is a strong paradigm for the theology at the present time.

There is a danger of theology losing its comprehension of being provisory and just like Israel, failing on its journey. Israel failed in its devotion to God, seeking other gods, imitating its neighbors. It was not concerned in being a sign and testimony of God's glory on earth but was more concerned with its own national grandness.

In Jesus Christ, God raised a new people and this was a message announced by the prophets and the New Testament testifies it. By God's acting in Christ God has surrendered to death on our behalf. This is the beginning of his reign. Justin the Martyr said: "He rules from the tree",[302] that is from the cross. Christ's cross is his throne and it is

---

[302] Justin the Martyr, Apology I,41 (transl. Ante-Nicene Fathers, Vol. 1. Edited by Alexander Roberts & James Donaldson, Buffalo, NY: Christian Literature Publishing Co., 1885). Also Tertullian, Against Marcion III,19 and 21 (transl. Peter Holmes. From Ante-Nicene Fathers, Vol. 3. Edited by Alexander Roberts, James Donaldson, and A. Cleveland Coxe. Buffalo, NY: Christian Literature Publishing Co., 1885); An Answer to the Jews 10 and 13 (transl. S. Thelwall. Ante-Nicene Fathers, Vol. 3. Edited by Alexander Roberts, James Donaldson, and A. Cleveland Coxe. Buffalo, NY: Christian Literature Publishing Co., 1885).

in this perspective that his kingdom overcomes the world. That is his glory. That is also the glory of his people in history: giving themselves up on behalf of the others and serving his creation.

To the Christian faith this alone might change society if the church acts this way. The crucified and resurrected Christ is the only hope for the world. This is the challenge of theological education: to train theologians to take the lead in this attitude of the church. Therefore, theological education faces today, as always, an urgent task, fulfilled only with joy and faith in total obedience to the Holy Spirit which rules the Church, guided through the Word of God and stimulated by the hope of His kingdom.

a. The Provisional Character of Theology

Theology, in its task, sees itself on a journey impelled to open up unceasingly to the future, because it knows that what it has already received is only a prolepsis of something greater that it is to come and to remember the promises, with the eyes on the Kingdom of God, which gives to theology the true sense and the true value to each step that has been taken on the way to faith and love. In this perspective, Moltmann wrote:

> *Therefore, there is a communio theologorum, a community of theologians, which spans time, space, cultures and classes, which is engaged in dispute, dialogue, and occasionally also interacts in mutual influence and enrichment. This is not that abstract perene theology of which we spoke. It is a concrete theologia viatorum, a theology of those on the way, who in the differing estrangements of this world and this history are searching for the one coming truth which will one day illumine everyone.[303]*

---

[303] Moltmann, Experiences, 61.

Continuing the eschatological message, according to a past understanding, according to a communion of love, Jesus inaugurated the Kingdom of God in his way to the cross and by his resurrection opening the way to the final fulfillment of God's love in human beings. This places the Church in the dynamism of being on the journey. Theology as wisdom will always be *theologia viatorum*.

Theology contemplates the labor in the struggles on this way of the Kingdom of God and must always do so with humility, because its word is always partial in the limitations of human history. Only the Kingdom of God is ultimate, when God will be everything in everybody. Christian faith has as its objective to contemplate God in the Glory of his acts, and it seeks to understand these; therefore theology must have a self-understanding of being provisory in its results, to see its own limits with humility as Moltmann wrote:

> *The theology of the people of God, wandering in the faith of Abraham and Sarah, is a theology of the journey – theologia viae – not yet a theology of exile and exodus, and in all its images and concepts it bears the stamp of the far-off land itself out of which these images and concepts are to lead us. The lament 'how shall we sing the Lord's song in a foreign land?' (Ps. 137:4) is the lament of theology, too, in this world, estranged as it is from God.[304]*

Theology that comes from understanding the revelation of God is not formed by the perspective of the present position of the Church in this world, but it moves forward in the direction of the Kingdom of God as manifested in the Gospel. That is a journey in time. Theology acts within the gift received through the resurrection and by the promise to be accomplished, and for this all theological activity is marked for the tenseness between "now" and "not

---

[304] Moltmann, Experiences, 50.

yet." For this reason, we can view the *viatorum* character of theology as the provisory fruit of its eschatological destiny.

It is in this condition of a pilgrimage that the activity of theology should interfere as wisdom of God, because it knows how always to be present in its goal and mission of summoning people to insert themselves into the people of God, as a light for the world, in spite of the shades of sin. The theological task operates in the tension between the first and second coming of the Lord, it contemplates and celebrates it in its services, linked to the whole hope of the Christian Church, which celebrates the banquet of Eucharist, the food of the Word, with the soul filled with gratitude, the signs of the coming glory. It contemplates with gratitude and passion the wealth of thought from the apostolic fathers to the last theological texts produced by so many voices, and in the expectation filled with hope for the execution of everything that has not yet been accomplished in the new creation that has already been promised and conquered by Christ.

The provisional character of theology gives it a relative character, because theology is not a purpose in itself, as if its conclusions were permanent, but it is an instrument and a means that points to Christ, the wisdom of God. So, theology lives in this world that groans as creation in process, waits as a community of the exodus, peregrinates to the earth of the promise, celebrating the signs of the new heaven and new earth. Theology should reject any perennial pretense, because it is summoned to renewal, the action of contemplating and teaching *in via et non in termino*. Theologians should see themselves within the people of God, who "were born at the foot the cross and were pilgrims throughout Good Friday which is the story of man on earth and who can never confuse the pale lights of human glory with the light of the promised Glory in the victory of Easter."[305]

The *viatorum* character of theology prevents theology from overlooking the relativity of theoretical greatness already reached by all thinkers of human history. There is always a risk that theologians see the great men of their own tradition as absolute authorities. Under the optics of being part of the people of the exodus, theology knows that everything is under the judgment of the promises of God.

Therefore, theology cannot, on behalf of any cultural contextualization, identify itself with any ideology or political forces, with any party or system. Under the truths of the revelation of God, it is aware of its critical conscience that transcends all of them always remembering its last destiny in the Kingdom of Jesus Christ, that is more critical than any critical political theory.

This does not mean, however, a lack of commitment. The conscience of being pilgrim and foreigner in the world is not an alienation of the truth, but a stimulating force to act better to the benefit of justice and universal *shalom*. In this sense, it can be stated that theology will always have a subversive character, because of the eschatological nature of the Church of Jesus Christ. Theology is a function of the Church, so it should understand its task as an accomplishment of the people of God and within the people of God. On behalf the eschatological promises, it acts in a critical way against the precarious accomplishments of human history. Forte writes:

> On behalf of this greater hope which encourages it, the Church then will be subversive and critical against all the myopic accomplishments of the hopes of this world: present in all human

---

[305] B. Forte, La Iglesia de la Trinidad. Salamanca: Secretariado Trinitário, 1995, 350.

situations; solidarity with the poor and oppressed, it won't be licit to identify its hope with one of the hopes of history. Even so this critical surveillance doesn't mean it is without any doubts, or lack of commitment or testimony of a cheap grace; it is, on the contrary, expensive and demanding. It is to assume the human hopes and verify them under the light of the resurrection of the Lord, which on one hand sustains every authentic commitment of liberation and human promotion, and on the other hand denounces all absolutism of earthly goals.[306]

b. Vocation and Sanctity in Poverty

The vocation of theology as a science of faith, hope and love is a universal vocation to the sanctity that should shine in its ecumenical character, for belonging in an unconditional way to God, who has elected a group of people exclusively as his property to peregrinate, in order to send these same people to peregrinate in history on a mission on his behalf for the whole world. In this eschatological horizon any intimate or individualist concept of the sanctity is overcome, as the apostle said: "But you are a chosen people, a royal priesthood, a holy nation, a people belonging to God, that you may declare the praises of him who called you out of darkness into his wonderful light" (I Pe. 2:9).

The Christian Church must shine in sanctity while executing its redeeming mission, to which all his children are summoned; it is above all a gift, grace, and free communication that comes from Jesus Christ as the Lord of life. Theologians in their acts as members of the body of Jesus Christ should answer to this gift with freedom; for that reason the sanctity is also a commitment, free adhesion and demanding option for the project of God for each of

---

[306] Forte, La iglesia, 351.

them. It is an answer that gives gratuitously what was gratuitously asked. The gift demands a welcome and an answer, in the measure that God works in each one, and its final objective is to serve the neighbor, especially to the excluded of the world.

In a relationship with faith in the work accomplished in Christ and with the hope for the divine homeland, theology moves forward in love and hope, seeking the purpose of being entirely within reach of the expectation of the future that is to come, cheerful and transformative. The idea of the transformative character links the theological task to always being purified and rejuvenated, because sin will always be present bringing new and challenging temptations and possible failures. This, however, should not cause despair, as if it trusted itself and was its own source and aim. Failures must not cause panic to theologians, but knowing that they failed and travel on a provisory way, they must come back in an incessant way to the Lord and its absolute lordship in all areas of its historical existence. "The approach of the true reform and authentic renewal consists essentially of increasing fidelity to its vocation."[307]

c. Theology is Directed to the Ultimate

The New Testament establishes clearly that theology is called to be ecumenical in its pilgrimage. The gospel is for the whole world as Jesus instructs his disciples (Matt. 28:19; Acts 1:8). This is not only geographically, but also comprehensive for the whole life. The wisdom of God in Christ penetrates each aspect of human existence and each social culture and the church is called to participate in this work. This ecumenical task needs to be practiced everywhere because it has to do with all human beings, the

---

[307] Forte, La iglesia, 357.

white and the black, the Northern and Southern hemisphere, the rich and the poor, the peasant and the proprietor. To accomplish this, leaving no doubts, it needs a wide and convergent strategy: it is a *docta* activity.

In order to understand the challenges of the current world in its alienation and dehumanization that oppress and exclude on behalf of progress and economic growth, the gospel challenges to a movement towards a new life. The incarnation in its integrative character means the revelation of the Glory of God, the identification of the Word of God with human beings as historical people. In the incarnation Jesus Christ assumes their place of humiliation. That is the reason why Paul the apostle places incarnation in the perspective of the cross. The core of incarnation is the cross. For this reason theology is not only an announcement of the identification of God with human beings in Jesus Christ, but his death in favor of the sinners of the world. From the point of view of theology as wisdom of God, the cross means redemption, offering substitution and reconciliation. So the cross becomes a symbol of victory. The cross has its greatest vindication in the resurrection. In fact, the resurrection is the source from where it derives the redemption and reconciliation power of the cross; it is the heart of all theological education of the Church. We shall always remember that the resurrection was the central theme of the apostolic *kerygma* (Acts 4:33). The resurrection is the dynamics that makes the Gospel the power of God for salvation.

The Latin American theologian Orlando Costas wrote:

"The resurrection is above everything else, the event by which the Church owes its existence and the base for the Great Commission."[308]

---

[308] Costas, Hacia una teología, 120.

It is necessary to affirm that Christ is not only the center of the evangelizing message, but also the heart of all theological education. He is the key for every strategy of theological education, because he constitutes the reason for the Gospel. The concept of Orlando Costas to the evangelization that only the Christological path can serve as guidance to us for an effective strategy should also be applied to theological training. And this path gives us three steps for a vigorous strategy: the way to incarnation, identification and participation.[309]

Affirming theology as wisdom of God among the paths of life as Christ's life was cannot be except from incarnational. A docetic theology that is not incarnated is a heresy to the theological education of the Church. The way of incarnation in theological teaching is essentially the path of an identification and authentic participation with those to whom we address our theology. If theology has as an end the encounter between Christ and the people, its presentation needs necessarily to take in account cultural characteristics. It should happen in the context of the culture given at a certain historical moment and geographical space. Every answer given by theology in its *viatorum* process is conditioned to a cultural transfuse. It is this encounter that takes the human beings to a state of ultimate concern. In this state the human being participates in its concern with those questions of infinite value: the meaning of human existence, in relation to the Creator, the neighbor, to himself and nature. Theological reflection should let us be conscious that Christ's encounter with culture reveals the existential and moral limitations of each human culture, while at the same time it summons a new opportunity for transformation.

---

[309] Costas, Hacia una Teologia, 122.

We must, however, realize that theology is made on the journey along the sidewalks of cultural life. Theology as wisdom is only possible if theologians or the theology teacher seeks to understand in depth the aspects of the culture where he intends to promote the effective encounter with the revelation of God in Jesus Christ. These are the depth of the cross and the cross bearers. Theological understanding of culture can only origin by participation in this cross bearing and investigating what the mechanisms are that people do suffer. Wisdom demands a strategy for theology, in order to let its influence reach people in a pertinent way where they live and act, and this means every social structure that has been affected by sin, impoverishing, enslaving, oppressing and excluding human beings, moving them away from being who they should be inside the purpose of God. Theology as *theologia viatorum* assumes Jesus Christ as an example and criticizes all inactivity. If Jesus Christ is the true Lord of theology, theological education has to take all the implications of incarnation seriously in its effort of confronting human beings of each generation with the good news of the Scriptures.

Theology on the way is theology of the cross, it is theology at service, and it is a strategy that takes the sacrificial acts seriously and focuses on a dynamic theological *praxis*. It is not an end itself, but a means at the service of the Kingdom of God, seeking to serve all human beings for the glory of God assuming the cost without waiting for applause. Theology as wisdom seeks a healthy balance between theory and practice, reflection and ethics, spirituality and life, manifesting signs and gestures of liberation to those oppressed.

It is characteristic for it as a *theologia viatorum* that it places itself in the eschatological perspective and impedes a short-term strategy. So it overcomes also the danger of falling slave to a context, because Christ is the global Lord, not just of a part of the world. He is the Lord of the whole universe. We see theology through the eschatological perspective, because any context will perish soon and be succeeded by a new time. Thus a *theologia viatorum* makes contextualization not only relevant but also relative. It declares the theological word to be just when it is waiting for the ultimate one that is the Lord to come. Jesus is, therefore, the heart and the center of Christian theology. Without him there is neither theology nor theological education, because he is the structural content of the Christian formation and the key to all interpretation of faith and acts of the people of God. Without this Christ centric character theology stops being wisdom and loses its effectiveness and authority.

Theology is a pilgrimage because it belongs to a community on the march, whose vision is in the future. It belongs to a community whose function and call is to live the present always in the hope of the execution of the word of promise. Therefore, it cannot rest even for a moment, because its mission is continuous.[310]

Faith, love and hope are paradigms of wisdom. Theology moves forward by the power and initiative of love, it takes place in reason of faith and is an existential opening for the continuity of hope; love takes us to the company of life with other human beings especially in the communion of the people of God; faith stimulates us to listen faithfully to historical memory, the reason why it welcomes the Word of revelation as a normative obedience, raises hope and feeds the Church on its journey according to its call to the *parousia*.

Without love theology would not begin, because it would lack stimulation of the reflection on the atrocities

---

[310] Costas, La Iglesia, 17.

of present life of human beings; without faith, it would not continue, because it would lack the original food of the Word of God; without hope, theology would not be lured to the future of Christ that evokes in the human today the fertile alliance of the Divine Revelation and movement of the exodus of the heart.[311] Therefore, each one of these three Christian virtues is indispensable to theological elaboration.

To propose theology as wisdom is the faith in which we live in our educational practice, a time with few safe references. To understand theology as wisdom is to have a well defined triple purpose – knowledge in the adoration of the Highest as practice of belief, human beings liberating knowledge for the practice of solidarity in love, and critical knowledge of the Church for the communion always more abundant between the exodus and the coming event in hope.

To do theology in the twenty-first century is like navigating in an ocean of changes, where there is a lack of gravity and uncertainty. It is up to theological educators to understand that making theology is to walk with our eyes fixed on the present that asks, on the past that encourages, and on the homeland anticipated by the preaching of the Church. For this, it discovers that it is not absolute in its convictions, it is just an instrument that points to the absolute; it is not ultimate but penultimate; it is not an end, but a means; its call is not to dominate, but to serve, and none of its certainties should obscure the heat of the expectation of the final victory. Their forms and conclusions can and must change with time – they will change little by little – theology is always the penultimate because it is *viae,* and this truth is that which always convokes an atti-

---

[311] Forte, Teologia, 194.

tude of humbleness and of always being a *studiosus theologiae*. Thus, it is asked to be free of all pride and presumption, because it has not arrived yet, it is still on the march. Christian theology was born at the foot of the cross, and starting from there it peregrinated through history, therefore, it does not have the right to confuse the light of any earthly honor with the brilliant light that waits for the coming of the Kingdom of God proclaimed and expressed in Jesus Christ.

A decisive character to theology as wisdom is that everything must undergo the cross and resurrection Jesus Christ, the Wisdom of God; it is under this approach that theological education must journey. Theologians who practice the necessary discernment in order to make theology will always put their critics within human situations in its needs, showing solidarity to the excluded from society. The wisdom as hope from practice of faith should never be identified with any ideological hope. It will always be an accusation against any ideology centered in human goals. We can apply what Forte states to theology as a practice of the church: "The church cannot identify itself with any ideology, political party or system. It should be a critical conscience of all of them, remembering its origin and its purpose, stimulating all that can benefit the development of humanity in each man according to the project of God."[312]

The practical and guiding sense for any enterprise in the *curricula* of theology courses is summarized decisively in these words. In the relationship with a sense of Christian hope, we can affirm that the eschatological character of the theological task demands an inconvenient and disturbing pedagogy, liberated by faith and served by love, not a theology of secular systems, committed to the alienating

---

[312] B. Forte, *La eternidad en el tiempo*, Salamanca: Sigueme, 2000, 335.

empires of an oppressed world or by the ultra modernity in a society of indifference and social apathy.

Finally, in the memory of its origin in the grace and purpose of God from whom it receives completeness, theological education is challenged to live in the triumph and hope of the promises of the Kingdom of God that is still to come in its power and glory. It is under the light of these promises that theology as Wisdom of God for the world today knows that its reflections are the anticipation of what was conquered, announced and expressed in Calvary and in Jesus Christ's Resurrection where he is seen as the Lord. Nothing can extinguish the power of hope of a faithful community and this is the message of Christian theology in its centrality.

Theology as wisdom can be summarized in the following theological articulation by Bruno Forte:

> *The last word is guaranteed in the paschal episode as a word of joy and not sin, life and not death. The eschatological ethos denounces all presumption of building a stairway to the skies, a new kind of Babel tower, of a world a prisoner of itself; it infuses peace and trust, because it is based on the certainty that the Spirit is acting within the time. Believers are in charge of living the mystery of what is to come in the heart of life and human history, welcoming with freedom the miracle of the eternity that has been invading history.[313]*

When seeking to understand theology as wisdom of God, we conclude, together with the Reformers and ecumenical theologians that "this encounter between eternity and time is salvation for human beings and it has a name on which everyone concentrates all paths and all works of the Living God: Jesus Christ, grace for the world, summary and "heart of every theology,"[314] therefore, every human

---

[313] Forte, La eternidad, 336.
[314] Van de Beek, Jesus Kyrios, 9.

being is summoned to "turn to God, Rejoice in Hope."[315] The Holy Spirit will always update the wisdom of God incarnated in Jesus Christ, which now means to touch again the context whose marks are globalization and social exclusion. But there is hope because the present and past are measured by the light of the future, which by faith is marked by the promise.

From this theological spectrum is necessary to design curricula and programs which have wisdom as paradigm. This is the major concern of the next chapter.

---

[315] This was the theme of the 8th WCC General Assembly, Harare, Zimbabwe, 1998. Plou, Together, 29.

CHAPTER 5

Teaching Theology as Wisdom

THE PRESENT RESEARCH IS a direct result of my vocation in teaching Systematic Theology for over two decades. I wanted to understand the reason why theological education had been so vital to my faith journey. At the same time, I felt frustrated over a contradictory series of relationships between the church and the academia, theory and practice and also between a holistic and a specific thinking about reality. These concerns have led me to see wisdom as a path to follow. Daniel Treier states:

> *If theology may be viewed as a pilgrimage, then Christian Theologians traveled the same road for hundreds of years. To be sure the road had its peaks and valleys, and was quite winding at points; nevertheless, the journey was undertaken on behalf of the church. Theologians were in hot pursuit of sapientia (wisdom), a kind of knowledge with teleology: the formation of virtue in God's people.[316]*

---

[316] D. J. Treier, Virtue and the Voice of God: Toward theology as wisdom, Grand Rapids: Eerdmans, 2006, 3.

In the present chapter I will address the following questions: What is the nature of doing theology as wisdom? What transformative implications can we find in theology as wisdom? What would be the basic features in the construction of a *curriculum* from the perspective of *sapientia*? Having sketched the sapiential character of theology, we now turn more specifically to theological training in the perspective of wisdom. The goal is to develop a viable way for theological education in the context of our contemporary societies. It is worth noting that in nowadays, generally speaking, theological education tends to fragment the classical disciplines to such an extent that the connection between exegesis and homiletics, for example, is lost in the process. As a result, the practice of theology derives its models more from successful preachers than from the holistic pastoral formation that should be taking place in theological schools.[317]

"Christians have begun reluctantly to admit their captivity to enlightenment rationalism," according to Daniel Treier.[318] Moreover, with Farley, many would now agree that:

> *The systematic exclusion of imaginative, tradition-oriented, and praxis perspectives has help produce a contemporary scholarship that is specialized to the point of triviality, preoccupied with technologies of method and with reworking already surfeited subjects with ever more ingenious procedures.*[319]

---

[317] See, for example, Daniel Treier's "Theology as the Acquisition of Wisdom: Reorienting Theological Education" in: Christian Education Journal (Spring 1999), 127-139, in which he argues that a similar process of fragmentation and 'instrumentalization' of theology can be felt in his North American context.

[318] Quoting the historian Mark Noll, Treier points out that it is "increasingly easy for evangelicals to treat the Scriptures as a 'scientific' text whose pieces [are] to be arranged by induction to yield the truth on any issue" (Treier, Theology as the Acquisition of Wisdom, 127).

[319] Farley, Fragility, 15.

By consequence church life and academic theology dealt with different subjects. Because theology was no longer relevant for the church communities, they went their way without theological reflection. What can be observed is that by seeking ecclesiastical relevance many schools have trained pastors to become 'institutional managers' or 'ministers of self help,' a kind of CEO (Chief Executive Officer) who becomes a specialist on ecclesiastical policies or a master of ceremonies. Richard Muller states that in order to "outmaneuver the Enlightenment and unify theology, American churches and schools often conspire to emphasize practice and define [it] in terms of ministry technique."[320] The situation is not different in Brazil. Ministers who have experienced formal theological training often display a shortsighted understanding of the theological task, thus rendering themselves unable to follow the tradition of Christian faith with a hermeneutics that gives this tradition consistency. Their approach to Scripture is arbitrary and private, focusing more on the need to "control" the flock than on expounding the biblical text in order to apply its timeless truths to contemporary issues.[321] This kind of pastoral theology more often than not leads to the formation of passive audiences. Thus, we need to search for a theological-pastoral model of theological education that would serve to promote the "recovery of theology's *sapiential* character — that is, its character as a form of wisdom."[322]

The Nature

What is theology as wisdom and how can it be defined? Doing theology requires an enlightened mind, perception,

---

[320] R. A. Muller, "The Study of Theology" in: Moises Silva, ed., Foundations of Contemporary Interaction, Grand Rapids: Zondervan, 1996, 556-7.

[321] Muller, The Study of Theology, 630-1.

[322] Treier, Theology as the Acquisition of Wisdom, 129.

science and wisdom in order to shed light on the task at hand.

From the point of view of its content, theology is always wisdom, i.e., knowing the supreme and divine things, even in the form of 'scientific theology' (wisdom as mere science). "From the perspective of its *form* of expression, only sapiential theology is wisdom, i.e., savory knowledge."[323]

In addressing the theme of 'theology as wisdom,' Clodovis Boff makes three methodological distinctions: wisdom and knowledge, mystical wisdom and theological wisdom and finally a distinction between sapiential theology and scientific theology. On the first distinction, he states that, "the ancient tradition, which comes from Aristotle, and runs through Cicero and Augustine and, through the latter, is assumed by medieval thinkers, clearly distinguishes though not rigidly between science and wisdom."[324] Augustine defined science as knowledge of things human and temporal, and wisdom as knowledge of things divine and eternal.[325] Wisdom would therefore mean knowledge of the ultimate, decisive, eternal ends. It would mean knowing the meaning of life, which regulates the ethical path.[326] Thus he is wise who knows the ultimate meaning of life, and seeks, as a result, to live ethically.

The Modern Age has provided a twist of things: it placed science above wisdom. It declared the end of theological wisdom (Descartes); then it decreed the end of metaphysical wisdom (Kant); and finally, it required of science to replace wisdom. It was the drama of a despotic

---

[323] C. Boff, O Método Teológico, 151.

[324] C. Boff, Método, 143.

[325] Augustine, On the Trinity XIII,15,23-25; XIII,1,3; The City of God, XII,12,17; 14,22. Cf. C. Boff, Método, 144.

[326] C. Boff, Método, 144.

kind of science, that was deprived of the guidance of wisdom (scientism).[327]

Clodovis Boff makes a second distinction between mystical wisdom and theological wisdom. He asks: how do we articulate these two wisdoms? The mystical wisdom is wisdom-as-gift, which is infused by the Holy Spirit in the hearts of the faithful. It is 'suffering God': because of the relation with God in Christ participate in a vulnerable life, with sensitivity for the sufferings of people. It is introduced by way of experience and apprehension. On the other hand, theological wisdom is wisdom-as-virtue: it comes by way of effort (*per studium*). It represents the labor of discourse. It is wisdom that, besides feeling, knows.[328]

Thirdly, Clodovis Boff calls our attention to the fact that the Latin word *sapere* means both to *taste* and to *know*. Therefore, true knowledge should be attractive to the senses. In other words, content and experience should go together, especially so in the realm of theology. Theoretical theology should be grounded in the practice of faith and vice versa. Arguments should be conveyed in terms of wisdom. As Clodovis Boff says, science produces knowledge whereas wisdom gives it warmth and movement.[329] Thus science and wisdom are not opposed; rather, they (should) complement each other. This dynamic synthesis should lay the foundation for the correct understanding of theology as wisdom. As a consequence, a competent theologian should awaken in his/her hearers an appetite for the knowledge of God that can be experienced in daily living. Only then can he/she be called a wise

---

[327] C. Boff, Método, 145, a summary of Jacques Maritain's lectures given in Rome in 1934, which were published in Science et Sagesse, Labergerie, Paris.

[328] C. Boff, Método, 146.

[329] C. Boff, Método, 148.

theologian. Theological knowledge gives wisdom its biblical foundation; therefore, there is no wisdom without
proper reflection and study. Scholarship and wisdom,
then, go hand in hand.[330]

Daniel Treier also raises questions about wisdom:

> *When the Bible speaks of wisdom, is it talking about cleverness
> or instrumental skill, about human moral judgment, about a
> quest to live in harmony with the order of creation, or about a
> prudence incorporating all of the above after beginning with
> 'the fear of the Lord' (Prov. 1:7; 9:10)? Did seeking wisdom
> keep us from the tree of life (Gen. 2-3), or is wisdom itself a
> tree of life (Prov. 3:13-18)?*[331]

Treier's answer is that in the Old Testament the literature of wisdom reflects on life in Israel and the order of
creation while in the New Testament the emphasis is
placed on the Spirit and the Word. He puts it thus:

> *The Bible manifests a pluriform unity on the theme of wisdom.
> There is a redemptive-historical thrust, as the OT consolida-
> tion of wisdom toward the Torah gives way to communication.
> In this communication what prior generations have heard
> from God and learned of God's creation persists. God's new
> communication, Jesus Christ, fulfills anticipations of OT wis-
> dom and reorders our lives so that we will keep the covenant
> and eat from the tree of life. This reordering includes a whole-
> ness of vision that glimpses a unity of canonical teaching by
> which to live in God's world.*[332]

Wisdom is difficult to define, says Van Leeuwen, because it is a *totality* concept. That is, the idea is broad as

---

[330] C. Boff, Método, 148.

[331] Daniel Treier, "Wisdom" in: Kevin J. Vanhoozer (ed.), Dictionary for
theological interpretation of the Bible. Grand Rapids: Baker, 2005, 844-847.

[332] D. Treier, Wisdom, 845.

reality and constitutes a culturally articulated way of relating to the entire world.[333] Van Leeuwen describes various aspects of wisdom in biblical thinking; they are fundamental emphases for the understanding of theology as wisdom. Firstly, wisdom presupposes the "fear of Yahweh/God" (Prov. 1:7). This concept has its origins in the numinous awe at God's mighty works (cf. Exod. 14:31), but becomes in the Old Testament tradition a term for "religion" as a whole: *all of life,* not just worship, as service to Yahweh, Creator and redeemer of the world through Israel.[334]

Secondly, wisdom entails insight into this practice of life, and becomes a norm for creation and creatures. "Knowledge of the cosmic order requires the knowledge not only of how things work, but also of how all things fit together and relate in one whole, all to the glory of God."[335] Therefore, wisdom has to do with the totality of things, with the complexity of life, which integrates itself because the whole cannot be realized as such as long as the parts do not come to fruition.

Thirdly, as Van Leeuwen has said, wisdom entails knowledge of and appropriate action with reference to particular circumstances, institutions, persons and other creatures. Wisdom behavior is always 'fitting' or appropriate to the concrete. In reference to Job's story, he states: "Part of the folly of Job's "friends" is that they know the general "rules" of the theological wisdom without recognizing that they do not apply to Job's particular, indeed unique, case. It is possible to speak the truth in ways that are false.[336] Information and knowledge are not by themselves wisdom.

---

[333] Raymond C. Van Leeuwen, "Wisdom Literature" in: Kevin J. Vanhoozer (ed.), Dictionary for theological interpretation of the Bible. Grand Rapids: Baker, 2005, 847-850.

[334] Van Leeuwen, Wisdom, 847-850.

[335] Van Leeuwen, Wisdom, 847-850.

[336] Van Leeuwen, Wisdom, 847-850.

Finally for Van Leeuwen, wisdom is traditional. Knowledge of common patterns and their re-cognition particular situations is mediated generationally, whether in professional or general affairs of life. Tradition enables us to discern new situations in view of past experiences. The Biblical image for tradition is the "way" or the path (Hos. 1; Prov. 1:9).[337]

Augustine appropriately indicates the following insight, which is markedly christological: "Though Wisdom (Christ) was Himself our home. He made Himself also the way by which we should reach our home."[338] With this insight Van Leeuwen points conclusively to Christology since it is in Jesus Christ that we find "all the treasures of wisdom and knowledge" (Col. 2:3). For the New Testament, the Redeemer of all things is the incarnate Word or Wisdom, through whom the Father created all things. Moreover, the life and teaching of Jesus embody and advance the principles of Old Testament wisdom.[339]

These ideas presented by Van Leeuwen, from the biblical wisdom literature, provide some of the key assumptions for the present research, and lead me to ask the following question: What are the characteristics of a curriculum of theological education that has wisdom as its method? For example, what characterizes a theological discipline that is taught as wisdom?

The emphasis of this discussion suggests that theology should encompass and integrate knowledge, feeling and practice. Next, we will suggest some examples that undergird our proposed model for the construction of a basic theological curriculum that has wisdom as its focus.

---

[337] Van Leeuwen, Wisdom, 847-850.

[338] Augustine, On Christian Doctrine 1:11.8.

[339] Van Leeuwen, Wisdom, 847-850.

Theological Education as Transformative Wisdom

The focus of the present research was born primarily out of the desire to make a contribution to systematic theology. In our context this discipline has resisted to listen to new voices, more than other fields of theology, by keeping to traditional textbooks from abroad. After decades of teaching this discipline, I nourish the hope that it is possible to propose a new methodological model, giving proper value to what has already been done. The proposal is to contribute methodologically to the new model as wisdom. We can see that other disciplines have developed faster with the new realities, for example, disciplines that relate to biblical, pastoral and missiological issues. However, after starting the present search for a living theology I realized that we could contribute not only to systematic theology itself but also to the actual construction of theological curricula, given the fact that theology is systemic. The whole cannot function if the parts do not operate as intended, since they are interdependent.

What caught my attention at an early stage in my research was the observation that Gustavo Gutiérrez himself, in his monumental A Theology of Liberation invests an entire chapter to the need for theology to rediscover itself as wisdom.

Thus, certain works serve as pointers for the direction of theological education. Von Rad says that wisdom has to do with all fields of life, integrating both theory and practice.[340] Peter Hodgson points to a theological education as

---

[340] In his study of Israelite wisdom, Gerhard von Rad draws attention to the experimental roots that underlie the human desire for knowledge. He explains that the Hebrew word for wisdom (hòkmah) does not demand any conceptual priority; it is the way of responsible and full life. The two terms hòkmah and t'bunã, both refer to 'intelligence,' but then intelligence not as abstract knowledge but as an intelligent way of life. There is also the word da'at (knowledge) that occupies a larger space. So does the word m'zimmã ('plan,' 'thought'). And finally we have the word musãr that means "correction," although it means mostly the result of the same word 'discipline,' which

wisdom that lead to transformative pedagogy — "wisdom that entails insight into teaching and practice is above all a call to the transforming vocation. The power of transformation is a sacred power.[341] Latin American theologians such as Gutiérrez[342] and Clodovis Boff challenge us to integrate both theory and practice.

During the last centuries, disciplines came to be compartmentalized in theological education. Compartmentalization has been an inevitable consequence of both the secularization of Western culture, which lacks unity due to a multitude of human opinions, and modern academic specialization. This has produced unfortunate consequences, such as the diminishing of pedagogical vision and the ghettoizing of theology. In the perspective of wisdom theology cannot be disintegrated but all its aspects should contribute to the fullness of life. In such a comprehensive approach theological education will have a liberating character.

Some themes are presented by Peter Hodgson in order to identify a "transformative pedagogy: education and life

---

approaches the Greek term paideia. G. von Rad, Wisdom in Israel, London: SMC Press, 1972, 4; "The primary meaning of hokmãh is 'superior mental ability or special skill,'" R. B. Y. Scott, The Way of Wisdom, in the Old Testament, New York: Macmillan, 1971, 6; G. von Rad, Weisheit in Israel, Verlag: Neukirchener, 1970, 77.

[341] Peter Hodgson, God's Wisdom, Toward a Theology of Education, Louisville: Westminster John Knox Press, 1999, 5.

[342] According to Gutierrez, all of the tasks of theology are permanent, but some arose earlier than others did. First, theology was seen as a kind of wisdom. Thus, one was initiated into theology along a path parallel to initiation into spiritual life, into mysticism. Although it may be tempting to leave things here, Gutierrez rightly moves ahead from here, realizing that this is a necessary but not sufficient part of the theological tasks. In addition to the spiritual function of theology as a kind of wisdom, there is a sense in which theology must be rational knowledge. In the work of Thomas Aquinas, both theology as wisdom and theology as rational knowledge were united, being "not only a science, but also wisdom flowing from the charity which unites a person to God" (4). For a theology of liberation, the rational aspect of theology will remain significant in that it lends itself to interaction with the social sciences, among other sources of dialogue. Gustavo Gutierrez: A Theology of Liberation: History, Political and Salvation, New York: Orbis Books, 1988.

formation; constructive and interactive knowledge; education as the practice of freedom, and connected teaching and cooperative learning."[343]

The education and life formation is one of the oldest and most persistent ideas, deriving from the primordial education human beings received (and still receive) at the hands of nature and life itself. *Torah* for the ancient Israelites meant instruction for living. It was Israel's worldview and way of life, and in this respect it has scarcely changed over three thousand years.

Torah is a form of teaching, knowing and learning issues for personal transformation and the attainment of a distinctive kind of virtue, the same is no less true of the Greek *paideia*,[344] most simply defined as "the formative process of the human personality."[345]

These ideas of the Greek pedagogy were incorporated by the first theologians of the Christian Church and for this reason they proposed an education that was wide and global, that is to say, an education that somehow may involve life as a whole. "Gregory of Nyssa in particular highlighted the concept of 'formation' (*morphosis*), which in Christian *paideia* became a 'transformation' (*metamorphosis*) of worldly standards, a reorientation to God. For Calvin education was at the heart of the Reformation and all that it had to say about scripture, church, sacraments, and the Christian life."[346]

It can be affirmed that the elements of a transformative pedagogy have to do with disciplined attitudes and critical thoughts. It is especially important to emphasize that such thinking has been a critical component of paideia from the

---

[343] Hodgson, God's Wisdom, 52.

[344] Paideia for Socrates combined knowledge and virtue, and it enabled persons to aspire toward the true aim of their lives. It was phronesis, practical wisdom, wisdom about life (Hodgson, God's Wisdom, 53).

[345] Hodgson, God's Wisdom, 52.

[346] Hodgson, God's Wisdom, 53.

beginning, and thus I am concerned about the situation that David Kelsey indicates: that deep tensions exist today between the "Athens" model of paideia and the "Berlin" model of Wissenschaft (critical, disciplined knowledge, or science).[347] Kelsey argues: "According to the 'Athens' model, theological education is a movement from source to personal appropriation of the source, from revealed wisdom to the appropriation of revealed wisdom as education in 'the faith' or more narrowly as education for church leadership."[348] According to the Berlin model, theological education is a movement from data to theory, and from theory to its application to practice.

It must be wondered if the opposition is as strong as Kelsey sketches. Also in the classic Greek (and Jewish) model a critical attitude is developed. There are sources and a critical evaluation of the contexts by clear application of scholarly methods. On the other hand was the ideal of the Berlin approach not mere theoretical knowledge that could be applied subsequently and separately. It was also an ideal of shaping a personality with an authentic attitude to life, the Bildung of a personality as a good member of society. We should not oppose both with the risk of playing down the critical aspects of classic education and the societal aspects of Berlin Wissenschaft. Tensions appear when one side wants to affirm that paideia is not so academically rigorous and the other that Wissenschaft excludes the subjective aspects. Theological education needs to have a multi-focus character in a productive interrelation among its models, because only this way it would escape from both the cold rigidity of reason and superficial pragmatism.

---

[347] D. Kelsey, Between Athens and Berlin: The Theological Education Debate, Grand Rapids: Eerdmans, 1993.

[348] Kelsey, Between Athens and Berlin, 19-22.

Such a theological education has the rhythm of life and thought or in the words of Peter Hodgson: theological education occurs rhythmically; moving through distinct stages or cycles and is thus a very old idea. It is embedded in the Socratic dialectic and in the Platonic dialogues. Through the art of questioning, Socrates was able to draw insight into the good, the true and the universal out of the experienced particularities of his interlocutors.[349]

Augustine and Thomas Aquinas made use of this dialectic method of teaching, and Aquinas elevated this method up to its highest point. They emphasized that only God teaches inwardly while humans teach outwardly as a secondary road.

The goal of this entire process, according to Whitehead (and emphasized by Hodgson), is the cultivation of mental power, which has the quality of wisdom, insight derived from principles and enriched by concrete experience.[350] A principle that has been thoroughly absorbed becomes a mental habit, which enables the mind to react in appropriate ways to various stimuli and situations.

Modern education has to a high degree retreated from the quest for wisdom. "The retraction from divine wisdom, which was the goal of the ancient people, to textbook knowledge of subjects which is achieved by modern theologians, marks an educational failure, sustained through the ages."[351]

What can be concluded from these arguments it is that the acquisition of knowledge requires discipline and involvement of students so that the mastering of knowledge in their minds becomes wisdom. Discipline and practice

---

[349] Hodgson, God's Wisdom, 60.

[350] Hodgson, God's Wisdom, 63.

[351] A. N. Whitehead, The Aims of Education and Other Essays, New York: Free Press, 1967, 29.

work as two indispensable legs to walk in search of wisdom. At this point, Peter Hodgson states:

> *As I understand it, this entire cyclic, rhythmic process is what constitutes paideia in the sense of the formation of human personality. It is important to stress that paideia includes the element of disciplined, critical thinking as well as the element of imagination and wonder, and that the two come together to form a kind of thinking called "wisdom," which construes the wholeness of things, their "being" or "truth," and learns how to apply principles of value and goodness in concrete situations. Human wisdom is evoked, empowered, and sustained by the divine wisdom, whose pedagogy is paideia... the rhythmic elements of this paideia are critical thinking, heightened imagination, and liberating practice.*[352]

Now we are led to another important theme of a transformative pedagogy, its own understanding as constructive and interactive knowledge. Education is not only made of built up concepts and data, but at the same time interacts with human relationships, and with its own world.

The true and authentic knowledge forms an interaction between professors and students, and together they build a new knowledge through interactivity with the world as a whole. Learning is a connected, cooperative process, and that tells us something about the nature of reality itself.

This approach leads us to the ethic aspect of transformative pedagogy. Education is the practice of freedom and has deep and ancient roots. Education is fundamentally liberation from the jail of ignorance and from the thought ghettos, wherein people are driven to short term advantages at the cost of themselves and other people. As said, Gregory of Nyssa emphasized education as a forming process (morphosis), through which human beings will become truly human; for him Christian paideia was even

---

[352]

more than this – it was a renewal, liberation, and transformation of human beings through the imitation of Christ.[353]

This establishes the necessity of engagement of all professors in the transformative teaching process. Only this way can students receive a quality of teaching based on the real wisdom of God, which will involve them in God's history project for the historical world.

This theme of connection and cooperation emerged in the classic theology tradition analogous to the connection that should exist between the revealed truth of God and the answer to human actions. In Jesus Christ as an educator, we find the greater expression of divine wisdom in its fullness.

Augustine suggest that instead of being preoccupied with "what the teacher thinks,' students should attend to the subject matters that are conveyed by the teacher. Thomas Aquinas invokes an ancient analogy: just as the physician heals a patient by the activity of nature, so the teacher produces knowledge in a student through the activity of the latter's own natural reason. Humans do not endow the mind with the light of reason but cooperate with it to help it reach the perfection of knowledge.[354]

To understand theological education as a process of wisdom in order to establish transformed habits constitutes a permanent challenge for every teacher and student involved in a pedagogic process. To teach is above all to change habits and understanding, from ignorance, illusion, fault, closure, isolation and condition of alienation to knowledge, truth, reconciliation, opening, connection and a state of reorientation. In sum, education theological as wisdom is a life formation; is a constructive and interactive knowledge; is education as the practice of freedom, and teaching as cooperative learning.

---

[353] Hodgson, God's Wisdom, 71.
[354] Hodgson, God's Wisdom, 81.

a. Wisdom and Teaching in the Old Testament

Teaching in the Old Testament is expressed by the word '*torah*'. The word *torah* has to do with the words used by parents and teachers giving instructions about the way a new generation must live according to God's purposes and in this sense it was very close to the Greek concept of *paideia*. "Torah" included information, instruction and the establishment of norms, which has to do with a committed obedience. It is a mistake to reduce *Torah* to simply "law." For the Hebrew tradition[355] the wisdom of God shines within the *torah* in full light. Therefore the study of the *torah* cannot be a purely intellectual activity, but one on the way to changes. *Torah* is not just knowledge as information, but knowledge as transformation of life. The God of Israel is involved day by day with his people's lives in a personal and encouraging way.

b. Wisdom in the Teaching of the New Testament

Jesus' teaching touches the reality of life in many ways. There is a practical proposition: "He who hears these words of mine and puts them to practice" (Mt. 7). The wisdom in Jesus as a method is a way of being and doing. Casiano Floristán says that Jesus did not teach like a temple priest or as a scribe of the law but above all as a prophet of God's Kingdom. Floristán contrasts between Jesus and the priests as follows:

> *Jewish religious law or the Torah was guarded and interpreted by the priests, then it would also be interpreted by the scribes.*

---

[355] The question of the place that should be assigned to the wisdom writings of the Old Testament in a work of Old Testament theology has not so far been accorded any widely recognized consensus. R. Clements, Wisdom in Theology, Grand Rapids: Eerdmans, 1992, 15.

Specifically the "high priest," who was the *custodian of the law and the temple, presided over the Sanhedrin and the worship. His dignity was as high as his economic status,* because of the *revenue produced by the temple. In Jesus' time, due to the nature of the office, the high priest was subject to* the *Roman ruler. His position was controlled by four families* of a *Sadducean inclination. Logically* [the high priest] *was an unpopular character. To help him carry out his function* there were *"chief priests,"* his own *relatives or friends,* who were *in charge of the cultus, the maintenance of the temple and of the treasury. The priests were in charge of the sacrifices. They numbered about 7,000,* and *were divided into weekly shifts, except in the three great festivals and pilgrimages, in which everyone was involved. Apart from the few weeks of priestly occupation, the rest of the time* they were *devoted to other trades. The priesthood was hereditary.*[356]

Floristán, furthermore, points to the fact that:

Throughout his public life, Jesus had little contact with the priests, except in moments of his passion. He dealt with a certain irony regarding the priestly concerns in the parable of the Good Samaritan (Lk. 10:31) and attacked the place of sacrifice at the scene called the cleansing of the temple, which can be found in the Synoptics (Mk 11:15-19; Mt. 21:12-17, Lk. 19:45-48) as well as in John (2:13-22).[357]

For Jesus there is no separation between the sacred and the secular; theological education happens in life. Floristán throws light on the issue as follows:

The expulsion of the merchants produced amazement [on the part of the onlookers] at Jesus' authority. He questioned the temple, at least as a place of bloody sacrifices. In view of the religious assertion that God is present in the temple, Jesus taught that God is everywhere, but in a special way in the new community of disciples ("Where two or three are gathered together in my name, there I am in their midst," Mt 18:20) and in the charity toward the poor ("Whenever you did this to one

---

[356] Floristán, Teología Practica, 24.
[357] Floristán, Teología Práctica, 25.

of these brothers of mine you did it to me," Mt 25:40). Jesus prayed in the countryside and in the mountains. For him there was no separation between the religious space and the sacred space, since all is holy because all is [part of] God's creation. The new temple will be the resurrected humanity since the essence of the new temple is the righteousness of the Kingdom.[358]

In terms of theological education one can deduce that the reliability of teaching comes not from the strength of institutions or their rituals but from Christ Himself as God's wisdom. In this view, Christian faith embrace life in all its breadth while it is surrender to God and to neighbor in his/her needs. Only in this perspective can we understand Christ's priesthood and thus build the pastoral perspective of Christian education. This must also be expressed in the Christian liturgy: it should not be reduced to rituals in temples; it is a service to God in a life to serve human beings, and most of all those who are powerless. Liturgy should not express the power of those who are in the office, but the ministry of compassionate servants of the Lord.

Floristán asserts that Jesus was not a scribe of the Law, and he sees a direct challenge to Christian education in its theological task as follows:

In Jesus' time, the scribes or teachers were the interpreters of the Law, explanation and update managers, taking the lead in interpreting and contextualizing its teachings according to the times and problems they encountered. They were a mixture of theologians and lawyers. Believing that the time of the prophets had finished, the scribes considered themselves their heirs until the messianic prophet would appear in the end times. Therefore, the giving of the title of prophet to John the Baptist or to Jesus amounted to an acknowledgment of the arrival of the end times. We should remember that Judaism became a Rabbinic [institution] after the destruction of the Temple in the year 70 and the disappearance of the ritual priesthood. In order to become a scribe the person had to go through long and meticulous studies, become an expert on both the law and the oral traditions. He earned the title at the age of forty. The scribes wore special robes, presided over meetings and were saluted, honored and appreciated by the people. Their presence was indispensable in various councils and courts, including the Sanhedrin. Most were characterized by their tendency toward Pharisaic ritual purity. As spiritual guides, their role was to promote faith in God and help in doing his will, according to the rules of ritual purity...

Jesus was not limited to teaching in the synagogues; he taught everywhere — in the open air, in the plazas, by the seashore. Among his pupils were women and children, sinners and tax collectors, farmers and fishermen — that is, simple people. Jesus taught according to the Jewish wisdom tradition through parables, proverbs, instructions and controversies.[359]

Floristán states unequivocally: "Jesus is a teacher who is akin to a prophet and a sage; he is charismatic and authoritative."[360] Finally, Floristán states that in this committed character of Jesus' can be found the prophetic perspective of the Kingdom of God. By way of its eschatological character of judgment it brings ethical, historical and contextual responsibilities. The model of wisdom here has a fundamental consequence of a historical commitment to life wherever it happens. Jesus is an eschatological prophet, rejected and persecuted, who proclaims the coming of the kingdom of God. In short, he is with an absolute fidelity to its mission and with a freedom without compromise, he announces the radical demands of God, with full awareness of individual and social events."[361]

At the end of his ministry Jesus gives his disciples a mission with a view to theological education and sends them to all nations (Mt. 28:18-20). The expression "all nations"

---

[359] Floristán, Teología Práctica, 26.

[360] Floristán, Teología Práctica, 27.

[361] Floristán, Teología Práctica, 28.

implies Christ's authority over the whole earth. The expression "everything" (or "all things" in some translations) applies to his authority over all aspects of life. "Make disciples" emphasizes the responsibility to apply the teachings of Jesus to all aspects of human life.

c. Wisdom in Teaching according to the Early Church Fathers

A fundamental concept of wisdom in terms of teaching is the idea of Paideia. Paideia is a conscious construction of man, in order to form in it the humane, an ideal of excellence (*arete*), an ideal formation of the human spirit, without any relation with the idea of training. Man is the center of the Paideia thought. The evolution of philosophical thinking is the evolution of the concern about the cosmos with anthropology as its core, which will culminate in the philosophy of Socrates, Plato and Aristotle. Philosophy for these thinkers becomes an exercise in educating man towards excellence. The essence of the Greek State, also, can only be understood from the point of view of the formation of man and his entire life.

The discovery of man is characterized by gradual understanding of the essence of this man and the laws that determine it. The Greeks meant by education to educate the man according to the true human form with your authentic self. However, this depends on your being deep rooted in community life. The man who is in the core of all Greek literature on education is the politician (zoon politikon). One could say that real men who represent and embody what the Paideia aims to attain are poets, philosophers, rhetoricians and orators; they are the men of state.[362]

---

[362] K. B. Dias, "Justiça e Arete como horizonte ético no pensamento de Aristóteles" in: Revista Jurídica da UniFil, Ano VI no 6, Londrina, 44-58.

Peter Hodgson, in his book God's Wisdom: Toward a Theology of Education, emphasizes this concept of Paideia in the early Christian educators:

Education as growth in wisdom is evoked by God's Wisdom (Sophia tou theou), which challenges the foolishness of worldly wisdom (Sophia tou kosmou) (I Cor. 1:18-2:13). This kind of education, I shall argue, can be characterized by the term paideia (the nurture, upbringing, disciplining of a child, pais), which according to Werner Jaeger was the central idea of Greek culture, designating, 'the formative process of the human personality.'[363]

Paideia also was used by the author of the Epistle to the Ephesians to characterize the upbringing of children, namely, "in the nurture (paideia) made admonition (nouthesia) of the Lord" (Eph. 6:4 KJV). Horace Bushnell commented that paideia is the "Lord's way of education" as opposed to the "ostrich nurture" (Lam. 4:3), which abandons offspring solely to the forces of nature.[364]

According to Hodgson, in the Christianity of the Greek-speaking world the classical idea of paideia was incorporated into a way of thinking that was influenced by Hellenistic Judaism and, in particular, by the figure of Jesus Christ. Hodgson argues on the basis of Clement of Rome as follows:

The letter of Clement of Rome to the Corinthians (from the last decade of the first century) is a fascinating blend of Greek and Christian ideas. At the end of the letter Clemente turns to the praise of paideia, thus suggesting that his epistle is a form of Christian education. Clement notes that the Septuagint (the Greek version of the Hebrew Bible) often speaks of paideia, meaning by this term the disciplining of sinners that produces a change of mind. But he specially notes the phase paideia tou kyriou ("nature of the Lord") used in the Epistle to the Ephesians (6:4), and undoubtedly he has this in mind when he

---

[363] Hodgson, God's Wisdom, 7.
[364] Hodgson, God's Wisdom, 7.

speaks of the 'paideia of God" or the "paideia of Christ" as the greatest force in the life of the divine paideia, and in his final prayer he gives thanks to God for sending us Christ, "through whom Thou hast educated and sanctified and honored us."[365]

During the second and third centuries, new pedagogical models came to light. Our focus is to consider the importance of the appropriation of Paideia on the part of the Christians with a focus on theology as wisdom. This appropriation culminated with the theologians of Alexandria and Cappadocia.

Clement of Alexandria (died c. 215) and Origen (c. 185-254) made use of philosophical speculation to support a positive religion based on divine revelation and teaching as mediated through a holy book. Thus they were consciously bringing paideia and *torah* under the figure of Christ.[366]

Clement of Alexandria's Paedagogus (The Instructor) is quite a remarkable work, with grandiose claims and vivid images. Clement's basic assumption is that Christ is the divine educator who transcends every other paidea.[367]

Clement dwells at length on the wisdom that characterizes the divine instruction, a wisdom marked by friendship, benevolence, persuasion, and consolation on the one hand, and exhortation, discipline, censure, and punishment (but never revenge) on the other.[368]

For his part, Origen[369] regards Christianity as the greatest educational power in history. He accepts the Platonic

---

[365] Hodgson, God's Wisdom, 21.

[366] Hodgson, God's Wisdom, 21.

[367] Hodgson, God's Wisdom, 22.

[368] Hodgson, God's Wisdom, 22.

[369] Hodgson refers to Origen's three kinds of wisdom: "Wisdom of the world" (poetry, grammar, rhetoric, geometry, music, and medicine), wisdom of the "princes of this world" (occult philosophies), and wisdom of God" (Hodgson, God's Wisdom, 23). The fundamental point for Origen was to understand Jesus Christ as the revealed wisdom of God, and the way Jesus Christ has manifested the divine wisdom in fullness. Origen states: "Wisdom infuses

idea that the seed of good is to be the found in everything, that the cosmos is an orderly process, and that God is the pedagogue of the universe. But something is needed to transfer these sublime ideas into reality, and this 'something' is Christ, the greatest of teachers. He associates Christ with the Wisdom of God in a suggestive way. Wisdom is the breath of the power and will of God.[370]

Two words define two cultures whose traditions have to do with wisdom: the Hebrew and he Greek cultures, and these words are pedagogic: *torah* and *paideia*.[371] Both were intertwined in the pedagogic model of the church fathers. These two traditions are the antecedents of a Christian theology of education, and they are embedded in it.

Both Jaeger and Hodgson agree with this interrelation between paideia and Christ in the thoughts of the first Christian theologians. While the primary concern of our first Fathers was to prove that Jesus Christ was the true wisdom in himself, and their apologetics were intended to lead people to believe in him as Lord and Savior, it is also clear that they incorporated the idea of Paideia — which means making someone truly human through the educational process, by teaching wisdom and virtue. The search for this pattern of what constitutes being human led them to Jesus Christ as the paradigm of Christian Paideia, i.e., wisdom as the pedagogical goal in the educational process.

Herein lies a conclusive reality: the teaching of systematic theology and other disciplines as well as the construction of a relevant curriculum for theological education will

---

and transforms the soul. This is a spiritual process, the pouring of the Holy Spirit into our heart in such a way that we freely receive the gift of the Spirit but at the same time are inwardly changed by it." (Hodgson, God's Wisdom, 24).

[370]   Hodgson, God's Wisdom, 23.

[371] Serene Jones, Calvin and the Rhetoric of Piety, Louisville: Westminster John Knox Press, 1995, 197. Paideia is the sum total of all that a human being is – his or her inner life, spiritual being, and culture."

have to take into account the human being in his/her context but, above all, as a target of God's purpose for human life, with Jesus Christ as the paradigm of the fully human. A relevant theology cannot ignore the contribution of theological education as wisdom that comes from the Early Church Fathers for whom wisdom was an essential part of the model.

Before we approach the construction of a relevant curriculum for a program of theological education as living wisdom it is necessary to realize that this understanding of theology affected the theological educators of the Protestant Reformation.

d. Wisdom in the Teaching of the Reformers

Continuing through the classic theological tradition, looking for traces of theology as wisdom, we come now to a period of a new rich contribution to the transformative pedagogic process, the Reformed theology. In this work is not possible to say everything about the theme, but the core is that the Reformation exposes an approach to theological teaching, not just as a discipline, but as *habitus* of wisdom. Calvin (1509-1564) was influenced by Bernard of Clairvaux.[372]

Against Plato, but in line with the Latin rhetorical tradition going back to Cicero, he believed that truth is a function of persuasive efficacy, employing a panoply of images, metaphors, rhythms, and discursive breaks. The sometimes chaotic rhetorical play of Calvin's writing 'opens up the possibility to the readers being grasped by a divine wisdom that can only speak to them in the fractured remains of their linguistic frameworks.'[373]

---

[372] W. Jaeger, Paideia: The Ideals of Greek Culture, Vol. 2, New York: Oxford University Press, 1943, 27-32, 37-39, 41-46, 59-70.

[373] Hodgson, God's Wisdom, 30. (Hodgson here quotes Serene Jones.)

As wisdom of God, Calvin emphasized the fact that theology is in charge of glorifying God and not of making speculations regarding the divine Being.

Peter Hodgson affirms in his book God's Wisdom, regarding the theological epistemology of Calvin, that there is in his work a Hebrew sensibility rather than a Hellenistic one. He gives the following instruction to read Calvin:

One way to read this work of 'instruction' is to follow the steps by which Calvin moves from (human) nature as a teacher to scripture as a teacher, to the Holy Spirit as a teacher. In all of these, it is really God who is both the teacher and the object of teaching.[374]

In this progressive understanding of Calvin's pedagogy, we observe the emphases that come from his thoughts. Firstly he wanted to affirm that all people have some theological perception and they ask for heaven's sake, but they need other teachers that will guide them through history, the Scriptures. For Calvin the Word of God in the Scriptures interprets the nature of the works of God.[375] It is surprising what Hodgson states:

> Calvin does not focus on the Institutes and the role of Christ as a teacher, although there are occasional references to him in this regard (Inst. 3.1.4; 3.20; 1; 4.8.8.). Rather Calvin's emphasis is distinctly pneumatic. Scripture obtains full authority among believers only when they regard it "as having sprung from heaven, as if there the living words of God were heard" (Inst. 1.7.1). This is a matter of seeing "as if," and believers come to see it as such through the inner witness of the Holy Spirit, which is higher than all proof, for here God speaks to us in person. The same Spirit who has spoken through the mouths of the prophets 'must penetrate into our hearts to persuade us

---

[374] Hodgson, God's Wisdom, 30.

[375] John Calvin, Institutes of the Christian Religion, Philadelphia: Westminster Press, 1960, I,6,3.

that they faithfully proclaim what had been divinely com-
manded' (Inst. 1.7.4). The Spirit does not compel or coerce but
persuades, draws, inflames us.[376]

It is for this understanding of the grace and power of
God as a single and exclusive work of the Spirit Saint of
God, that Calvin is seen as a Holy Spirit theologian, pene-
trating this way into the territory of this thesis: theology is
wisdom of God, and as Jesus Christ is the revealed wisdom
of God in human history, wisdom is the very heart of theology. Christ, however, is not present as a teacher of rules
or an example only. He is far more present in his Spirit
who shapes the lives and thought of Christians. Under Calvin's optics, "the way to the Kingdom of God is open only
to him whose mind has been made new by the illumination
of the Holy Spirit."[377] Without the light of the Spirit, all is
darkness; thus God gives to us "the Spirit of wisdom and
revelation" (Eph. 1.17).[378]

But, and this "but" is important, for Calvin we need one
more teacher, the Church. That is not in contrast to the
Spirit as teacher. It means rather that the Spirit works by
the means of the church.[379] The Spirit is not 'spiritual' as
something abstract, but present in the concrete work and
life, and thus in the concrete teaching and life, of those
who educate. It is through the community of the church
that we are freed from individualistic dangers, fanatics, ty-
rants, and psychopaths.

It is important to stress this approach of Calvin in the
context of the beginning twenty-first century. Some people think they have a special revelation of God, becoming
dominant over whole communities as owners of the truth.

---

[376] Hodgson, God's Wisdom, 32.

[377] Calvin as quoted by Hodgson, God's Wisdom, 32.

[378] Calvin quoted by Hodgson, God's Wisdom, 32.

[379] Calvin, Institutes IV, title.

In the beginning of this millennium our cities are periodically frightened by moonstruck and false mystics, bringing abuses of spiritual authority and new heresies. We need the Church as a teacher. Through its institutions and schools and in its activities the Church shows itself as a school of the Holy Spirit.[380] This school has people appointed to specific offices: apostle, prophet, evangelist, shepherd, and teacher. It is through these ministries that the Church becomes a master, leading the people of God to a living wisdom. The future of pastoral theology needs to deepen the essential dimensions of all these ministries and not just to concentrate in some of them, as it has been done.

Theology as wisdom is pneumatology in its essence and it is, therefore, transformative. Thus we join Calvin to attend "the school of that best schoolmaster, the Holy Spirit, in which we so advance that nothing need be acquired from elsewhere."[381] According to Hodgson:

> For this reason, education, the schooling of the Holy Spirit, is at the heart of the Reformation. Without it, nothing is effective; with it, in the final analyses nothing else is needed. Calvin's understanding of the role of the Spirit in the education-event represents a breakthrough on our journey toward a theology of education.[382]

To summarize the thought of Calvin: the Spirit completes pedagogy as the pedagogy of God. The Father of Lights illumines our minds; the Word and sacraments confirm our faith by setting before our eyes the good will of the Father while the Spirit engraves this confirmation in our minds and makes it efficacious. In my opinion here lies the very heart of theology as wisdom.[383] In the perspective

---

[380] Calvin, Institutes IV,1,5.

[381] Calvin, Institutes IV, 17, 36.

[382] Hodgson, God's Wisdom, 35.

[383] Calvin, Institutes IV,14,10.

of this faith in God who enlightens human beings we must train people in the knowledge of God who reveals Himself in Christ, who is the Light of the world (John 8:12). Our task in the present research is to explain how a curriculum that is theologically responsible and relevant can be constructed from this faith. In the paradigm of Christ as the Light of the world by whom God enlightens us human beings can be trained to become lights of the world themselves (Matt. 5:14, 16).

We have seen that the challenge for theology in its pedagogic function is to understand that information is not enough, but that transformation is its aim, too. Theology teaching in colleges and theological seminaries demands integration between knowledge and transformation (conversion), between intellect and change of condition with ethical commitment, as inseparable dimensions.

For Christian theology human beings are not the measure of all things. Paul the Apostle has something to say about wisdom, as we can read in I Corinthians 1:18-31. He quotes the Prophet Isaiah: "I (the Lord) will destroy the wisdom of the wise, and the discernment of the discerning I will thwart" (Is. 29:14, in the Greek). For Paul this means God has "made foolish the wisdom of the world," or, more precisely, that "the world did not know God through wisdom" (1 Cor. 1:20-21). Paul assumes that this weakness of human wisdom must be part of the divine plan or purpose so that God can bring about salvation through "Christ crucified" – who is "a stumbling block to Jews and foolishness to Gentiles" (1 Cor. 1:23).[384] Teaching this wisdom of God is the challenge for any theological training. By this wisdom theologians will be transformed and become participants of transformation of the church as a transforming power in society. Let us see which features are essential in

---

[384] Hodgson, God's Wisdom, 87.

theological education as a result of having wisdom as its model.

Characteristics of Theology as Wisdom in Search of a Theological *Curriculum*

At this point in the present research a question arises: What are the features in understanding theology as wisdom that point to the construction of a curriculum for theological education? How can we adopt a basic model of a curriculum within the space of a Reformed tradition?

a. Practical Characteristics

Theology as wisdom is the most demanding task every theologian can have. It is also the most relaxed task one can imagine. For wisdom knows about human limitations. Wisdom will not use these as an excuse, but as a disclaimer against frustrations. Theology is practiced before the face of God and then we know that we are limited and dependent beings. We live in a world that is too large for a human being, in a city that is too complicated. We can only contribute a little stone to God's building, a piece of gravel to the road of justice. That is enough for a little human being. Theology is *theologia viatorum*, going on a way that is not yet paved. We can only give small contributions. That is enough for human beings. Humility is wisdom's partner.

Humility is wisdom's partner. She is so because humility is the opposite of resignation. Resignation means that we give up because we cannot solve the problems. Humility is the wisdom that knows that nothing is done at random, but as a step on the way of God. Therefore theology is wisdom: it is *docta fides* as the solid ground of the things we hope (Hb. 11:1); it is *docta spes* as the hope that does not disappoint (Rm. 5:5) and it is *docta caritas* as the love that many waters cannot quench and rivers cannot wash away.

In the present research, the proposal is that theological education should and must return to the idea of theology as wisdom, present in the old thoughts and forgotten in modern times. Thus, as Jesus healed a man with a withered hand, we too have in the theological passage to extend a withered hand. Many times we show our good hand; there are marvels being taught in our theological seminaries.

We have in Brazil, for example, great exegetes, excellent biblical scholars and renowned historians but the problem is not here. The question is what is lacking; we still have a withered hand. We need to integrate wisdom with the life of the people in each context. There are many models that have sought this integration but there is still a deep gap, especially when it comes to teaching Systematic Theology. We still face a great challenge; there is much still to walk in this direction. It is necessary to extend the withered hand from exclusionism so that it does not fall on the deaf ears of society, fruits of confessional narcissism.

Wisdom illuminates reason. A rational intelligence is necessary and also affection, sympathy, compassion and existential involvement. A purely rational theology would be a contradiction as it would be empty of life and not a life full of emotion, passion, joy and love. "Passion is necessary for the humanization of reason which prevents falling into a delirious abstraction. Reason and passion should be rectified amongst themselves."[385]

Wisdom in theology is to acknowledge the need for courses in which the whole cannot function properly if the parts do not operate together as they should. Most difficulties come from the instructors' own antagonisms and

---

[385] Morin, Ética, 136.

from their vices and weaknesses, that are products of ideologies that in some form influence theological constructions. It is also necessary to perceive the complementary that we find among reason and passion as a greater challenge for theological education. It is this that could be called dialogue as theology as living wisdom is dialogue. To live for theology is to live with perception of social reality, this implies integrating love, faith and hope to the reality of the human existence.

The art of life for theology is a living in Jesus Christ and in him to be forever regenerated – that which is not regenerated, degenerates. Theology as the wisdom of God in Jesus Christ is a permanent poly-regeneration. To know is to put into practice. Knowledge that cannot be lived is lost in time and has no value for future generations.

Theological education that forgets the cause of its past failures is condemned to repeat them. He who forgets the lessons of oppression in history will not hesitate to oppress. Wisdom, however, in our theological schools should take us to *ars theologica*. This, today, demands a reform of the contents of the theological course. It is a reform that integrates knowledge, disciplines and the various contributions of science.

The current mission of theological education consists of training minds capable of connecting knowledge, recognizing global and fundamental problems and of assuming the implicit challenges in the revelation of Jesus Christ in His message. Theological education has a permanent challenge to acquire the tools to investigate as only then will there be progress and the concepts to be applied to the needs of the context will be renovated.

The theologian in his investigation has a calling to be the spokesman of hope as he believes in the promises of God and waits decisively for such promises. He is also somebody woven with faith in God's Word as the instrument that weaves the contents of his teaching and proclamation as threads taken from the Sacred Scriptures. He is permeated by the spirit of love, which celebrates new challenges in order to render a better service to the world.

Theological education as wisdom deals with all aspects of life. Therefore it is always contextual. This is even more the case if we consider that theology is founded in God's gracious acting in Christ. Jesus Christ is the key to theology as wisdom. The Christological approach is the most encouraging as a guide for theology as the wisdom of God. At least we point to an efficient method that could reward us with vigorous transforming guidelines.

Christian theological education provokes an efficient encounter between Jesus Christ and the real situation. As Orlando Costas says:

> *The incarnation of Christ shows us the aspect of this way of identification and participation. Not only is identification with the cultural ambient necessary but also the concrete and existential situation and in which men to be evangelized are found.*[386]

For theological education this implies that the presentation of the contents should never lose this incarnate aspect.

Theology is about God incarnate. It is about God who is present in the bodily, material world of human beings. It is in this reality where the Spirit dwells. Therefore we will now focus on the way theological education should be modeled in the concrete situation where we have our first responsibility: the city of Londrina as we depicted it in the first chapter. Certainly many aspects will be applicable in other situations as well, because they have to do with the relation of tradition and context, of praxis and theory, of

---

[386] Costas, Hacia una Teologia, 123.

understanding and critique. They will be also applicable in other contexts because it is one Lord about we speak all over the world and one humankind with hopes and despair, with happiness and sorrow, wherein we can understand each other in the unity of humanity and in the unity of faith.

Each city has its own configuration. Therefore, we have to focus on a specific context, being aware of the fact that many cities and countries as well have similar challenges and hopes and that we belong to a worldwide community. However, precisely because of this worldwide community we can and must focus on this city now, so that theological education is not a mere abstract enterprise, without real bodily and material life. It is in Christ that the human being glimpses his future. For this, you can already live in hope. Boff thus affirmed:

> In faith, however, and in a correct hermeneutic we can see the manifestation of the only mystery of Christ that, for being a mystery and for being rich of the richness of God you do not tire of any image nor get lost. He continues to perpetuate his incarnation, while penetrating in our schemes of understanding in each generation.[387]

We have argued that theology as wisdom in a Christian perspective tries to lead the student to takes on the shape of *docta fides*, *docta spes* and *docta caritas*. Theology as critical reflection may people show the way to the Christian life in faith, hope and love. It is in this perspective that we will deal with theological education in Londrina.

Paul, when speaking about these three basic aspects of Christian life, says that the most of the three is love. Love is the end of God's acting towards the world. Faith and hope will end up in the vision of God's love, which will be

---

[387] L. Boff, "As Imagens de Cristo Presentes no Cristianismo Liberal do Brasil" in: J. Maraschin Quem é Jesus Cristo no Brasil, São Paulo: ASTE, 1974, 34.

in everything and all. Therefore the primary focus of theological education as training how to speak about and reasonably live with God must be on love.

Love is not an abstract idea. Love is relational. Love has to do with persons. A loving person is nothing if there is not another person whom he or she loves. Love has to do with the real embodied and socialized life of the other one.

That is where theological education has to start: the consciousness of the real presence of human beings in your city, in their concrete material and social embedding. If it is not about these human beings it is not about love and thus not about wisdom nor about theology as reflecting on the incarnate God.

A theology that goes to the encounter of life in an ample manner will have a future in Brazilian reality because it will give human beings an expectation of hope through love. John Mackay affirmed having two perspectives, theology from the balcony and theology along the way. For Mackay *the balcony* is this platform of wood or stone that is above the façade and with high windows in Latin American houses. It is the place from where the family can ponder everything that is happening in the street. It could also be the place to gather to see the sunset or even marvel at the stars in the sky. It is the symbol of a perfect spectator to whom life and the universe are permanent objects of study and contemplation. A person can live his whole existence on the *balcony* even physically having the capacity of knowing about various worlds. Mackay speaks of this as a constant temptation for the thinker of Christian theology, remaining in this place of contemplation and analyzing the evil of the world.[388]

On the other hand, the street, its sounds, congestion and danger present another perspective to man. The street

---

[388] J. Mackay, The Other Spanish Christ, New York: Macmillan, 1932, 22.

is where life is lived intensely, where thoughts are born from conflict and serious interest, where options are presented and decisions taken. The street is the place of action, of the crossroad and real life. In the street one seeks a goal and runs the risks in order to reach it.

Mackay warns us not to interpret the street in purely material terms. Many people go along the street, never very far from their office or pulpits, their hospital or their workshop but have traveled far along the journey of life. For them, both the street and the balcony provoke a feeling of excitement.

With these models, Mackay arranged an agenda for a mission with obligatory participation. The Church is a companionship for those who live in the street and not a group of observers who spend their lives lamenting the sad successes of life from the safety of the balcony. A Christian cannot only be a contemplative being who is wrapped up in himself. The work of God can only be carried out in the street in company with the resuscitated Christ. A Christian as a pilgrim is seeking a pearl of great value, and this is why Mackay affirms:

> *A man exists when for him the eternal converts to the active beginning within a storm. When the eternal produces such an impact on the life of man in its finitude and in the real situation wherever it speaks, man is completely dominated by this impact on all parts of his being, so this man exists and really starts on his way.*[389]

So the first challenge for students is to know the social reality where people live in. That implies also that theology cannot do without sociology, without such bare matter as statistic figures. What are these people with whom we live and whom we want to serve as theologians? What is their wealth and what is their poverty? Theology will

---

[389] J. Mackay, El Otro Cristo Español, Buenos Aires: Aurora, 1988, 57.

not get body if students are not impressed by the reality of life as expressed in statistic figures. They must know reality.[390]

The vision of theological education has as much to do with individuals as with society, as individuals cannot be separated from social systems. The conflicts and problems of social injustice affect individuals directly. He who says he serves the Lord should fight for social justice, for love and for liberty of the Kingdom of God. The Christian faith has the function of expressing visible signs of economic and social life as signs of hope for those who are hopeless, which will have also consequences for dealing with politics. If Christians, who say they possess the truth of the Gospel and confess to living under the lordship of the resuscitated, do not take their responsibility in history seriously, how can we expect anyone else to take this seriously?

Sociological studies and interpretations, however, are not sufficient for *docta caritas*. Statistics can be an eye-opener and can display the extent of problems, but in the end they are only generalizations. It is totally different if you know a person who lives in a poverty situation. It is different, also, if that percentage if reflected in the face of a mother who lacks the means to buy the food she needs

---

[390] This is the whole problem Clodovis Boff dedicated in the early 80s. Problem is what sociology should we theologians chose to rely on and to offer us a reliable picture of reality? Clodovis proposes a dialectical explanation, a socio-analytical mediation. "Liberation theology uses Marxism in a purely instrumental way. It does not venerate the Holy Gospels nor does it feel the obligation to report to social scientists the use it makes of Marxist words and ideas (whether it uses them correctly or not), except to the poor, their faith and hope in the ecclesial community. Freely it uses some of Marxism's 'methodological indications' that prove fruitful for understanding the universe of the oppressed, including: the importance of economic factors; attention to class struggle, the mystifying power of ideology, including religious ones, and so forth" (Clodovis Boff & Leonardo Boff, Como Fazer Teologia da Libertaçao, Petropolis: Vozes, 2010, 44-45).

for her child or the face of a young man dying of AIDS.[391] Many people resent it when theological education appears to be focused more on political and social programs than on the personal wounds of human beings in all their necessities. Many people, again, feel that they are used as objects for humanitarian projects whose purpose may only be to give Christianity a good image rather than helping people at the point of their need.

Love has to do with relations and therefore students must not only know figures, interpretations and causes (they must know these as well), but they must know people. They must see the faces of those who are excluded and of those who have no hope. They must also see the faces of those who are powerful and wealthy and it might be more difficult to trace the reality of the life of precisely those people because they are able to hide their sorrows behind the gladness of their faces, the walls of their houses and the security systems that surround them in the prosperous quarters of the city. A student in theology should know human beings and learn to know them in such a way that it is not mere intellectual knowledge but knowledge that fuels love and is fueled by love.

Theology as wisdom is *docta caritas*. That implies at least two things. First of all it means that it is critical. Theologians must learn to discern what is really at stake. People can hide themselves, both in wealth and in poverty. People who are exploited can themselves exploit those who are entrusted to them. The poor father who has no job and stays in his hut for the whole day can exploit his daughter and oppress his wife. Many examples in this field can easily be found. Students must learn to discover the slings and twists of human relations and of the human mind.

---

[391] S. Frossard, "A Ação Social da Igreja", in: Muzio, A revolução, 130.

Docta caritas means also that theologians are challenged to find solutions. They are trained to help people how to cope with their situation. As liberating wisdom of love theology searches for ways to the future for those people who did not have any perspective. Know-how as such is not yet love, but love challenges to know-how, finding ways where no way could be.

Theology as wisdom is comprehensive, taking into account God's revelation and the whole of life. Nothing can be excluded. That implies also the person of the theological teacher. The teaching for an intellectual life is finally, an instrument for an objective to be existentially undertaken or, in other words in life, in an effective way.

An effective life is not a professional life only, as a professional life is abstract. It is only an aspect of life. A professional life is only the role played in certain parts in front of certain people, but that cannot be undertaken in another place in the presence of other people. Theology is about the whole life and not as a merely professional activity. This implies dominating the function of the professional teacher in theological education, theology is life and all of life and only thus will it be wisdom.

No other science has the function of affecting the complete reality of human life more than theology, affecting not only the life present but also the eternal. This demands a spirit of humbleness and service from the theologian. It is a barefooted messenger facing the sanctity of God walking through the avenues of history in the direction of the Kingdom of God that comes with power and glory. The theologian *that is truly a theologian* "remains a student of theology until death, even with old age or he will never have been."[392] The whole project of theology of wisdom

---

[392] K. Barth, Introdução à Teologia Evangélica, 9th ed., São Leopoldo, 2008, 108.

will collapse if the teacher is not wise in love, hope and faith. The teacher of wisdom should be a wise person.

First of all teachers of wisdom must be wise in love. They must express this towards their students and in the way they speak about God and human beings. That does not mean that they cannot be strict. True love is very strict, precisely in the interest of the other one. Teachers of wisdom should lead their students on solid ways in a *habitus* that fits to their calling as theologians.

Love as *docta caritas* implies that one is also self-critical. The professor is not his or her own end. They live and work at the interest of the students and to their service and by doing so they are an example for a new generation of theologians to devote their lives to the service of people in the church and in society. Thus theology as *docta caritas* is not only a model or a *curriculum* but first of all an attitude, as we can learn from old teachers of *torah* who gathered their students and trained them in way of God. Theologians are a community of students and teachers in search for the ways of life.

Teachers of theology as wisdom must also be an embodiment of hope. They must point to the future and open new ways, new perspectives where students can go. They must be faithful so that students can trust them and find a solid base for their thought. They on their turn must trust the students even if a student does not come to the standards. In the latter case they must open ways to the student that fit to his or her capabilities. But most of all they must challenges the student's talents so that he or she can develop hope as a contribution to transformation.

Above all, theologians of wisdom must be a sign of hope by their patience and perseverance. The perseverance is hope's closest friend. By going on in troubles and setbacks the teacher shows a solid, imperishable hope. They must express this facing the concrete situation of Londrina, with its scattered and wounded members of the church, with its exploited poor people and exploiting rich people, with its hope and its despair. They should not give up when the struggle for transformation of human life is tough and falls back again and again. The character of the teacher of wisdom, therefore, will rise from a theological exercise that combines both being and doing. In other words, the theologian of wisdom will become a model of the values he/she teaches because he/she has found the source of wisdom in the merging of theological reflection and Christian action.

In order to become a strong reference point of *docta spes* a theologian must have a passion for life and be in close contact with the needs of the people in his/her context of ministry. Only in a sound embedding in the Scriptures and the faith of the church of all ages it is possible to hold on to life without bitterness and frustration. The Scriptures witness to Christ, who 'when they hurled their insults at, did not retaliate; when he suffered, he made no threads. Instead, he entrusted himself to him who judges justly' (I Pe. 2:23). In all situations, we must trust in God and his wisdom and the wisdom of God is Christ.

b. Objective: What to Expect from a Wisdom Model?

We have said that approaching theology as wisdom could have several consequences for a teaching project for a course in theology. It is commonplace in education in general to speak about skills and competences as the larger goal of any given course. Theological education cannot escape this objective.

What is expected as a result of a wisdom approach in curriculum construction is a challenge to all — a theological education that integrates scholarship and practice. As Mendonça states, theological education is experiencing a deadlock between pastoral action as a whole and theological scholarship. He says: "Theology today, in Brazil, is being called upon, and even challenged, to leave its church niches to enter the broader universe of the debates about human problems that until recently were confined to the areas of science and philosophical reflection, almost always limited to an anthropocentric ethics."[393] He asks: "How can we, on one hand, meet the pastoral needs [of the people] and, on the other, accepting the challenge of academia?"[394]

Our proposal in the present work is to contribute to a curriculum in theological education that generates the following consequences:

To exercise a role in communities of faith, especially in the evangelical.

To implement community projects of Christian faith in different ethnic and cultural contexts, from the perspective of the Missio Dei;

To develop relevant research in Theology, Exegesis, Literature and History of the Christian Religion, Pastoral and Mission Action, Philosophy and related areas – notably in the areas of Psychology, Sociology and Anthropology.

To reflect theologically on the bible text and the issues of human existence, in a constant inter-disciplinary dialogue in the pursuit of religious knowledge to be applied to the common welfare.

To promote the potential of different religious groups with a view to developing concrete action on behalf of society.

---

[393] A. G. Mendonça, "Currículo teológico básico" in: Marcio Fabri dos Anjos (org.), Teologia profissão, São Paulo: Soter/Loyola, 1996, 123-147.

[394] Mendonça, Currículo, 123-147.

To acquire a taste for scientific research, the study of various sciences related to the phenomenology of religion.

To understand the complexity of human beings, particularly in their religious behavior, so as to live the faith with tolerance and social responsibility.

Similarly, the competences to be developed include:

To read critically, biblical texts, theological and literature traditionally religious, especially the Reformed, keeping the necessary distance that a reader-interpreter should have in relation to the text in such a way that a compromise with a naive or mistaken point of view is presented.

To develop historical and biographical research on texts from Theology, the Bible and historical documents making use of adequate methodology.

To reflect critically with sensitivity, tolerance and affection.

To understand the methodological principles adequately that allow reading and the relevant interpretation of the Bible, Christian Theology and religious phenomenon.

To understand the religious diversity and its consequences of living the faith in a postmodern pluralistic society.

To work in a team, developing a sense of co-operation and respecting each other's limits.

By understanding these skills and competences mentioned, the course intends to express a liberating character in context, toward a committed pastoral and theological education academically consistent and therefore academic and contextually relevant.

This kind of theology would be relevant to the social reality, where models of theologies emerged with all their variants, involving race, gender and socio-economic differences.

c. Towards a Curriculum Construction

The Revista do Núcleo de Estudos e Pesquisa do Protestantismo (NEPP, the Journal for the Study and Research of Protestantism of the Escola Superior de Teologia) under the theme "O novo rosto do ensino de teologia no Brasil: números, normas legais e espiritualidade" [=The new face of teaching theology in Brazil: figures, legal norms and spirituality] discusses the curriculum question. After a presentation of statistics on the reality of theological education in Brazil, the reader is informed that there only 29 study programs in theology (as of 2002) that have been accredited by the Ministry of Education. "The available data on the accredited theological courses show that the higher education system offers 2,000 student placements to 2100 potential applicants [every year]. Actual enrollment fills a little over half of these vacancies. Every year, fewer than 300 theologians graduate with a Bachelor's degree in theology in Brazil."[395] The dropout rate of theological students is quite high. These figures indicate that for every four students entering the first year, only one completes his theological training. Since being a theologian in Brazil is not a "recognized" profession, there is "no need to establish curriculum guidelines that pertain to the teaching of this discipline."[396] Thus the construction of any curriculum of theology is a free enterprise.

---

[395] E. L. Pauly, "O novo rosto do ensino de teologia no Brasil: Números, normas legais e espiritualidade," in: Protestantismo em Revista, volume 10, May-August. NEEP – EST, Escola Superior de Teologia, São Leopoldo, 2006, 20-35.

[396] Pauly, O novo rosto, 20-35.

Theology at the present time needs to seek ways of interaction with issues that were hitherto demonized, for example, economic issues and party politics - especially within the segment of 'mission Protestantism.' Certainly any theology that seeks to insert itself in society will be highly contextual, but not all theologies encompass appropriate methodologies.

The challenge outlined for Theology as Wisdom and more specifically within the 'mission Protestantism' segment is to break confessional barriers. Doing theology requires dialoguing with other social and theological segments. Another need is to dialogue with the theological tradition of the First Fathers. Theology as wisdom must be able to influence the teaching of Systematic Theology and the construction of curricula in theological education. It should focus on four poles: ratio, memory, praxis and hermeneutics. In other words, it should be scientific, reproductive, productive and practical. It should be highly dialogical — in order to overcome the culture of the ecclesial ghetto — opening up to dialogue with other voices of the theological spectrum, the voices of ecumenical theology and liberation theologies. This dialogical character, especially in relation to the wisdom of the Apostolic Fathers, the Middle Age theologians and the Reformers, as well as theologians of today, is a task that cannot be postponed any longer.

Liberation theology, for example, has an extremely efficient methodological and theological corpus and we still reap the rewards of their mature reflection. I emphasize here the wisdom in the proposed biblical reading of Carlos Mesters,[397] and the accurate, growing and mature contribu-

---

[397] Through his "Parable of the Door," Mesters defends the idea that the theologian, in order to be authentic and relevant, should integrate the following dimensions in his theological work: the life of the people, the exegetical

tions of Clodovis Boff, whose work "The Theory of Theological Method," deserves a more accurate analysis by those who are responsible for theological education.

Theology as wisdom has a comprehensive and challenging agenda — to seek a balance between the poles; it must be productive and reproductive, rational-scientific and practical. In all models there are theologians who seek that balance. We want to affirm wisdom as an integrating factor in the doing of theology.

We seek this integrative character across disciplines thus overcoming the fragmentation that exists between the various fields of study. A challenge will be to face the difficulties inherent to the status of theology itself, since the concept is very fragmented and easily confused with doctrines and dogmas. Theology has been a speech directed to the church and not properly to society.

In the Protestant case, this issue is even more aggravating because there is a distancing from culture due to an excessive emphasis on "regeneration" and "sanctification" of the individual, which turns human behavior into the hermeneutical key to determine whether a converted person does or does not have faith in Christ. The consequence of this is the omission towards popular culture and towards politics in various sectors of society.

When we think beyond the walls, there is another problem. Missionary activity is seen as a territorial breakthrough by making use of a military language, where established temples are synonymous with the Kingdom of God. In this case, a proposal of a theology that favors life in all its spheres, which is inserted in social systems, could still meet with suspicion, but on the other hand there is a

---

science and the faith of the church. All of these should be placed at the service of life, which was created by God and saved in Christ so that it may become, at last, "abundant life" (Jn. 10:10; cf. Carlos Mesters, Por Trás das Palavras, Petrópolis: Vozes, 1999).

desire for a type of theology that integrates the content of the Christian faith with human life in its dimensions.

There is a need for theological education, especially in the Protestant case, to go through a process of theological decolonization due to the fact there is excessive consumption of foreign theological literature, mainly North American.

In Clodovis Boff we find clues for a new curriculum, as pillars that are applicable to the teaching of theology as wisdom. His contribution can be summarized as follows:

> *"Three essential moments comprise the theological discourse in its productive process, i.e., as a practice - listening to the faith (fideism auditus), explaining the faith (intellectus fidei), applying the faith (fidei applicatio). As one can see, there are three major operations in the theological process — hermeneutical, to listen to the faith; speculative, to explain the faith; practice, to apply faith in life. The hermeneutic moment seeks to understand the very meaning of the message of faith, as recorded in sacred Scripture, in Tradition and in the dogmas of the church.*[398]

In a first moment, among the witnesses that the theologian must listen to, there are 'primary' [elements], which are the Sacred Scripture and Tradition, 'secondary' [elements], which are the other ecclesiastical witnesses (Creeds, Liturgies, the Magisterium, the Fathers, the Doctors and the Theologians) and, finally, there are elements, which, even as outsiders can be appropriated by theologians (religions, philosophy, ideologies, sciences, history and the signs of the times).[399] This affirms that listening is always active. In particular, it listens to the Scriptures. "Scripture is the 'soul' of every theology. It is not that Scripture is at the service of theology; it is theology that is

---

[398] C. Boff, Teoria do Método Teológico, 199.
[399] C. Boff, Teoria, 228.

at the service of the Word of God."[400]. It has to be a prayerful and obedient listening to the Word. To C. Boff, theology is the theoretical unfolding of the Bible.[401] He next emphasizes the value of tradition, and distinguishes the true tradition, which is a living process, both dynamic and creative, from traditionalism, which seeks to reify and mummify tradition. "Without tradition, people or communities become victims of change, of the general unfolding [of the world] and they flounder in nihilism."

There is a second moment, which C. Boff calls *intellectus fidei*, i.e., the 'theoretical moment' or the explanatory moment in theological construction. That moment unfolds in three steps: (1) An analysis that explains the logical reasons or the internal nexus of the faith, its roots or its own reasons, showing the why and the how of the mysteries believed; (2) A systematization, which joins all analyses in an organic synthesis. "However, all theological synthesis is an open synthesis because of the ever greater Mystery;"[402] (3) Creation, which means developing new connections and hypotheses that the truth in question may have with other mysteries and with the human condition and destiny.[403]

In his next methodological moment, Boff states: "The third great moment of theological production is the confrontation of faith with life. Here we approach the faith ad extra, as projected outward to mission."[404] "Theology must necessarily be open to life and the pastoral [ministry]. It is better to speak of ['updating'] the faith in life than just the application of faith. This has been done by classical theology, however, for [this classic theology] the social

---

[400] C. Boff, Teoria, 228.
[401] C. Boff, Teoria, 229.
[402] C. Boff, Teoria, 277.
[403] C. Boff, Teoria, 266.
[404] C. Boff, Teoria, 282.

practice did not have the complexity it has today, and therefore, it did not require the theoretical mediations we need to understand it properly.[405]

Speaking about theology as wisdom implies speaking about "life," with all its implications. This resonates with Clodovis Boff's proposal that, when re-dimensioning the "multiple levels of confrontation,"[406] theology itself is challenged today, i.e., the inner life, the place of decisions, of faith, of spirituality; the psychic life, which is the space of emotions and feelings; interpersonal life, which is family, community and everyday oriented; social life, the field of civil society; economic life: work, labor union struggles; political life, the sphere of citizenship, the political party, the State; cultural life: leisure, art; religious life, the sphere of multiple expressions of faith; ecological life, the common house of the enormous stream of life; planetary life, in the relation of humankind with the entire cosmos.[407] The methodological conclusion is that the updating of the faith has its own logic: the logic of acting.

Regarding the Protestant itinerary, Antonio Gouveia de Mendonça, speaking from his Reformed tradition, describes a similar concern about this task under a theme "Toward a core curriculum of theology". He writes:

> *Protestant theology in Brazil is at a crossroads today. The messianic message of waiting has lost its meaning, and the historical Protestantism has not been capable of taking up another form of messianism, just as it has not been able to develop a more open theology which is more concerned about social issues, because of the fundamentalist pressure from outside. How, therefore, can we organize an objective theological education? Nowadays the Brazilian Protestant churches do not know what to do with their seminaries because they are*

---

[405] C. Boff, Teoria, 283.
[406] C. Boff, Teoria, 284.
[407] C. Boff, Teoria, 285.

not capable of building the profile of the pastor in view of the new religious landscape.[408]

Mendonça says that the Christian tradition has found it difficult to reconcile theology, as technical or speculative knowledge, with the proclamation of the Gospel pure and simple and the parallel function of shepherding the flock. He says that the missing element has been to study theology in order to connect the theologian with his/her life.

> *"What happens is that in teaching theology we have the habit of dissociating the biography of the theologian from his/her thinking or at least from the setting and the challenges of the world in which he/she lives". This creates a dichotomous understanding between the scholarship of the theologian and the spirituality of the proclamation. "When we examine the work of the theologian from the perspective of his/her biography and the reality of his/her time, it is very difficult not to find in it the spirituality that inspired it, whether or not we agree with their viewpoints."*[409]

Mendonça advocates a balance between academic rigor and pastoral principles.

> *"Our experience in graduate school, with students coming from Protestant seminaries who cultivate their piety more than their than intellect has shown in many cases the difficulty in adapting to critical approaches, a factor that prolongs the graduation of the student besides the conflicts of conscience it causes. A curriculum that would introduce critical approaches from the beginning could reduce these difficulties and conflicts."*[410]

Therefore, how should a core curriculum look like in order to meet the challenges of the moment? It should meet three specific but complementary areas, that should

---

[408] Mendonça, Currículo, 140.

[409] Mendonça, Currículo, 141.

[410] Mendonça, Currículo, 144.

be integrated in the midst of their complexity. We should synthesize a formula that consists in the confrontation between Faith and Life. This is the essential core in the curriculum construction of theological education.

Thus the new *intellectus amoris* is not opposed to the classical *intellectus fidei*; they fit together perfectly. This way, theology can be synthetically called intellectus fidei formatae amore (the intelligence of faith informed by love), or even, in Pauline and Augustinian times, intellectus fidei quae per caritatem operatur (cf. Gl. 5:6): an understanding of the faith that operates through love.[411] This involves thinking on a broad ecumenical dialogue with other religions, seeking convergence in relation to social construction — seeking justice, fighting political oppression— believing that another way of doing things in society is possible and necessary. It also involves a deeper understanding of the plurality of ideas and exegeses in the form of an interreligious dialogue, which would result in an amazing human growth.

Now considering the disciplines in particular, we must say that we all should put into practice the aforementioned confrontation, and thus we should emphasize methodologically those various moments. For example, Biblical Theology, in its introduction and exegesis, must develop the pole of faith as lived in the community of faith, and through *auditus fidei*, in connection with life, it seeks an update of the meaning of the texts. Systematic Theology also develops more strongly the pole of faith, in its *intellectus fidei* moment, but it should not fail to take into account the projection into life of the truths of the faith, expressing hope (*docta spes*). Pastoral theology, practical theology, the theology of spirituality and related disciplines that emphasize the reading of life, the *applicatio fidei*

---

[411] C. Boff, Teoria, 288.

(i.e., the living out of the faith), also takes into account the theoretical truths of the content of the faith — which includes Church History and the history of the Christian Thought), while developing a creative dialogue with Systematic Theology and Biblical Theology.

We have to agree with Clodovis Boff that if such confrontation Faith-Life[412] is non-existent, the theological discourse remains unfinished. Theological education must be aware of this potential gap. C. Boff strongly proposes that, "there is an intersection between the two, a link, a *perichoresis.*"[413] Not theory "or" practice, but theory "and" practice; the interface is marked by "and." Therefore, a core curriculum, according to Mendonça, should answer to three distinct but complementary areas, as dogmatic and pastoral, general Christian tradition and supporting sciences. The first would meet institutional and ecclesiastical needs and objectives; the second would offer the students the basic elements of the *depositum fidei* that is common to Christianity; and the last would consist in the disciplines of general scientific education, whose main purpose would be to give the students a needed contact with scientific methodology.[414]

Clodovis Boff discusses the systems of theological disciplines in two dimensions, internal and external. In order to do this we must grasp the higher unity of theology and at the same time its diversity. "Theology has an organic unity of principle, which, being the unity of a living organism, articulates itself in many functions."[415]

---

[412] "The pole 'Faith' equals 'Theory' and refers to faith-narrative or faith-doctrine. The pole 'Life,' in turn, corresponds to 'Practice.' [They] are not necessarily connected, as they are relatively autonomous. They are called upon to join themselves, which takes the form respectively of 'Lived Faith' and 'Life of Faith'" (C. Boff, Teoria, 292).

[413] C. Boff, Teoria, 294.

[414] Mendonça, Currículo, 145.

[415] C. Boff, 610.

I will proceed on the track that Boff opened. I understand that the construction of a curriculum should include four areas:

(1) Theology and History;

(2) Biblical Theology and Exegesis;

(3) Pastoral Theology and related disciplines;

(4) Supporting disciplines (or sciences).

This will give the necessary balance that is sought by the present study, so that, in its task, theological education may express its functions (cf. the second chapter), which are: reproductive, productive, scientific-rational and the practice of theology. Therefore, the end product will be *docta fides, docta caritas* and *docta spes* (cf. the third chapter).

> 1. Theology proper (which can be called either Systematic Theology or Thematic Theology) covers the major theological themes in dialogue with the Christian theologians of the past two thousand years while listening, at the same time, to biblical theology in its current new contributions of faith. It should do so without losing its look on life. Therefore, it should have an ecumenical character, contextual as well as practical. Because it is involved with the *depositum fidei*, theology needs among its disciplines the History of Christian Thought, covering the Christian traditions of the West, as a minimum. Patristic Studies would be a key component in this.[416] We must be aware that it is necessary to open a dialogue with so-called 'genitive' theologies: feminist theology, Black theology, African theology, Asian theology, etc. In order to do it, we must have an open mind, an open heart and an open will.

> 2. In the area of Biblical Theology and Exegesis, we need to be aware that this is the soul of theology per se. Every

---

[416] Mendonça, Currículo, 145.

theologian and every professor of theology, as well as the students, must be impregnated with Scripture. The following disciplines should be included: Introduction to the Old and New Testaments; Biblical Exegesis of several books; Greek and Hebrew studies. Hermeneutics is indispensable at this point. A discipline contextual hermeneutic is essential since the unity of theology is established and sustains itself on the foundation of biblical truth, as its source, and its actualization in life, as its end.

3. The third segment comprises the disciplines related with pastoral theology. Practical Theology is facing a strong challenge today, which has to do with articulating itself between the truth of faith and the call to life. Pastoral theology, one of its disciplines, is gaining increasingly importance in the curriculum as it promoted a dialogue between faith and social sciences. Here there is room for creativity: public theology, theology of citizenship, *diakonia*; nonprofit organizations, Christian education, church and society, homily, rhetorics, sign language, spirituality, theology and economics, liturgy.

4. Finally, especially the disciplines which are related to other academic disciplines would give attention to scientific methodology, social sciences, applied sciences and philosophy. I agree with Mendonça in that "it would be useful to abandon the so-called 'introductions' in favor of content that gives support to theological studies — for example, the study of the great schools of thought."[417] I would also emphasize the growing space that has been appropriated by the applied sciences in our time — for example, by management, marketing, law and economics —, which call on theology to dialogue. This would make for a highly enriching and needed experience. We must remind ourselves that spirituality and value-built organizations are the current theme in the corporate world. A constructive and entrepreneurial theological education will hear the cry of its generation and will act accordingly.

---

[417] Mendonça, Currículo, 146.

However, it is necessary to point out that this proposal
carries the marks of the Protestant experience, as the fruit
of the biography of its author. Still, I hope that it will be
widely suggestive to other segments that also work in theological education. I am aware that the path is in the practice of balance, because a bird with weaker wings will fly
in circles.

Theological education, which is wise and relevant to
our context, will have to be inspired by the great principles of past educators, not repeating them but being inspired by them. What is expected is a theological
education that will be open, mobile, laborious, and even if
often hesitant to walk in the face of new dangers, it shall
preserve the humility to correct itself and update itself
time after time.

Theology must be traditional and contemporary at the
same time; Christ centered and dialogic; theoretical, scientific and practical; pastoral, committed to memory, contemporary society, and prophetic action. Theology would
thus be both intellectual and servant, and at the same time,
cognitive, constituent, and critical. It would always express a reminiscent perspective, a reflexive perspective,
and a prospective perspective. The theological task is, at
the same time, faithful to its historical memory, faithful to
its call in Jesus Christ and faithful to its hope. Reminding
and proclaiming to Jesus Christ's Church, that it has a mission in the world and an eternal destiny, which is the reason that the theological task of the Lord's Church is a
permanent challenge that needs to be answered with devotion, humility and faith. Theology constitutes itself in a
permanent task of the Christian Church, a hermeneutical
community which has received as its responsibility a still
expanding mission that should take place according to its
postulates of faith.

The challenge of theology is how it should be practiced in such a way that it can serve this task best. We have argued that the functions of theology cannot be isolated and that not one of those can be practiced at the expense of the other ones. This requires a specific competence and attitude of theologians, especially in a time of social challenges that leave people in deep uncertainties. That is the question we deal with in this research.

Theology is a service of the Church to the world — as it lives out its faith in practice its path is marked by signs of hope. There is an alternative to the powers of the world. And this alternative community must be nourished, empowered to its task, criticized and corrected where needed in order to be light in the world. The church is a community of hope. She is so even when she is endangered, oppressed and persecuted. Theology must support her most of all when facing this contested position of the church. Theology must empower her to hold on and not to give up her love and hope. She must persevere even when Christians are excluded from high society, or in other cases imprisoned or killed.

Love and hope are embedded in the church and so is faith. The anamnesis of faith is not a lonely reading of old texts in a study room. Certainly it is this as well. But it is so not in isolation. In a theology of wisdom it is so only as part of a participating listening to the Scriptures relates directly to the confessed faith of the church. We are not the first readers and we are not the only readers of Scripture. The reading of the Scriptures is focused on the celebration of the Word in the worship in a hendiadys with the anamnesis of the Eucharist. It is one and the same anamnesis of Christ by the community, which is his body. The core of theology is in this celebrating community in faith, hope and love, so that she can hold on in love, which is the most of all and so be light of the world.

This implies not only that the theologian must be present in the church, but also that the life of the church must be present in the classrooms. When doing exegesis or historical research continuously the community of Christians with their challenges, problems, hopes, weaknesses and power must be in mind and that means: must be explicitly reminded as theologians easily forget their participation in the whole. As theologians bring in the whole tradition into the church by means of anamnesis, so they must consciously bring in the local church and the wounded memories of its members into the classroom. And continuously the question that must be in their minds is this: how can this community be a light to the world so that she mirrors the Light of the world? Thus the streets and houses, the meeting rooms and the markets of Londrina must be present in the classroom. The wise theologian will learn and share what it means to be a living Christian community both at the heart and at the periphery of the city.

Final Considerations

THE THESIS THAT has guided us is that Christian theology is above all wisdom from God and the encounter between this concept and Christian education produces a clear enrichment in the task of theological education.

In the last decades of the twentieth century, upon the initiative of the Latin American Theological Fraternity, many meetings and conferences were held to reflect on "New Alternatives in Theological Education." The challenge that was proposed in the official document in 1985 in Quito, Ecuador, is still relevant. The conclusion of that consultation can be summarized in one sentence:

> "After all, we are willing to continue the search for new alternatives in theological education, the theme for which we have been encouraged by our consultation, for which we depend on the grace of God."

This work was based on the persuasion that it a new way of studying theology and developing the theological curriculum is both possible and necessary. In agreement with the Latin American Theological Fraternity, we can say that we seek reflective theologians who live closely with the marginalized sectors of society and who articulate the Gospel in the socio-cultural contexts in which the majority of the Latin American people live. Liberation theologians had already responded unanimously that God's gift of salvation from sin consists in an integral and holistic liberation.

Considering the fact that "salvation is the fullness of humanity while, on the other hand, poverty and oppression are social manifestations of sin —which is the fundamental alienation" both in relation to God and in relation to humanity, the task of doing theology and practicing theological education is a challenge that seeks a model forged in dialogue with the people and reflects their struggles, suffering and aspirations.

Without a continuous dialogue between Bible and context, the message proclaimed will lack relevance. Hence the importance of a theological education that is based on God's Word and is guided towards the world and what happens in it —because theology arises from the dialogue of the people of God about the meaning of faith in its concrete historical situation. The theological method is conceived as a concrete pilgrimage, i.e., a contextual re-enactment of the praxis of Jesus, not merely a reflection about praxis. Thus many dualisms disappear, such as the separation between process and content, between theory and praxis, between faith and history, between spirituality and theology. As the saying goes that life which is unexamined is not worth living, Christian education that is not practiced and will not evolve is not worth pursuing.

The aim of this study is to contribute to new approaches in theological education toward the formation of thinkers and practitioners of a living contextual theology. The challenge is to propose a viable integration between classic theology and life, content and context, which can be called wisdom. The outcome that is intended for the study programs under scrutiny is the development of a model of theological education from the perspective of the wisdom theology.

The objective of this studies is to be an introduction of a corrective action regarding the teaching of Reformed theology, in particular that of systematic theology. It is intended as a challenge to take up the need to correct the current curricula in theological education and, at the same time, serve as a guide to new educational projects in theological education.

The historical memory of theological education in Brazil, for example, points to the fact that the pietistic roots of Reformed theology in this country, in broad terms, have emphasized an individualistic approach to faith, and therefore theology has not been able to deal with the social reality of suffering, poverty, social exclusion, violence and corruption, so evident and still growing in Latin American society. Moreover, Liberation Theology with all its valuable analyses, relevant contributions and incisive prophetic statements, has not satisfactorily influenced the Protestant theological seminaries, having had little effect on theological education, especially in the area known as Systematic Theology. In other words, it can be said that the dialogue between Liberation Theology and the Reformed Tradition has proven fragile in terms of theological education, as if they were mutually exclusive.

In this thesis I have sought to emphasize the proposal of a living theology, and for that I have proposed a paradigm: theology as wisdom. As Daniel Schipani rightly says, "Jesus the Christ incarnates the wisdom of God." Jesus can be seen from the perspective of the Gospels as a wise teacher who models the living parable of the life and wisdom of God. From below, his ministry can be seen as the incarnation of God's wisdom and, from above, as God's wisdom in the flesh. Jesus reveals the true meaning of God for life and he empowers human beings to discover truth in their own circumstances, while challenging them to pursue transformative practices.

Although it is difficult to define because of its complexity, wisdom encompasses not only the personal level but also the social and cultural levels. I reaffirm here, in harmony with Schipani, that "the sources of wisdom include both internal resources (commitment to learning, a desire to grow, positive values, social competencies, positive identity and self-esteem) as well as external resources (support and encouragement, autonomy, boundaries and expectations, guidance and direction)."

To establish this connection between the concept of wisdom and Christian education is appropriate as well as necessary, in view of the historical background and the detected continuity, which dates back to centuries of tradition in the biblical world and the development of Christian doctrines. Lastly, wisdom is a concept that "implies a holistic view of life and human behavior in the broader context of family and society, nature and the world as a whole." This concept is of a very high value in theological education because wisdom approached from a holistic perspective involves seeing the human being as a whole and stimulates integrity and consistency between knowing and doing, encouraging a path towards the emergence of the truly human within the Divine purpose. This model provides an interdisciplinary dialogue, due to its close connection to the context.

The crux of the problem resides in finding a contextualization that is appropriate to the teaching of Reformed Theology in Brazil. This sounds like a growing and vital challenge and it is urgent and necessary in our present time of institutional distrust.

We have sought to introduce some Latin American theologians whose constructive contribution can make this correction possible. As far as theological education is concerned, the proposal of curricula must be illuminated by the Scriptures and take into account the historical, cultural, social and ecclesiastical contexts in which the students will develop their ministries. These curricula should not be a slavish imitation of foreign contexts neither should they be inflexible or immutable; they must be updated to reflect the reality of their social concreteness. In view of the personal and social complexity of human beings we know that no curriculum is perfect or final. There will always be a point of arrival and a point of departure in this endeavor, as every curriculum will be a product of pedagogical experimentation. However, there will always be elements of permanent value in any such curriculum because of the historical basis in the tradition of the faith. Such an endeavor is and will always be a complex task in permanent motion; it will always be an invitation toward an engagement in the multiple tasks of observing empirically, reflecting thoughtfully and applying its tenets in concrete practice.

The answer to this complex moment in theological education in Brazil is a formulation in the way of doing and teaching theology, which can be called Theology as Wisdom —which consists in integrating four basic functions of theology as an academic science: the reproductive function of theology (anamnesis), where it is essential to dialogue with the traditions of historical Christianity; the productive function of faith (hermeneutics), which updates to each new generation the eternal truths, as it courageously faces new questions from new situations and circumstances of social reality; the practical function of faith (praxis), which has to do with the pastoral ministry, with its mission "grounded" in the social locus —whether political, ethnic or spiritual; and finally, the scientific and rational basis of faith (ratio), implying here an exegetical

seriousness of biblical texts, a sociopolitical and socioeco-
nomic mediation of society, always open to new scientific
discoveries, with bold determination and love, humility,
creativity —sacrificially seeking meaning and applicability
of the transforming Gospel in its mission.

There is no doubt that these features are typical of the
theological methodology in any context and they should
always be sought by a Theological Education that seeks to
be faithful to its task. This having been said, it is necessary
to honor what has been proposed by Latin American theologians and their relevant contributions, which still warrant renewed research. I recognize the ocean of wealth in
the theological world that has already been reached and
still is in progress in Latin America (Brazil included) and I
am aware that there is a call to continue this enriching dialogue in the years to come.

The challenge that remains is the need to continue to
listen to the voice of theologians from all continents on
the part of those who seek to build educational projects in
implementing new courses in theology —not only as projects in themselves but also for the day-to-day theological
education that is lived out in the classroom.

The act of listening to the theological voices should be
a theological habit, in every subject, in every dogma, in
every new topic that arises from social and ecclesiastical
realities. From the point of view of this thesis, this act requires an act of listening that arises out of an integration
of all functions and mediations proposed here and this
should be done with an open mind, an open heart and an
open will —i.e., with an ecumenical spirit.

I have sought to bring out the question: do the theological education models in our context satisfy the four functions of theology? Do their pedagogical projects appear at
least implicitly to resonate with the present methodology
model that calls for a theoretical-practical integration?

I am convinced that the four functions can be a way of approaching all disciplines in a theology program, be they systematic, biblical, missiological or pastoral theology. When speaking of theology in three dimensions —the theoria, poiesis and praxis model (Bosch) — or the socio-analytical mediation, socio-hermeneutic and practice model (L. Boff and C. Boff), or listening to the concepts reflected in Chapter III —docta fides, docta spes and docta caritas—, it is possible to find room for the four functions of theology: anamnesis, hermeneutics, ratio and praxis. The question that could or should always be raised by each new project is this: Are these triple distinctions sufficient to meet the four functions of theology as described here?

Theology is a glorious adventure of the faith community and should always be faithful to its nature, which consists in expressing the wisdom of God as part of its task, whether in the classroom, or in the church, or in the world, as it should always be aware of their origin in God, God's mission in the world and God's pointing to the eternal destiny of human beings as a goal.

Amid the complexities of life, there is hope in pointing to the comprehensive character of theology as wisdom, always challenged to perform a hermeneutic task of the Christian faith, which will provide a clearer contextualization by generating a prophetic role and transforming its own theological discourse in the midst of human suffering, which addresses both oppressive and oppressed human beings.

What is expected of those who articulate Christian education is a wisdom that proposes a reflexive bold relevance, which is repentant because it knows that it is sinful and can only walk in the grace of God. Since it is a sojourner, this reflection should be known as tentative in its responses to a changing world and especially prophetic in the face of dehumanizing ideologies and an idolatrous consumer society.

What is expected for the future is the creation of new studies in this direction by comparing themes that are articulated in different social contexts, with a view to different policies and ethnic variables. This will prove highly enriching and creative because it will deliver us from theological exceptionalism. Thinking of theology as wisdom avoids any stagnation in its originality. It is a way of appreciating an increasing dialogue with various contexts at different times. It is also a way of listening to theological voices without any limitations of time or place. As recommended by David Suazo Jimenez, Latin American theological education must take three steps: firstly, it should start by "analyzing the models that have shaped evangelical theological education in Latin America; secondly, it should provide open spaces for the consideration of new models; thirdly, it should adopt or create these new models."

As a consequence, new avenues are open and the rhetorical wisdom of philosophers and theologians such as Cicero, Augustine, Aquinas and Bonaventure are waiting to be considered. The wisdom of native peoples, who have their "feet" firmly grounded, as they are reached by a simple message of the Gospel, calls for studies to enrich our theology. Thus, there is a need to continue on this journey that will tread this wonderful science called theology, the most beautiful among all sciences studied in academia, since it reflects upon is the entirety of the human life — which makes us ever-learning apprentices.

Finally, it is hoped that the instructors will take up wisdom as a way of thinking about the design of their curricula and the development of their content. Wisdom should not be ever present in all disciples but it should permeate the whole, because the whole and its parts are intertwined. My desire is that the investigation of theology as wisdom and its implications for theological education would motivate an approach to theological education that would result in enthusiastic Christian teaching and action-oriented mission.

It is hoped that the ideas presented here will serve as a stimulus for new researchers to analyze and reflect on the reality of the summons of theological education that finds its inspiring presence in its manifold contexts, always challenging its thinkers to change. A living theology is what we seek.

Ultimately, we need divine wisdom in order to apply wisdom to theological education. The grace of it all is the understanding that the wisdom of God is available to us so that we can turn our theological task into a living activity.

Bibliography

General

ALFARO, Juan. *Revelación Cristiana: Fe y Teología,* Salamanca: Sígueme, 1985.

ALVES, Rubem. *Towards a theology of liberation: An Exploration of the Encounter Between the Languages of Humanistic Messianism and Messianic humanism,* Ph. D. dissertation, Princeton Theological Seminary, May 1968.

_____*Theology of Human Hope,* Washington: Corpus Books, 1971.

AQUINAS, Thomas. *Summa Theologica,* Madrid: Biblioteca de Autores Cristianos, 1990.

ARAUJO, João Dias. Imagens de Jesus Cristo na Cultura do Povo Brasileiro. In: MARASCHIN, Jacy. *Quem é Jesus Cristo no Brasil?* São Paulo: ASTE, 1974, 39-54.

ARAYA, Eugenio. *Introduccíon a la Teología Sistemática,* Santiago: CTEC, 1983.

ARIAS NETO, José Miguel. *O Eldorado: Representações da Política em Londrina – 1930-1975,* Londrina: UEL, 1998.

AUGUSTINE. Homily in John 27,9, *Homilies on the Gospel according to John and his first letter,* translation by H. Brown, A Library of the Fathers of the Holy Catholic Church Anterior to the Division of the East and the West, Oxford: Parker/ London: F. and J. Rivington, 1848._

BARREIRA, José. Revelando a Cidade para os Teólogos. In: MUZIO, *A Revolução,* 77-92.

BARTH, Karl. *The Epistle to the Romans,* London: Oxford University Press, 1933.

_____*Church Dogmatics,* Edinburgh: T. & T. Clark, 1956-1981.

_____*Fides Quaerens Intellectum: Anselms Beweis der Existenz Gottes* (1931), Zurich, 1958.

_____*Dogmatics in Outline,* New York: Harper & Row, 1959._____

_____*Einführung in die evangelische Theologie,* Zürich: EVZ Verlag, 1962.

_____Dádiva e Louvor: Artigos Selecionados, São Leopoldo: Sinodal, 1986.

_____ Evangelical Theology: An Introduction, Grand Rapids: Eerdmans, 2000.

_____Carta aos Romanos, São Paulo: Novo Século, 2003.

_____ Fé em Busca de Compreensão (Fides Quaerens Intellectum: Anselms Beweis der Existenz Gottes) [1931], São Paulo: Novo Século, 2003.

_____Credo: Comentário ao credo apostólico, São Paulo: Novo Século, 2005.

_____Esboços de uma Dogmática, São Paulo: Fonte Editorial, 2006.

_____Introdução à Teologia Evangélica, São Leopoldo: Sinodal, 2008.

BAVINCK, Herman. Teologia Sistemática, São Paulo: Socep, 2001.

BELL, George K. Allen. The Stockholm Conference 1925. London: Oxford University Press, 1926.

BERGMANN, Sigurd. God in Context: A Survey of Contextual Theology, Burlington: Ashgate Publishing, 2003.

BERKHOF, Hendrikus. Christian Faith: An Introduction to the Study of the Faith, Grand Rapids: Eerdmans, 1985.

BERKHOF, Louis. Teologia Sistemática [1949], São Paulo: Cultura Cristã, 2001.

BEVANS, Stephen B. Models of Contextual Theology, New York: Orbis Books, 2002.

BLOCH, Ernst. Das Prinzip Hoffnung, Frankfurt: Suhrkamp, 1959.

_____The Principle of Hope. 3 vols., Cambridge MA: MIT Press, 1986.

BOEHNER, Philotheus & GILSON, Ethiene. História da Filosofia Cristã, Petrópolis: Vozes, 2003.

BOFF, Clodovis. Teologia e Prática: Teologia do Político e suas Mediações, Petrópolis: Vozes, 1978.

_____ Teoria do Método Teológico. Petrópolis: Vozes, 2007.

BOFF, Leonardo & BOFF, Clodovis. Da Libertação Libertação: O Sentido Teológico das Libertações Sócio-Históricas, Petrópolis: Vozes, 1982.

_____*Como Fazer Teologia da Libertação,* São Paulo: Vozes, 1986.

BOFF, Leonardo. As Imagens de Cristo Presentes no Cristianismo Liberal do Brasil. In: MARASCHIN, Jacy. *Quem é Jesus Cristo no Brasil,* São Paulo: ASTE, 1974, 11-38.

_____*Fé na Periferia do Mundo,* Petrópolis: Vozes, 1979._____

_____*Teologia do Cativeiro e da Libertação,* Lisboa: Multinova, 1976._____

_____BOSCH, David J. The Nature of Theological education. In: *Theologica Evangelica* 25 (1), 1992, 8-23.

BRAVO GALLARDO, Carlos. *Jesús, Hombre en Conflicto,* México: CRT, 1988.

BROMILEY, Geoffrey William. *Introduction to the Theology of Karl Barth,* Grand Rapids: Eerdmans, 1979.

BROWNING, Don S. *Practical Theology.* San Francisco: Harper & Row, 1983.

BRUNNER, H. Emil. *Dogmatics: The Christian Doctrine of God,* Vol. 1,. Philadelphia: Westminster, 1950.

_____*Teologia da Crise.* São Paulo: Novo Século, 2004.

_____*Dogmática: A Doutrina Cristã de Deus,* São Paulo: Novo Século, 2004.

_____*O Escândalo do Cristianismo,* São Paulo: Novo Século, 2004.

_____*O Equivoco da Igreja,* São Paulo: Novo Século, 2004.

CALVIN, John. - *Institutes of the Christian Religion,* Philadelphia: Westminster Press, 1960.

_____*True Christian Life,* Grand Rapids: Baker Book House, 1952.

_____*Institutes of the Christian Religion,* [1536] (transl. by Ford Lewis Battles), Grand Rapids: Eerdmans, 1986

CANO, Melchior. *De locis theologicis,* Salamanca: M. Gastius, 1563.

CHAFER, Lewis Sperry. *Teologia Sistemática,* São Paulo: Hagnos, 2003.

CLEMENT of Alexandria, *Stromata* V,1, in the translation by William Wilson, Ante-Nicene Fathers, Vol. 2. Edited by Alexander Roberts, James Donaldson, and A. Cleveland Coxe. Buffalo, NY: Christian Literature Publishing Co., 1885.

CLEMENTS, Ronald. *Wisdom in Theology,* Grand Rapids: Eerdmans, 1992.

COMBLIN, José. *O Tempo da Ação: (Ensaio sobre) O Espírito e a História.,*Petrópolis: Vozes, 1982.

CONGAR, Yves M.. *La Tradizione e la Vita della Chiesa,* Roma: Paoline, 1983.

COSTAS, Orlando. *Hacia una Teologia de la Evangelización,* Buenos Aires: Aurora, 1973.

CYRIL of Jerusalem, *Catechetical Lecture* 5,4, translation by Edwin Hamilton Gifford, Nicene and Post-Nicene Fathers, Second Series, Vol. 7. Edited by Philip Schaff and Henry Wace. Buffalo, NY: Christian Literature Publishing Co., 1894.

DEMO, Pedro. *Metodologia do Conhecimento Científico,* São Paulo: Atlas, 2000.

DE SANTA ANA, Julio. *Pelas Trilhas do Mundo a Caminho do Reino.* São Bernardo do Campo: Imprensa Metodista, 1985.

DIAS, Silas Barbosa. *Doctrine Divides, Service Unites – The Universal Christian Conference on Life and Work, Stockholm, 1925.* Geneva: Unigeve, 2001.

DOS ANJOS, Marcio Fabri (org.), *Teologia profissão,* São Paulo: Soter/Loyola, 1996.

DUCH, Lluís. Hermenêutica. In: SAMANES, C. F. & ACOSTA, J. T. (eds.), *Dicionário de Conceitos Fundamentais do Cristianismo,* São Paulo: Paulus, 1999, 326-331.

ECHEGARAY, Hugo. *A Prática de Jesus,* Petrópolis: Vozes, 1984.

FARLEY, Edward. Theology and Practice Outside the Clerical Paradigm. In: BROWNING, Don S. (ed.), *Practical Theology,* San Francisco: Harper & Row, 1983, 21-41.

_____Theologia: The History of a Concept. In: HODGSON, Peter & KING, Robert (eds.), *Readings in Christian Theology.* Minneapolis: Fortress Press, 1985, 1-15.

_____*The Fragility of Knowledge: Theological Education in the Church and de University,* Philadelphia: Fortress Press, 1988.

_____*Theologia: The Fragmentation and Unity of Theology Education,* Philadelphia: Fortress Press, 1989.

FERREIRA, Franklin & MYATT, Alan. *Teologia Sistemática, uma análise histórica, bíblica e apologética para o contexto*, São Paulo: Vida Nova, 2007.

FINNEY, Charles. *Teologia Sistemática*, Rio de Janeiro: CPAD, 2002.

FLORISTÁN, Casiano. *Teología Práctica: Teoria y Praxis de la Acción Pastoral*, Salamanca: Ediciones Sígueme, 1998.

FLORISTÁN SAMANES, Casiano & TAMAYO ACOSTA, Juan José. *Dicionário de Conceitos Fundamentais do Cristianismo*. São Paulo: Paulus, 1999.

FORTE, Bruno. *A Teologia como Companhia, Memória e Profecia*. São Paulo: Paulinas, 1991.

_____*La Iglesia de la Trinidad*, Salamanca: Secretariado Trinitário, 1995.

_____*La Eternidad en el Tiempo*, Salamanca: Sígueme, 2000.

FROSSARD, Selma. A Ação Social da Igreja. In: MUZIO, R. (ed.), *A Revolução Silenciosa: Transformando cidades pela implantação de igrejas saudáveis*, São Paulo: Sepal, 2004, 123-142.

GADAMER, Hans Georg. *Truth and Method*, London: Sheed and Ward, 1979.

GEFFRÉ, Claude. *The Risk of Interpretation: On Being Faithful to the Christian Tradition in a Non-Christian Age,*. New York: Paulist Press, 1987.

GONÇALVES CÉSAR, Emerenciana. *Dados Históricos da Primeira Igreja Presbiteriana Independente de Londrina*, Londrina: IPILON, 1988.

GONZÁLEZ, Justo & MALDONADO PEREZ, Zaida. *An Introduction to Christian Theology*, Nashville: Abingdon Press, 2002.

GORRINGE, Timothy J. *Karl Barth Against Hegemony*. Oxford: Oxford University Press, 1999.

GREGORY NAZIANZEN, Oratio XXVII, The First Theological Oration, A Preliminary Discourse against the Eunomians, part III. In: Philip Schaff and Henry Wace (eds.), *The Nicene and Post-Nicene Fathers*, second series, vol. VII: Cyril of Jerusalem, Gregory Nazianzen. Edinburgh: T&T Clark, 1867.

GRUDEM, Wayne. *Teologia Sistemática*. São Paulo: Edições Vida Nova, 1999.

GUTHRIE, Shirley C. *Christian Doctrine,* Revised Edition, Louisville: Westminster/John Knox Press, 1994.

GUTIÉRREZ, Benjamin & CAMPOS, Leonildo Silveira. *Na Força do Espírito: Os Pentecostais na America Latina,* São Paulo: Pendão Real, 1996.

GUTIÉRREZ, Gustavo.*A Força Histórica dos Pobres,* Petrópolis: Vozes, 1982.

_____ *La Verdad los Hará Libres,* Lima: IBC-CEP, 1986.

_____*A Theology of Liberation, History, Politics and Salvation,* Mariknoll (New York): Orbis Books, 2000.

HODGE, Charles. *Teologia Sistemática,* São Paulo: Hagnos, 2001.

HODGSON, Peter C. *God´s Wisdom: Toward a Theology of Education,* Louisville: Westminster John Knox Press, 1999.

HODGSON, Peter C. & KING Robert H. *Readings in Christian Theology,* Minneapolis: Fortress Press, 1985.

HOWELL, Leon. *Fé en Acción,* Ginebra: CMI, 1982.

IANNI, Octavio. *A Era do Globalismo,* Rio de Janeiro: Civilização Brasileira, 2002.

JAEGER, Werner. *Paideia: The Ideals of Greek Culture,* New York: Oxford University Press, 1943.

JIMÉNEZ, David Suazo, *La Función Profética de la Educación Teológica Evangélica em América Latina,* Barcelona: Editorial Clie, 2012.

JOHNSON, Elizabeth A. *She Who Is: The Mystery of God in Feminist Theological Discourse,* New York: Crossroad, 1992.

JONES, Serene. *Calvin and the Rhetoric of Piety,* Louisville: Westminster John Knox Press, 1995.

JUSTIN THE MARTYR, *Apology* I, translated by Marcus Dods and George Reith. Ante-Nicene Fathers, vol. 1, edited by Alexander Roberts, James Donaldson, and A. Cleveland Coxe, Buffalo. New York: Christian Literature Publishing Co., 1885.

_____*Apology* II, translated by Marcus Dods and George Reith. *Ante-Nicene Fathers*, vol. 1, edited by Alexander Roberts, James Donaldson, and A. Cleveland Coxe, Buffalo. New York: Christian Literature Publishing Co., 1885.

KELSEY, David. *Between Athens and Berlin: The Theological Education Debate*, Grand Rapids: Eerdmans, 1993.

KINNAMON, Michael & COPE, Brian. *The Ecumenical Movement: An Anthology of Key Texts and Voices*, Geneva: WCC, 1997.

KINSLER, R. & CAMPO, I. M. (ed.). *Educacion Teologica en situaciones de sobrevivência, uma consulta latinoamericana, Managua 1991*, an Jose: CMI-SBL, 1991.

KLEIN, Carlos Jeremias. *Curso de História da Igreja*, São Paulo: Fonte Editorial, 2007.

LATOURELLE, René (s.j.). *Théologie Science du Salut*, Paris: Cerf, 1968.

LEE, Sang Hyun. *The Philosophical Theology of Jonathan Edwards*, Princeton, N.Y: Princeton University Press, 1997.

LIBÂNIO, J. Batista & MURAD, Afonso. *Introdução à Teologia*, São Paulo: Loyola, 1998.

LIMA, Eber Ferreira. *Apóstolo Pé Vermelho: Jonas Dias Martins e a Evangelização do Norte do Paraná*. São Paulo: Pendão Real, 2002.

LOSSKY, Nicolay and others. *Dictionary of the Ecumenical Movement*, Geneve: WCC, 1991.

LUTHER, Martin. *First Principles of the Reformation or the Ninety-five Theses and the Three Primary Works*, London: John Murray, 1883.

MACKAY, John. *The Other Spanish Christ*. New York: Macmillan, 1932.

_____*El Otro Cristo Español* [1919], 2a. ed., Buenos Aires: Aurora, 1988.

MACQUARRIE, John. *New Directions in Theology Today*, Philadelphia: Westminster Press, 1952.

_____*Principles of Christian Theology*. New York: Charles Scribner's Sons, 1966.

_____*God-Talk: El Análisis del Lenguaje y la Lógica de la Teología*, Salamanca: Sígueme, 1976.

MARASCHIN, Jaci Corréia. *Quem é Jesus Cristo no Brasil,* São Paulo: ASTE, 1974.

_____*Tendências da Teologia no Brasil,* São Paulo: ASTE, 1977.

_____*Sillabus in Teologia Sistemática,* Universidade Metodista de São Paulo.

MASCALL, Eric Lionel. *Christ, the Christian and the Church: A Study of the Incarnation and its Consequences,* London: Longmans, 1963.

MELMAN, Charles. *L'homme sans gravité,* Paris: Donoel, 2002.

MENDONÇA, Antônio Gouvêa. *O Celeste Porvir: A Inserção do Protestantismo no Brasil,* São Paulo: Aste, 1995.

_____Currículo teológico básico. In: ANJOS, M. F., (org.), *Teologia profissão,* São Paulo: Soter/Loyola, 1996, 123-155.

MESTERS, Carlos. *Por trás das Palavras,* Petrópolis: Vozes, 1974.

_____*Flor sem Defesa,* Petrópolis: Vozes, 1983.

METZ, Johann Baptist. *Faith in History and Society: Toward a Fundamental Practical Theology,*New York: Seabury, 1980.

_____*Faith Seeking Understanding,* Grand Rapids: Eerdmans, 2002.

MILLER, Donald E. & YAMAMORI, Tetsunao. *Global Pentecostalism: The New Face of Christian Social Engagement,* Berkeley: University of California Press, 2007.

MOLTMANN, Jürgen. *The Power of the Powerless,* S. Francisco: Harper & Row, 1983.

_____*Jesus Christ for Today's World,* Minneapolis: Fortress Press, 1995.

_____*O Espírito da Vida: por uma Pneumatologia Integral,* São Paulo: Vozes, 1999.

_____*Experiences in Theology,* London: SCM Press, 2000.

_____ *Trindade e Reino de Deus,* São Paulo: Vozes 2002.

_____*A Vinda de Deus: Escatologia Cristã,* São Leopoldo: Unisinos, 2003.

_____*Experiências de Reflexão Teológica: Caminhos e Formas da Teologia Cristã,* São Leopoldo: Unisinos, 2004.

_____*Vida, Esperança e Justiça, um testamento teológico para a América Latina,* São Bernardo do Campo: Eiteo, 2008.

MORENO, Tomas. Algumas Conclusões e Propostas para a Transformação da Cidade de Londrina. In: MUZIO, R. (ed.), *A Revolução Silenciosa: Transformando cidades pela implantação de igrejas saudáveis.* São Paulo: Sepal, 2004, 163-168.

MORIN, Edgar. *Ciência com Consciência,* 2nd ed. Rio de Janeiro: Bertrand Brasil, 1998.

_____*O Método,* v. 6: *Ética,* Porto Alegre: Sulinas, 2005.

MORIN, Edgar & Le MOIGNE, Jean-Louis. *A inteligência da complexidade,* São Paulo: Petrópolis, 2000.

MULLER, R. A. The Study of Theology. In: SILVA, Moisés (ed.), *Foundations of Contemporary Interaction,* Grand Rapids: Zondervan, 1996, 537-666.

MUZIO, Rubens. *A Revolução Silenciosa: Transformando cidades pela implantação de igrejas saudáveis.* São Paulo: Sepal, 2004.

NESTOR, Jaén. *Hacia una Espiritualidad de la Liberación,* Santander: Sal Terrae, 1987.

NÚÑEZ, Emilio Antonio. *Teología de la Liberación: Una Perspectiva Evangélica,* Miami: Caribe, 1987.

OGILVIE, Matthew C. *Faith Seeking Understanding: The Functional Speciality 'Systematics' in Bernard Lonergan´s Theology,.* Milwaukee: Marquette University Press, 2001.

OLSON, Roger. *The Story of Christian Theology,* Downers Grove: InterVarsity Press, 1999.

PADILLA, C. René. *Nuevas Alternativas de Educación Teológica,* Buenos Aires: Nueva Creación, 1986.

PARKER, T. H. L. *Calvin: An Introduction to His Thought,* London: Continuum, 1995.

PELIKAN, Jaroslav. *The Christian Tradition: The Development of Doctrine* vol.1: *The Emergence of the Catholic Tradition (100-600),* Chicago: University of Chicago Press, 1971.

PLOU, Dafne. *Together in the Way: Official Report of Eighth Assembly of the World,* Geneva: WCC Publications, 1999.

_____*Juntos en el Camino,* Informe oficial de la Octava Asamblea el Consejo Mundial de Iglesias, Geneva: WCC Publications, 1999.

PREISWERK, Matias, *Educación Popular y Teologia de la Liberación*, San José, Costa Rica: Editorial DEI, 1994.

PROENÇA, Wander de Lara & SOUZA, Raimundo Soares. Formação e Desenvolvimento das Primeiras Igrejas Evangélicas na Cidade de Londrina. In: MUZIO, R. (ed.), *A Revolução Silenciosa: Transformando cidades pela implantação de igrejas saudáveis*. São Paulo: Sepal, 2004, 41-61.

RICHARD, Lucien J. *The Spirituality of John Calvin*, Atlanta: John Knox Press, 1974.

RITO, Frei Honório. *Introdução à Teologia*, Petrópolis: Vozes, 1998.

SANDER, Luis Marcos. *Jesus, o Libertador: a cristologia da libertação de Leonardo Boff*. São Leopoldo: Sinodal, 1986.

SATHLER-ROSA, Ronaldo. *Cuidado Pastoral em Tempos de Insegurança*, São Paulo: Aste, 2010.

SCHILLEBEECKX, Edward. *Mensen als verhaal van God*, Baarn: Nelissen, 1989.

SCHIPANI, Daniel S. *Teologia del Ministério Educativo: perspectivas latinoamericanas*, Buenos Aires: Nueva Creación, 1993.

_____ *El reino de Dios y el ministério educativo de la iglesia: Fundamentos y princípios de educación Cristiana*, Costa Rica: Editorial Caribe, 1983.

_____ *O caminho da sabedoria no Aconselhamento Pastoral (translation of The Way of Wisdom*
        in Pastoral Counseling, IMS: Elkhart, Indiana, 2003*)*, São Leopoldo: Sinodal, 2013.

SCHREITER, Robert J. *Constructing Local Theologies*, London: SCM, 1985.

SCHÜSSLER FIORENZA, Elisabeth. *Jesus: Miriam's Child, Sophia's Prophet: Critical Issues in Feminist Christology*, New York: Continuum Publishing Co., 1994.

_____ *Wisdom Ways: Introducing Feminist Biblical Interpretation*, Maryknoll (New York): Orbis Books, 2001.

SCHWARZ, Lilia M. (org.), *História da vida privada no Brasil 4: contrastes da intimidade contemporânea,* São Paulo: Companhia de Letras, 1998.

SCOTT, Robert Balgarnie Young. *The Way of Wisdom in the Old Testament,* New York: Macmillan, 1971.

SOBRINO, Jon. *Christology at the Crossroads: A Latin American Approach,* London: SCM Press, 1978.

SPROUL, Robert Charles. *Verdades Essenciais da Fé Cristã,* São Paulo: Cultura Cristã, 2000.

STACKHOUSE, Max L. and others. *Apologia, Contextualization, Globalization, and Mission in Theological Education,* Grand Rapids: Eerdmans, 1988.

STROMQUIST, Nelly P. *Education in a Globalized World,* Lanham, Md.: Rowman & Littlefield Publishers, 2002.

STRONG, Augustus Hopkins. *Teologia Sistemática,* São Paulo: Hagnos, 2003.

SUNG, Jung Mo. Cinismo e solidariedade na globalização. In: *Espaços* 8(1): 2000: 37-47.

TEIXEIRA, Alfredo Borges. *Dogmática Evangélica,* São Paulo: Pendão Real, 1958.

TERTULLIAN. *On the Praescription of Heretics,* translated by Peter Holmes. Ante-Nicene Fathers, vol. 3. Edited by Alexander Roberts, James Donaldson, and A. Cleveland Coxe, Buffado, NY: Christian Literature Publishing Co., 1885.

_____*Against Marcion,* translated by Peter Holmes. From Ante-Nicene Fathers, Vol. 3. Edited by Alexander Roberts, James Donaldson, and A. Cleveland Coxe. Buffalo, NY: Christian   Literature Publishing Co., 1885.

_____*An Answer to the Jews,* translated by S. Thelwall. Ante-Nicene Fathers, Vol. 3. Edited by Alexander Roberts, James Donaldson, and A. Cleveland Coxe. Buffalo, NY: Christian Literature Publishing Co., 1885.

_____*On the Testimony of the Soul and on the 'Prescription' of Heretics,* Translated into English by T. Herbert Bindley. London: SPCK, 1914.

THIELICKE, Helmut. *A Little Exercise for Young Theologians,* Grand Rapids: Eerdmans, 1999.

TILLICH, Paul. *Systematic Theology,* vol. I, Chicago: University of Chicago Press, 1951.

_____*Teologia Sistemática,* vol. I, II, III, São Paulo: Sinodal Paulinas, 1984.

TOMBS, David. Latin American Liberation Theology: Moment, Movement, Legacy. In: Patrick Claffey and Joe Egan (eds.), *Movement or Monument? Assessing Liberation Theology Forty Years after Medellin,* Studies in Society, Theology and Culture, vol. 1. Bern: International Academic Publishers, 2009, 29-54.

TRACY, David. *The Analogical Imagination: Christian Theology and the Culture of Pluralism,* New York : Crossroad, 1981.

TREIER, Daniel. Wisdom. In: VANHOOZER, Kevin J. (ed.), *Dictionary for theological interpretation of the Bible,* Grand Rapids: Baker, 2005, 844-847.

_____*Virtue and the Voice of God: Toward Theology as Wisdom,* Grand Rapids: Eerdmans,

2006.

TRIGUEIRO, José. *Alvorada: Negros e Brancos numa congregação em Londrina.* São Paulo:

Mackenzie, 2002.

VAN BUREN, Paul. *The Secular Meaning of the Gospel,* New York: Macmillan, 1963.

VAN DE BEEK, Abraham. *Jesus Kyrios: Christology as Heart of Theology,* Zoetermeer: Meinema, 2002.

VAN DER BENT, Ans J. *Historical Dictionary of Ecumenical Christianity,* London: The Scarecrow Press, 1994

_____*Commitment to God's World: A Concise Critical Survey of Ecumenical Social Thought,* Geneva: WCC, 1995.

VANHOOZER, Kevin, and others. *Dictionary for Theological Interpretation of the Bible,* Grand Rapids: Baker Booker House Company, 2005.

VAN LEEUWEN, Raymond C. Wisdom Literature. In: VANHOOZER, Kevin J. (ed.), *Dictionary for theological interpretation of the Bible,* Grand Rapids: Baker, 2005, 847-850.

VILANOVA, E. Teologia. In: SAMANES, C. F. & ACOSTA, J. T. (eds.), *Dicionário de Conceitos Fundamentais do Cristianismo*, São Paulo: Paulus, 1999, 793-798.

VISSER 't HOOFT, Willem Adolf. *Memoirs,* London: SCM Press, 1973.

_____*The Gospel for all Realms of Life,* Geneva: WCC, 1975.

VON BALTHASAR, Hans Urs. *Meditaciones sobre El Credo Apostólico,* Salamanca: Sigueme, 1997.

VON RAD, Gerhard. *Weisheit in Israel,* Neukirchen-Vluyn: Neukirchener Verlag, 1970.

_____*Wisdom in Israel.* London: SMC Press, 1972.

WALDENFELS, Hans. *Teologia Fundamental Contextual,* Salamanca: Sígueme, 1994.

WHITEHEAD, Alfred North. *The Aims of Education and Other Essays,* New York: Free Press, 1967.

YOUNG, F. The critic and the visionary. In: *Scottish Journal of Theology,* Volume 41(3), 1988, 297-312.

ZALUAR, Alns. Para não dizer que não falei de samba: Os enigmas da violência no Brasil. In: NOVAIS, Fernando A. (coord.); SCHWARZ, Lilia Moritz (org.), *História da vida privada no Brasil 4: Contrastes da Intimidade Contemporânea.* São Paulo: Companhia de Letras, v. 4, 1998, 245-318.

References in Newspapers and Periodicals

DE WIT, Hans. Muerte cotidiana y creación teológica en Chile. In: *Vida y Pensamiento,* Seminario Biblico Latinoamericano, San José, Costa Rica, vol. 8, n. 2, 1988 , 117-124

DIAS, Kleber Barbosa. *Justiça e Arete* como horizonte ético no pensamento de Aristóteles: *Revista Jurídica da UniFil,* Ano VI númeor 6, Londrina, 2009, 44-58.

ERLOZA, T., Londrina cresceu 13% em 10 anos. In: *Jornal de Londrina,* 30 November, 2010.

_____Renda na RML cresce 133% em dez anos. In: *Jornal de Londrina,* 3 July 2011.

GONÇALVES, Alonso. Pastoral Pública: a possibilidade de uma práxis a partir da Teologia Pública. In: *Protestantismo em Revista* [São Leopoldo], v. 27, January-April 2012.

KINSLER, F. R. Kairós en la educación teológica: Un cambio de perspectiva desde abajo. In: *Vida y Pensamiento.*Seminario Biblico Latinoamericano, San José, Costa Rica, vol. 8, n. 2, 1988, 16-28.

LANGE de MORRETES, F. O *Pinheiro na Arte. Ilustração Brasileira - Edição comemorativa do Centenário do Paraná,* Rio de Janeiro, n.224, dez. 1953.

LUQUE, P. M. & CONDORI, R. M. Identidad y transformación: Nuevos rumbos de educación teológica en Bolivia. In: *Vida y Pensamiento,* Seminario Biblico Latinoamericano, San José, Costa Rica, vol. 8, n. 2, 1988, 111-116. PAGURA, F. J. Formación espiritual contextual. In: *Vida y Pensamiento* [Seminario Biblico Latinoamericano, San José, Costa Rica], vol. 8, n. 2, pp. 7-15, 1988.

PAULY, Evaldo Luis. O novo rosto do ensino de teologia no Brasil: Números, normas legais e

espiritualidade. In: *Protestantismo em Revista,* volume 10, May-August. NEEP-EST, Escola

Superior de Teologia, São Leopoldo, 2006, 20-35. Available at <http:// www3.est.edu.br/nepp/revista/010/ano05n2.pdf> Accessed on December 31st, 2012.

PIEDRA, Arturo. Investigación socio-religiosa y educación teológica. In: *Vida y Pensamiento,* 8 (2), 1988.

ROLLIN, F. El Pentecostalismo a partir del pobre. In: *Cristianismo y Sociedad* [Mexico], n. 95, 1988, pp. 51-69.

TREIER, Daniel J. Theology as the Acquisition of Wisdom: Reorienting Theological Education. In: *Christian Education Journal* (Spring 1999), 127-139.

UNIFIL. Theology Pedagogical Project, Londrina, 2004.

UNIFIL. Educational Project of the Theology Course re-designed and updated in 2010.

Internet Sources

AUGUSTINE. City of God. http://www.logoslibrary.org/augustine/city/0801.html, accessed 10 December, 2008.

_____On the Trinity. http://www.logoslibrary.org/augustine/trinity/index.html, accessed 28 September, 2013.

_____On Christian Doctrine. http://www.logoslibrary.org/augustine/doctrine/index.html, accessed 28 September, 2013.

BENEDICT XVI, Spe Salvi. http://www.vatican.va/holy_father/benedict_xvi/encyclicals/documents/hf_ben-xvi_enc_20071130_spe-salvi_en.html, accessed on March 21, 2013.

Gaudium et Spes. http://www.vatican.va/archive/hist_councils/ii_vatican_council/documents/vat-ii_cons_19651207_gaudium-et-spes_en.html, accessed 10 December 2009.

ABOUT THE AUTHOR

Silas Barbosa Dias lives in Londrina, Brazil. He holds a PhD from Vrije Amesterdan University in Reformed Theology and a Master's degree in Ecumenical Studies from the Ecumenical Bossey Institute (World Council of Churches/University of Geneva). He is graduate in Theology, Philosophy and Psychotherapy. Since 1984 he has taught in several Reformed institutions Systematic Theology, Ethics and Philosophy.

Printed in Great Britain
by Amazon

27374972R00155